T0358766

TRAVELING THE OLD SKI TRACKS
OF NEW ENGLAND

TRAVELING THE OLD
SKI TRACKS OF
New England

E. JOHN B. ALLEN

BRIGHT LEAF
BOOKS THAT ILLUMINATE
Amherst and Boston
An imprint of University of Massachusetts Press

Traveling the Old Ski Tracks of New England has been supported by the Regional Books Fund, established by donors in 2019 to support the University of Massachusetts Press's Bright Leaf imprint.

Bright Leaf, an imprint of the University of Massachusetts Press, publishes accessible and entertaining books about New England. Highlighting the history, culture, diversity, and environment of the region, Bright Leaf offers readers the tools and inspiration to explore its landmarks and traditions, famous personalities, and distinctive flora and fauna.

ISBN 978-1-62534-673-5 (paper); 674-2 (hardcover)

Designed by Deste Roosa
Set in Calluna, Dazzle Unicase, and Acumin Pro Condensed
Printed and bound by Books International, Inc.

Cover design by Deste Roosa
Cover art by John Ryland Scotford, *Dartmouth Winter Carnival, February 9-10,* 1940.
Trustees of Dartmouth College. https://doi.org/10.1349/ddlp.1297.

Library of Congress Cataloging-in-Publication Data
Names: Allen, E. John B., 1933- author.
Title: Traveling the old ski tracks of New England / E. John Bedford Allen.
Description: Amherst : Bright Leaf, an imprint of University of Massachusetts Press, 2022. | Includes bibliographical references and index.
Identifiers: LCCN 2022022437 (print) | LCCN 2022022438 (ebook) | ISBN 9781625346742 (hardcover) | ISBN 9781625346735 (paperback) | ISBN 9781613769539 (ebook) | ISBN 9781613769546 (ebook)
Subjects: LCSH: Skis and skiing—New England—History. | Winter—New England. | New England—Social life and customs.
Classification: LCC GV854.5.N35 A56 2022 (print) | LCC GV854.5.N35 (ebook) | DDC 796.930974—dc23/eng/20220630
LC record available at https://lccn.loc.gov/2022022437
LC ebook record available at https://lccn.loc.gov/2022022438

British Library Cataloguing-in-Publication Data
A catalog record for this book is available from the British Library.

An earlier version of chapter 1 was previously published as "Millions of Flakes of Fun in Massachusetts," in *Sports in Massachusetts: Historical Essays*, ed. Ronald Story (Westfield: Institute of Massachusetts Studies, 1991), 69–95. Courtesy of *Historical Journal of Massachusetts*. An earlier version of chapter 2 was previously published as "'Skeeing' in Maine: The Early Years, 1870s to 1920s," *Maine Historical Society Quarterly* 30, no. 3&4 (Winter, Spring 1991), 146–63. Used by permission. An earlier version of chapter 4 was previously published as "The Making of a Skier: Fred H. Harris 1904–1911," *Vermont History* 53, no. 1 (Winter 1985): 5–16. Courtesy of Vermont Historical Society. Aspects—especially on the mechanization of skiing—were previously published in *From Skisport to Skiing: One Hundred Years of an American Sport, 1840–1940* (Amherst: University of Massachusetts, 1993); parts of chapter 7 have previously been published in *The Culture and Sport of Skiing from Antiquity to World War II* (Amherst: University of Massachusetts, 2007). Both used by permission.

CONTENTS

ACKNOWLEDGMENTS

In a way, this book has been forty-five years in the making. My skiing life began seventy years ago, but the academic side of it only in 1976. I was on a sabbatical leave in Innsbruck, Austria, working on a book on European Renaissance diplomacy, when, quite by chance, I visited a small exhibition of old skiing prints. This pivoted me, as unlikely as it sounds, from sixteenth-century ambassadors to nineteenth-century skiers. Over seventy articles and a dozen books later, here is *Traveling the Old Ski Tracks of New England*. These tracks stretch from New Sweden in Maine to Milford in Connecticut and take in various aspects along the way. In the course of this wandering, I have many people to thank: Sofia Yalouris for permission to use an article I wrote in the *Maine Historical Society Quarterly* 30, (Winter–Spring 1991): 146–65; Paul Carnahan for permission to use an article I contributed to *Vermont History* 53 (1985): 5–16; and Dr. Mara Dodge for permission to use a chapter in *Sports in Massachusetts: Historical Essays* (Westfield: Institute of Massachusetts Studies, 1991), 69–95. This institute no longer exists but has been superseded, in some ways, by the *Historical Journal of Massachusetts*. I am also grateful for permission to use material in *From Skisport to Skiing: One Hundred Years of an American Sport, 1840–1940* (1993) and *The Culture and Sport of Skiing from Antiquity to World War II* (2007), both published by the University of Massachusetts Press. Seven of the images are from the collections of the New England Ski Museum. I am indebted to director Jeff Leich for making them available to me. For insights into New England's ski history, I have been fortunate to have help, foremost from Jeff Leich, whose knowledge and assistance have proved invaluable. Other members of the New England Ski Museum who have critiqued chapters and answered questions are Brian Fowler, Meghan McCarthy McPhaul, Sally Seymour, Glenn Parkinson, and Jeremy Davis:

my deeply felt thanks for your efforts. Others to whom I owe thanks for helping in various ways are Kathe Dillmann, Rick Moulton, Philip Palmedo, Bo Adams, Tom Eastman, Theresa Stranahan, and Meredith Scott. Special thanks to Dana Sprague for allowing me to look over his personal Brattleboro collections for an entire day.

On the technical side, I am always in debt to various people connected with the Plymouth State University Library in Plymouth, New Hampshire. I want to acknowledge the students and staff of the help desk who have always been unfailingly patient with my technical difficulties. Mike Cosma has, seemingly, always been at hand to help. Joyce Bruce, as in the past, has worked her interlibrary loan marvels for me. I have also had help from Tim Shuffleton, Henry Krause, and Megan Shuffleton in straightening out printer and laptop technical misuse. Louiselle St. Laurent has put me on the right Internet track many times, for which I am extremely grateful. I am grateful for the advice and help from Brian Halley, Rachael DeShano, and Ivo Fravashi of the University of Massachusetts Press. My wife, Heide, has had a major share in our ski-about and has contributed to this book in too many ways to enumerate. Errors that remain are my responsibility.

TRAVELING THE OLD SKI TRACKS
OF NEW ENGLAND

INTRODUCTION

If you are a skier with any experience, you will know exactly what a chairlift will do, even one that will hold six of your breed. Now that ski areas have turned into summer recreation centers as well, a lot of nonskiers discover the mountaintops with a minimum of physical effort. In winter, our skier will sit on the chair and put his fiberglass skis on a footrest. The skis will be colorful and of varying shapes. Back in the shop where he bought the skis, he might be forgiven for not instantly realizing which was the front end and which the back. But now he has placed his boots made of fairly stiff plastic into the bindings by clicking into the system designed to secure them to the ski. You do not just buy a pair of skis today, you buy an entire system of skis, click-in bindings, and compatible boots. You will hold a high-tech and extremely light pole in each hand, most likely straight, some with a crook in them—those are for the racer types. This basic equipment of skis, bindings, boots, and poles has made an extraordinary difference to the way that we ski and to the pleasure economy on local, national, and international levels.

Arriving at a snowsports center—the term "ski area" is fading owing to the snowboarders—you will be greeted with clouds of descending snow from a vast number and variety of what are called snow guns. They use seventy-five thousand gallons of water for a six-inch snow cover of a 200-by-200-foot area overnight. Simple snow guns cost $5,000 and up, the more powerful fan guns anywhere from $28,000 to $35,000. The actual cost of producing a good snow cover for a weekend of skiing depends on weather, terrain, and the type of snow-making machinery. That new snow will be groomed, again overnight, by a fleet of machines, each costing about $150,000 in 2020, providing corduroy skiing. All this is now expected and demanded. Where snowmaking did not occur, there may be a sign such as I have seen at the top of the Hardscrabble trail at Cannon, New Hampshire, warning, "Danger. Natural Snow." Danger! Natural Snow! You may be inclined to return to your rented condo. Real estate on a large scale has been an impetus to development in many areas. In 1966 Snowmass, Colorado, became the first purpose-built ski area to serve a condo clientele.

You will be dressed in efficient clothing, made with fashion in mind. You will be helmeted and goggled, and your insulated gloves may not always keep your hands warm to thirty below, as advertised, but you can insert handwarmers. Besides, if you do get cold, the building at the bottom of the chairlift—now called the "base lodge"—may well be an architectural showpiece while supplying warmth, food, and even a kind of mall experience. The chapter on advertising is particularly instructive here.

All this is extremely expensive. Daily lift tickets at resorts such as Sugarloaf in Maine and Bretton Woods in New Hampshire cost $105. At Stowe, Vermont, the daily pass is $147. Stowe is now owned by Vail Associates in Colorado, one of their twenty-seven (and counting) areas stretching from Perisher in Australia to the U.S. West Coast, through the Rockies, and into the Midwest. In the east, Vail's holdings also include Okemo and Mount Snow in Vermont, and four areas in New Hampshire: Mount Sunapee, Crotched Mountain, Attitash, and Wildcat. Most people do not pay per day, of course. There is the seasonal Epic Pass (covering fifteen areas in the United States, including Stowe, Okemo, and Mount Sunapee in New England), and passes good for weekdays only. Seniors get a break; so do military personnel on active duty. There are 2-for-1 days, and students at the University of Vermont pay $99 for the season at Jay Peak in northern Vermont. Even so, skiing, alpine skiing, is not for the less well-off, and never has been.

In part, the high expenses of alpine skiing provided a reason for the increase in cross-country skiing—but only in part. Three other factors contributed to the rise of the popularity of cross-country skiing in the 1970s. First, Brattleboro-born and Putney-educated Bill Koch unbelievably won a silver medal in the 30K at the Winter Olympics in Innsbruck in 1976. This became an advertising gift to those promoting cross-country skiing. Second, it coincided with the popularity of what was at first considered a fitness fad that proved to have lasting health and economic benefits. And third, the 1972 oil embargo took its economic and social toll on the alpine ski business as well as its clientele, some of whom turned to cross-country skiing.

How this modern skiing, with its accompanying economic ups and downs, its oft-changing equipment and ready use of new materials, got its start is told in the venues visited in this book. The early skiers in New England, although often lone individuals, and "skeeing alone, all, all alone, alone as a wide territorie," as noted by Fred Harris, Dartmouth, class of 'II, were not, in fact, as isolated as they might have experienced or imagined. By 1900, there were groups of Scandinavian immigrants in New England who brought with them not only their knowledge of making skis but also the technique of using them. Skiers could be found in all the New England states except Rhode Island. Not only did these immigrants attract notice by their tracks across the local fields and roads, but their skis were on view at the Maine State Fair in 1885. Immigrant communities tended at first to be quite restrictive when forming organizations such as their churches and clubs. For example, you will read how the ski club minutes of Berlin, New Hampshire, were written in Norwegian. These immigrants were also working men, so naturally loggers in the woods of northern New England took to skis. Once this utilitarian activity was noted, and then passed on to college men, it assumed a very different aspect: skiing became a sport. Some of the chapters chronicle this change in detail; the example of Dartmouth is a primary focus.

This is not to say that the Scandinavians were uninterested in skiing as a sport. For them, Jump Day quickly became an unofficial national holiday. In New England it also became something very special for the immigrant communities. Jump Day required a lot of preparation. A jump had to be constructed, special regulations had to be followed, and spectators came to cheer the "Knights of the Sky." This was not just a sporting event but a major social happening, frequently the central part of an annual winter carnival, managed by local club and town fathers. The best jumpers were the stars of the day and of the season because they were invited from Berlin and Brattleboro, Newport and Salisbury. Some towns made great efforts to build a spectacular jump, because the best jumps, meaning those you could get a good distance from, attracted the better skiers. Frequently it was Norwegian immigrants such as the Satre brothers from Trysil in Hedmark who sparked an initial interest that enthused the local public to make northwest Connecticut the major jumping enclave that exists to this day.

So much for immigrant enthusiasm. But a notable fact was that there were not that many Scandinavian immigrants in New England. They were spread out, some in Maine, some in New Hampshire, a few in Vermont, and others in Massachusetts and Connecticut. Most of their confreres had gone to the Midwest, where they dominated the ski sport—a direct translation of *ski-idræt* (Norwegian) and *ski-idrott* (Swedish). Scandinavians had no word for "sport," but they did have *idræt*, a word that by the late nineteenth century meant healthy outdoor living relying on ancestral games and perceived simple pleasures. Such would benefit not only the man who practiced them but would also influence his wife, children, village, region, and even—it is difficult to believe—the country itself.

These notions were put into practice and then publicized by Norwegian explorer-scientist Fridtjof Nansen, who had crossed the southern part of Greenland in 1888 and who published what can best be described as an outdoorsman's bestseller in 1890. Four years later he attempted to reach the

North Pole by ship and then, when icebound, by ski. He failed gallantly, but he was the man who had been "Farthest North," as he titled his account of that trip. By this time Nansen had become the fulcrum around which Norwegian freedom from Swedish control turned. That happened in 1905, just at the time when Scandinavian immigration brought thousands to the American shores. "I know of no sport," Nansen wrote,

> which so evenly develops the muscles, which renders the body so strong and elastic, which teaches so well the qualities of dexterity and resource, which in an equal degree calls for decision and resolution, and which give the same vigor and exhilaration to mind and body alike. Where can one find a healthier and purer delight than when on a brilliant winter's day one binds one's ski to one's feet and takes one's way out into the forest? Civilization is, as it were, washed clean from the mind and left behind with the city atmosphere; one's whole being is, so to say, wrapped in one's ski and the surrounding nature. There is something in the whole which develops soul and not body alone.

And then the clincher: "The sport is perhaps of far greater national importance than is generally supposed."

It was not that these immigrants necessarily had such lofty ideas in their minds and firm muscles in their bodies as they strapped on their skis. But their skiing was bound up with health-giving enjoyment that could only better body and soul. This was the Scandinavian ideal of Western Europe's Renaissance idea of *mens sana in corpore sano*, a healthy mind in a healthy body. At the height of immigration, the Victorians had transformed this ideal into a social Darwinian nationalistic cult. Its modern equivalent, containing some of those basic tenets, you will find in Norway today: it is called *Friluftsliv*—open air living.

In the United States around 1900, the ski sport was changing. It appealed to an increasing number of native-born

Americans, and therefore Scandinavian exclusiveness began to give way to the promotion of Norwegian skiing for "men of all nationalities of good character." Even so, Carl Tellefsen, a major figure in Midwestern skiing, reminded his Ishpeming Club in 1904, "[I] will earnestly ask you not to bring the nationality question or any other question foreign to the sport into the club." It was the immigrants themselves who made this demand. However, as remembered by one non-Norwegian youngster from Berlin who went on to captain Dartmouth's team in the late 1930s, sometimes you had to have close ties to the Norwegians to be picked for the meet. Nansenesque backing became increasingly lost in myth as young men of means, now at New England colleges and universities, took to skiing as sport. It was not that Norwegians were simply pushed aside—how could they be when they skied better than anyone else? They were the winged Vikings of the air. What they said was accepted as holy writ. In 1912, when an undergraduate received a pair of poles to try out, he experimented with them in the dark because Norwegian practice was clear: one pole or no pole was the right way to ski. He did not want to be accused of needing any help for this masculine sport.

Sport—organized sport—requires many aspects in winter that play little or no part in simply putting on your boards to go visiting or fetching milk. In an analysis that is now forty-three years old and hallowed as definitive, Allen Guttman's *From Ritual to Record* analyzed how the nature of modern sports requires certain fundamental conditions. These are: secularism, equality of opportunity to compete, equality in the conditions of competition, specialization of rules, rationalization, bureaucratic organization, quantification, and the quest for records. Guttman's analysis runs from the Maori *teka* (*guessing game*) to Vince Lombardi. Skiing is hardly mentioned!

What you will find lurking in *Traveling the Old Ski Tracks in New England* is how skiing became in some ways secular, in some ways not. If you consider nationalism as a secular religion, then surely it has played a role in the harrowing tale of the Austrian Hannes Schneider and his imprisonment during the Anschluss, the takeover by Nazi Germany of his homeland. His statue stands at the entrance to Cranmore Mountain, commemorating how the *Skimeister* to the world ended up in the White Mountains of New Hampshire and what that meant for Austria and for the United States.

Patently, the opportunity to compete was a much-probed ideal. Opportunities covering geographical conditions are not the same in Rhode Island—the Ocean State—as they are in wooded and mountainous Maine. Americans living near Scandinavian immigrant communities had far more opportunity to compete than those who might only read of those exploits in a Boston newspaper. These geographical opportunities were open to those of European heritage. White Europe gave America its ski beginnings, it was white America that lived in the snow belt. White immigrants taught Americans how to ski—even though many had been on the opposite side in the war. Skiing was a white winter culture promoted by images advertising fashions, venues, and personal relationships. It was not that skiing entrepreneurs or practitioners were against Americans of color or of Asian origin (though some were antisemitic); it was that the continuation of the immigrant heritage, the imperial arctic adventuring of Nansen, the reigning superiority of the Austrian Arlberg technique, and the influence of the British way of skiing had only to do with what Annie Gilbert Coleman characterized as "the unbearable whiteness of skiing." The Alpine image was European—not just the geographical regions of mountainous France, Switzerland, Northern Italy, Austria, Germany, and northern Yugoslavia, but a culture that did not include any who were not white.

In 1972, the Black National Brotherhood of Skiers was founded to bring minority city kids to the white hills for winter fun and health. The Brotherhood's first "week" the following season was in Aspen, and in 2022 they are booked into Snowmass, Colorado, around the corner from Aspen. The organization comprises about fifty clubs in over forty cities, with a membership of about 3,500. They have difficulty in making it all work not because of lack of acceptance on the ski slopes and in the resort towns but because advertisers' dollars continue to support the Germanic Alpine ambience.

It is this historical background of 100 percent whiteness that makes the foundation for New England's ski tracks immediately apparent as skiing reached the college set. Dartmouth, Middlebury, Williams, Harvard, Yale, Norwich, the University of Vermont, and the University of New Hampshire, formed their outing clubs, following Dartmouth's lead, and became well established. Once the members graduated, they spun their collegiate winter pleasures into the Dartmouth Outing Club of Boston and the Dartmouth Outing Club of New York. Roland Palmedo, on the Williams team prior to World War I, was responsible for founding the Amateur Ski Club of New York, and the Schussverein comprised fifty Harvard graduates. These were people of wealth for whom skiing was a recreation. To compete at the college level, you needed equipment sent east from the Midwestern factories of Lund and Strand or, from 1905 as detailed in the Maine chapter, manufactured by Theo A. Johnsen of Portland. The world of making your own skis, of practicing on local golf course and meadow, of jumping off jerry-rigged structures, of enjoying the fun and games of an obstacle race during winter carnival, was passing. As many joined in, the standard of skiing rose. What had once been simply a pile of snow stamped down to produce a level and fairly firm takeoff for a jump now required some wooden framework. The race was on to see from which jump men would get the longest leap—perhaps the magic of one hundred feet! Today's record is 832 feet. In many of the chapters, the construction of the jump provides insight into why and how it all happened; Brattleboro and Berlin are the best exemplars. Jumps at colleges on carnival weekend, the winter equivalent of the summer prom, were the centerpiece of the seasonal social extravaganza.

Jumping rules owed much to the Norwegian ideal of a long jump but with good form. Both were given points based on actual length and particular form that had to be described to the growing number of spectators who relished length rather than agreeing with the mathematicizing of aesthetics. Rules in the early days were agreed on, and by the 1920s it was still the Norwegian point system that held sway.

For cross-country races, obstacle events, and the like, the organizers relied on the ready-made rules for track and skating. There was little argument over all these, as there was in fact little support. The problem was that a cross-country race of ten kilometers took place far from the viewing crowd. Competitors would be cheered off and certainly cheered again on arrival, but for the most part they were out of view. Compare that with the heroic high-flying Norsemen who seemed like birds.

If length of jump was so important, as was time for the cross-country racer, then there had to be some record of the event. "Any fool can make a record," I can remember sports historian Stephen Hardy saying, "but it requires hard data to beat the record." Bureaucracies—officials—set the rules, administered and certified the results, all to the end that what was once a free-for-all sporting event for the competitor and an enjoyable pastime for the spectator became an organized day in which norms were expected and hoped for and frequently advertised as probable. A hundred-foot jump provided a fascinating goal, and, once reached, a newspaper reporter would declare that this jumper was bringing fame and, perhaps, if not fortune, then at least an economic boost to his town. New England organizers also tried to attract Canadians to come south from Montreal; the farther competitors had to travel, the more it increased the importance of the venue.

The quest for records is bound up with quantification, of course. A record is, after all, something that has to be recorded, so it is also very much a bureaucratic necessity. In the long run, these records are also part of a heritage. Visitors to the New England Ski Museum, after their tram ride to the top of Cannon Mountain, having been told that Bode Miller's five Olympic medals are on view—that's what they want to see, the actual artifacts of his outstanding record.

Why are we interested in the heritage of skiing? Interest peaks at times when it appears that something is going to be lost. In the case of skiing, the organization of the sport was being managed by second- and third-generation Norwegian Americans in the Midwest. They had little understanding of the attractions of the alpine skiing world of New England and the Rockies. A necessity was seen to preserve the Midwestern skiing of their forebears, so the ski-minded Midwesterners founded the National Ski Hall of Fame in the Upper Peninsula of Michigan at Ishpeming in 1954.

In New England's case, its preeminent place in American skiing was confined to the 1930s and the years immediately following World War II. We can take the alpine events sanctioned by the Fédération internationale de ski (FIS) as the last major fling of New England as the powerhouse of American skiing. On Cannon Mountain, Jean-Claude Killy swept the New Hampshire meet in 1946, and Toni Sailer triumphed in the Stowe competition in 1948. Increasingly, the West, with its higher mountains and the allure of its destination resorts, pioneered by Sun Valley, Idaho (opening in December 1936), provided greater sporting and social temptations for those with disposable wealth. The FIS World Championships in 1950 were held in Aspen, Colorado. And Europe, too, the home of right-minded alpine skiing, home of Schneider's Arlberg technique, offered spectacular skiing along with the *Gemütlichkeit* provided by an exotic accent, an accordion lilt, raclette, and foaming *Bier*.

So New England's moment in American ski history had passed. And, passing too, was the Arlberg crouch, *Vorlage* (lean forward), and *Geländesprung* (terrain jump). What was taking its place was . . . snowboarding! And snowboarders, with their youth, their grungy outfits, their seemingly uncontrollable single board, their attitude of flaunting organizational orders from the ski patrol, appeared a threat to New England skiing traditions. Time, then, to save those traditions. Thus, in the 1970s, hesitant steps were taken to find a home for cups (you wouldn't believe how many were awarded in the 1930s), wooden skis, cotton parkas, and googly-eyed goggles, not to speak of leather ski boots, safety bindings of questionable efficiency, how-to books galore, and films. The desperately serious instructional films on snow-ploughing competed with *Schlitz on Mount Washington*. It all had to be saved in order to preserve the very sport of skiing that seemed under siege by raucous snowboarding youth. Prospective donors felt that the grand glories of their past were slipping from their grasp—hence ski museums would ensure them forever.

A further development has recently taken place. In addition to the ski museums in Maine, New Hampshire, and Vermont, and an exhibit in Massachusetts—all well worth a visit—there is talk of a northern New England ski history trail in the making. It is planned to run roughly from Sugarloaf in Kingfield, Maine, south and east to both of the New England Ski Museums, at North Conway and Franconia, New Hampshire, then further west to Stowe, Vermont. Along the way, viewing interesting relics of the past, some mentioned in this book, travelers can have their fill of New England's skiing history. It has been a good trip:

> My skis are long and lithe and fleet,
> Pagan wings for questing feet.
> They take me to forbidden lands
> Where King Winter's temple stands
> And pilgrims of the Northland meet.

CHAPTER 1

"MILLIONS OF FLAKES OF FUN IN MASSACHUSETTS"

BOSTON AND THE BERKSHIRES, 1870-1940

Nowhere is it more certain than in the development of skiing that America was a nation led by immigrants. The early clubs were all immigrant inspired, the manufacturing was done by an immigrant workforce, and rules were copied from the old world, as were the competitions. How all this fared in the United States makes an interesting study. The emphasis on skiing came from nordic immigrants, especially Norwegians, who had gained their freedom from Sweden only in 1905; from Swedes; and from Finns, who, prior to the end of World War I, were part of a duchy of Tsarist Russia. They settled mostly in the Midwest, a term in general use from the 1880s on.

New England, too, had communities from northern Europe, but comparatively few. However, these were often led by individuals who played major roles in the development of skiing. In 1887, for example, a man identifying himself as a Norwegian wrote to the *Boston Globe* wondering why "skeing" had not been brought to the northern states of the United States. More practical were men such as Dr. Andreas Christian of Boston, Massachusetts; Theodore Johnsen of Portland, Maine; Strand Mikkelsen of Greenfield, Massachusetts; and the Satre brothers of Salisbury, Connecticut. Boston, New England's Shining City upon a Hill (with an average annual snowfall of forty inches over the winters from 1910 to 1930), had a population of 250,000 in 1870, and some of the 1,255 Scandinavian immigrants (Finnish excluded) registered in the state must have lived in town. By 1910, 5,434 was the total number in the state—a small number when compared to over twenty-five thousand in Minnesota. Yet that year the *Boston Globe* and *Herald* interviewed Dr. Andreas Christian, photographed at the Belmont Country Club, performing "some high jumping stunts which were loudly applauded," and now touting himself as gaining a second place in the Holmenkollen competition, Norway's most prestigious ski event in 1898 (when there was no competition due to lack of snow) and as its winner the following year, which was also not true. Dr. Christian rejoiced at the hundreds of skiers swarming over the Newtons and Brookline, over Middlesex Falls and Blue Hills. Skis were stacked on shop counters in Boston for even more people to enjoy the sport. Although he believed the New Hampshire countryside fifty miles north of Boston was perfect for skiing across field and dale, the Berkshires were not to be belittled. The article also instructed neophytes on how to ski. It was accompanied by eight large photos of Trygve Frølich, "a conspicuous performer" at the Holmenkollen competition (whose name is not on the list of prizewinners), and included customary asides on the sport's appeal to children, its inexpensiveness, and its benefits to the physical and mental health of men. For women, Dr. Christian assured his readers, skiing was also "a great antidote for corsets."

It is difficult to believe Dr. Christian's entire assessment, especially the number of participants and the availability of equipment. But the *Herald* article does indicate what was important to those who skied prior to the advent of steel edges, ski lifts, and ski areas: by 1910, skiing provided both sport and sociability in the Boston area, another outdoor winter diversion enjoyed on the undulations of suburbia and the odd golf links and country club grounds:

> Hurrah for the ski! and the taut snow-shoe
> And the swift skate's shrill refrain!
> When the world's enwrapped in its mantle new
> And winter awakes again!

Nor is it a coincidence that it was a Norwegian who was interviewed for skiing. Norwegians had brought the culture of *ski-idræt* with them to America—an ideal of all-around exercise and expertise in nature's outdoors, something they claimed their ancestors had passed on to them. It engendered sound body and a sound mind; as a result, any man who took to the ancestral ways would have an effect on kith, kin, village, town, and even nation. Fridtjof Nansen himself had written that skiing was of national importance. This ideal held dominion over the "ski sport," a direct translation of *ski-idræt* until challenged by the fast-paced, downhill *Schuss*, imported from the Alps at the end of the 1920s and in the early the 1930s.

Norwegian immigrant Lars Petersen is the first recorded skier in the state. He came from the old country in around 1873 and settled in Concord. The winter of 1876 being particularly snowy, Petersen made his own skis to get out and about. Subsequently he made some skis for others. Peter Severinsen is believed to have started a ski factory in 1890, also in Concord. If so, this would be very early; the first in the world was in Norway in 1882. Back in Concord, there may well have been skiers right through the 1920s; there is one report of a Norwegian team training on Punkatasset Hill in 1927. Wilmington was singled out as offering good skiing grounds in 1905, and in the 1930s was described as one of the finest skiing centers for beginners and moderates. The Brookline Country Club saw skiers in 1906, the Belmont Spring Country Club in 1909, and when the cold snap hit in February 1917, many were out on the grounds of the Oakley Country Club in Watertown. The Wellesley Hill woods attracted an English skier in 1914. In sum, throughout the Boston area, there are reports of skiers enjoying the snow.

If Mr. Petersen had made his skis for purely utilitarian purposes, Dr. Christian was an advocate of their use for social sport. As such, his appeal was to those who had leisure time enough to learn and then enjoy their newfound winter activity. Others in the state who commented on early skiing were from the well-to-do sector of society, including students off to Dartmouth and Harvard. Early ski activity also occurred in the Boston-based Appalachian Mountain Club. Originally a club for scientifically oriented gentlemen, the AMC embraced the environment as much for its spiritual qualities as for recreational enjoyment. In 1882, a snowshoe section was formed, and in the 1890s members delighted in the challenge of a winter climb. A "skee-man" was on an AMC trip to Fryeburg, Maine, in 1895. Although we know little of this trip, a photograph of the impressive array of webbing in front of the hotel includes a pair of skis. The AMC "has done much to spread winter sporting," commented the *Boston Globe* in 1912. "Snowshoe tramps now give way to winter mountaineering on snowshoes and skis." One of the more expensive winter hostelries in northern New Hampshire that was open for winter sporting (and very few remained open during the winter) was Pecketts on Sugar Hill, New Hampshire, in 1911 hosting a party of seventeen from Boston. The Northfield Friendship Club put on an annual house party, a kind of winter carnival for a semireligious group of about seventy guests between 1912 and 1920 that included moonlight sleigh rides, snowshoeing, tobogganing, and skiing. Parties came from New York and Brooklyn, from New Britain, Connecticut, Langbourne, Pennsylvania, Boston, and eight other Massachusetts communities. Williams College was first attracted to skiing in 1914, and after the war, the Williams Inn advertised that it pleased "particular people" attracted to "those alluring Berkshire Hills."

The point is obvious: wealth was attracted to the challenge of winter out of doors. President Theodore Roosevelt's strenuosity appealed to those who could afford to escape urban confines. Roosevelt himself was an enthusiastic skier, and his skis may be seen in the Smithsonian Museum in Washington, DC. Some traveled far in their quest. The "fur-clad society girls . . . motor-coated men of fashion and affairs—all amateurs—who hope to become really proficient before the season ends" included a Mr. Greenough of Boston, in attendance at the ski competitions at Cary, Illinois, in 1913. These were men, and a few women, who took their runs across the countryside. Pittsfield locals were reported skiing to their camp in 1916 near Tower Mountain, some six miles away. Other young people sported on skis around town in January 1918. During the big snows of March 1920, when mail delivery was halted in Stockbridge, a dozen miles from Pittsfield, skiing for pleasure was enjoyed, reported the *Berkshire Evening Eagle*. Yet much of the attraction of skiing lay in the excitement of jumping. Although "thank-ee-ma'ams" might be constructed on Massachusetts hillsides, there was no attempt to indulge in what the Norwegian communities called the real riding, spectacular leaps of over one hundred feet from carefully constructed jumps (today's world record stands at 831 feet and eight inches for men, and 656 feet for women). In the Midwest, these spectacles brought thousands into town on jump day and were an immediate economic boon to the hosting community. In 1910, at the Lexington Minute Men's Outdoor Festival, the crowd waited for John Rudd, Chicago's flying policeman who "turns somersaults backwards or forwards." Massachusetts was, however, generally slow to realize just how a star jumper could bring in the crowds, but there was, as Dr. Christian pointed out, an increasing awareness of what would become winter tourism. In the 1920s, these two factors—the Norse high-flying jumpers and the possibility of winter tourism—combined successfully.

Individual inns remained open for the winter in the years after the Great War, such as the already mentioned Williams Inn, and the *Boston Globe* in 1918 suggested that there was skiing as well as snowshoeing, tobogganing, coasting, and sleighing. The Toy Town Tavern's "longest ski jump" was included in the advertisement. Railroad officials discussed schedules for special events, and in the summer of 1921 a brochure was prepared by the New England Winter Sports

Committee specifically "to invite our summer visitors to come back next winter." The *Atlantic Coast Merchant* believed that one and a half million dollars of new business could be generated. Maine and New Hampshire dominated the preliminary listing of inns in the brochure, but Greenfield, Swampscott, Gloucester, and Williamstown were included. None, however, was advertised as a skiing venue! That soon changed. Greenfield's 1923 winter carnival showcased the "fastest toboggan chute in America, ski jumping for amateurs, [a] chinook dog team bound for the North Pole, skijoring, and ski races." When the Massachusetts Hotelmen's Association was headquartered at the Weldon Inn with a capacity of two hundred at Greenfield in 1926 for their annual winter meeting and outing, sugaring-off parties were organized, snowshoeing and ski hikes taken, and ski jumping exhibitions were added to the festivities.

Norwegian immigrant Strand Mikkelsen represented something special at the Weldon Inn in Greenfield as the inn's resident instructor. For the first time in the East, the Weldon advertisement in the *Boston Herald* pictured a jumper. Here was the attraction, and Mikkelsen was the state's premier competitor on the national circuit in the late 1920s and in the 1930s. New York winter motorists in 1929 could read the headline, "New England Offers a Royal Welcome." In fact, most of the article was about the attractions of Greenfield, Massachusetts. As noted, Northfield provided some competition, and in the 1930s produced postcards of skiing out of the inn along with advertisements in the *New York Herald Tribune*.

In the 1920s, skiing became two different yet related activities. The jumping competitions produced the star excitement, and thus the sport became a spectacle. Yet urbanites could themselves enjoy the more prosaic runs on skis across the fields. In 1920 one young Boston skier could find no one to accompany him on ski excursions. Ten years later, the Appalachian Mountain Club—and others—were discovering that skiing was entering a boom phase.

A number of factors reinforced the boom. In spite of, and in some cases because of, the Great Depression, there was more leisure time for more people with unexpended energy, to use Scott Fitzgerald's phrase, to channel toward sporting activities. And from the Alps came a new way to ski, characterized by a love of speed and taught by men with highly valued exotic accents. The traditional nordic Telemark turn was about to be replaced by the low-crouch Arlberg technique. The AMC found Otto Schniebs, from the Black Forest in Germany, to initiate the club into the mysteries of "the supple crouch, with its elastic knee," as *Appalachia* recorded in its 1928–29 season. Schniebs's "unusual skill as an instructor, made the more effective by his engaging personality," enticed not only club members—from twenty-five skiing members to over three hundred in 1931—but also people from clerical and professional groups. Schniebs reached a wider public in 1929 with an illustrated article in the *Boston Evening Transcript*.

There were other clubs in the Boston area. None was so important in the development of skiing as a sport as the Ski Club Hochgebirge. The German name was picked from *Wunder des Schneeschuhes*, the most important book—and film—to promote what was becoming known as Alpine skiing, as opposed to Nordic skiing; here is where the two disciplines of skiing down hills and skiing across the countryside divide. Many of the Hochgebirge members had skied when they were in college, and they had traveled to enjoy the snows of the Bavarian Alps, the Black Forest, Switzerland, and Austria. The racing technique of the Arlberg crouch was de rigueur. In naming the Ski Club Hochgebirge, members were acknowledging the influence of the German high mountains. Others quickly followed suit. In Massachusetts alone could be found the Sargbetrueger (Coffin Cheaters), Edelweiss, Schneehaserle (Snow Bunnies), Schussverein, and Smith College's Hochalm played off Boston's Hochgebirge. Although the Norse heritage continued to have some influence in skiing matters, there was a remarkable, quick, and general adoption of German downhill as the way to skiing enjoyment. The language reflected this sporting speed skiing from its alpine roots. Many *Skiläufer* might have to revert to a *Stemmbogen* on the *Steilhang*—especially if their *Vorlage* did not permit a secure *Geländesprung* before starting their *Schuss* across the *Firnschnee*. Even if they made a *Sitzmark*, they would still be able to attend the *Preisverteilung* with the *Stimmung* provided by the *Amerikanerin* of the *Damenmannschaft*. These are words picked at random from the *American Ski Annuals* from 1934 to 1939. It was the language of the new foundation for alpine skiing, and it had to be learned. Indeed, necessary for understanding a ski lesson in 1937 were the terms *Langlauf* (cross-country), *Dauerlauf* (long distance cross-country), *Geländesprung* (terrain jump), *Quersprung* (cross jump), *Vorlage* (forward lean), and *Bahnfrei* ("Track!" Yelled to alert a person in front of you to get out of the way). *Abstemmen* (stem the lower ski), *Stemmbogen* (stem turn), *Passgang* (simultaneous thrust of the same side pole and ski), *Vorläufer* (forerunner), and *stemmfahren* (snowplow) were in use as well. The one remaining word still used today, and even now is going out of use, is *Schuss*. *Ski Heil!* was the American greeting to fellow skiers in the 1930s. All this had been learned by well-to-do club members who went to three venues in particular: Saint Anton am Arlberg, where Hannes Schneider, *Skimeister* of the modern world, taught his Arlberg technique; to Mürren in the Berner Oberland of Switzerland, where Arnold Lunn's upper-crust English amateurism was combined with a devil-may-care dash; and to Wengen, across the Lauterbrunnen valley from Mürren, where the British Downhill Only (always the DHO) held that taking it straight, redolent of the fox hunt, was the proper way to ski.

The Hochgebirge club—Hochies, as they were immediately called—sponsored and gave panache to downhill racing, built trails, fostered the growth of tows, and were the impetus behind the first U.S. aerial tramway at Cannon Mountain in New Hampshire. They were responsible for the Inferno Races. Most of the Hochie members and those of the AMC, along with college alumni now in the Dartmouth Outing Club of Boston had enjoyed the social and athletic attractions of skiing at college. Once graduated, this educated elite wanted to continue their winter muscularity. Skiing offered an aesthetic experience along with adventure, in addition to the pleasures of discussing failed Christiania turns and linked somersaults. The new jargon helped set the skiing fraternity apart from sedentary urbanites.

Many who entered college had already had ski experience at private schools. Cushing Academy (in Ashburnham) had a recreational ski program as early as 1920, Eaglebrook (in Deerfield) in 1922, and Mount Hebron (in Northfield) in 1930; so did Phillips (in Andover) and Williston (in East-hampton). Competitions were arranged with private schools in Vermont, New Hampshire, and Connecticut. When Cushing Academy produced a captain at Dartmouth, 1932 and 1936 Olympians, an intercollegiate jumping champion, and a number of leading coaches, the elite ski fraternity became an in-group. Indeed, when the snow-train masses left Boston, the hills became like "Coney Island" as the old guard attempted "to preserve the remnants of what was once a glorious Kamaraderie," now being swamped with "society buds and their anemic escorts." The Arlberg, it was feared, might be replaced with "the Saks Fifth Avenue and other Borax schools." Of thirty-three charter members of the Old Carriage Road Runners, twenty came from Massachusetts.

Patently, skiing was a social as well as physical sport. Though clubs and their outings were male-dominated—the Schussverein was "entirely men." As members married, "the wives were brought in, obviously, but they're not referred to as members; they're always members' wives," remembered one stalwart. There is no woman listed in the first ten years of the Ski Club Hochgebirge. In fact, while women at Smith and Mount Holyoke College—Wellesley students preferred "yar-ting" (sliding on trays) in 1926—already had ski experience, it was the social drive of the Hochies and the Dartmouth men that impelled Smith women to compete for the Hochgebirge Cup in 1931 and to join in racing with the Dartmouth men in 1932. "This is a sport for ladies certainly," and it was hoped that Miss Hoyt would "stir up an interest in Smith" and bring the Hochalm along on outings.

Mount Holyoke emphasized skiing within the confines of the Physical Education Department's program. An instructor was available in 1935, and points on skijoring (being towed behind a horse) were given by the equestrian teacher, Mrs. Henry Beaumont. In 1936, about a hundred students from the sophomore class chose winter sports as their physical education subject. In 1937, the number rose to 120, and "advanced members" planned to blaze a trail in order to be ready for skiing when the snow came; an unnamed local school instructor and "winter sports expert" temporarily helped the physical education staff. At Northampton, too, that snowless year, recreational skiing rose in popularity: from fifty-six enrolled for lessons in 1935 to two hundred in 1937. Harriet Aull of the Smith physical education staff was the second woman to be granted professional ski instructor status, in December 1938. By 1939 skiing was popular at Smith because it was "a social asset." There were also those "girls who go to the winter sports centers with no 'ulterior motive'—they just plain love to ski." But one has a feeling that was best done with a Hochie or Dartmouth man.

Also significant in these years were the introduction of the snow train and the publication of the *Ski Bulletin*. Trains had, of course, carried skiers even before the Boston and Maine Railroad (B&M) took 197 from Boston to Warner, New Hampshire, on January 11, 1931, for the specific purpose of skiing. AMC members had experienced snow trains leaving Munich for the Bavarian Alps, and this inspired Park Carpenter to pressure the B&M to institute a similar service. Although the B&M's annual report made no mention of it, 8,371 took the train that season. Most of the trips were to New Hampshire, but on February 15, 938 descended on

Greenfield, eighty to one hundred of whom were employees of the Harris Forbes Bank, "as guests of the company." Here are those clerical groups referred to earlier. They were, it was reported, "mostly young folks in a wide variety of costumes, and on the way back musical instruments appeared." They were out for amusement and sociability, determined to enjoy themselves in the few hours available to them—rather different from the healthy collegians who sported a touch of muscular Christianity in their efforts. In 1932, other trains left from Framingham, Worcester, and Springfield, and the indication was (even though the service was soon discontinued) that skiing was appealing to urbanites across the state other than just the well-to-do in Boston.

The B&M had first promoted the idea of taking the train north to attend winter carnivals, where "the breath-taking thrill of the ski-jumping contests with the daring leap from dizzy heights" was the major attraction. In other words, the B&M saw itself running spectator specials. By the end of the 1930s, spring snow trains were being touted as "Sun Tan Specials." In spite of the enthusiasm for the snow trains, the B&M reported total passenger revenue down by 20.5 percent in 1931, and in the Depression years there were further declines of 29.2 percent in 1932 and 18.7 percent in 1933. Only in 1934 was there a 2.5 percent increase, the first since 1923. Weekend and Sunday snow trains certainly raised revenue on those occasions; in the years 1936, 1937, and 1938, the increase rose annually by 4.4 percent, 7.7 percent, and 6.2 percent, respectively, and there were very small increases in 1939 and 1940. The apparent success of the B&M's winter venture spawned the idea of the Snow Plane, a regular air run on weekends from Boston, including "night flights in heated cabin" to Pittsfield.

Snow train passengers left their money mostly in New Hampshire. Massachusetts communities first benefitted from snow train business in 1935, when the New York, New Haven and Hartford Railroad ran a special carrying 447 from Grand Central Station to Pittsfield, G-Bar-S at Great Barrington, and Stockbridge. The following figures indicate the growing popularity of skiing in the Berkshires:

1935	3,658
1936	11,945
1937	463
1938	2,445
1939	2,466
1940	7,682
1941	5,410
Total	34,069

The *Ski Bulletin* was the most important seasonal publication for Boston skiers and for others in the state. First issued on December 25, 1930, it appeared weekly until the middle or the end of March, for a dollar a season. It started as a six-by-nine-inch information sheet giving snow conditions and the weekend forecast for an area covering Lucerne-in-Quebec (of the Chateau resort in Montebello, halfway between Ottawa and Montreal) in the north to Salisbury, Connecticut, in the south. The report from Groton, Massachusetts, for instance, on Thursday, December 15, 1932, was "5 inches, 1 inch fluffy over breakable crust. Temperature 20." The adoption of British ski tests and the Greenfield Winter Carnival were listed, as was Cushing Academy's interscholastic tournament and Eaglebrook's invitation meet; the Massachusetts State Championship was scheduled for Lancaster on Washington's Birthday. Of twenty-seven events, these were Massachusetts's contribution. The *Ski Bulletin* often carried insider remarks: "a very hush-hush secret of this year's plans—for the benefit of ski runners only" and the like. There was a section called "Brevities," and also short articles such as "The View from Toronto." In short, the *Ski Bulletin* was a publication printed by skiers for skiers in 1930, when just about everyone knew everyone else. But by December 1934, its circulation had risen to 1,300, by the end of the 1935 season to 2,100, by

1936 to 3,000, and by 1939 to 4,000. From 1936 on, it was an expanded, glossy publication with photos, views, and commentary. The price went up to ten cents a copy, or about two dollars a season.

For those who cared to ski only occasionally during the winter, a column, "Old Man Winter," appeared regularly beginning in December 1934 in the *Boston Evening Transcript*. In most ways it did for the interested what the *Ski Bulletin* did for the committed. It was written by journalists, and the *Evening Transcript* had to sell, so there was heavy reporting of race results and human interest stories. Fashion was a constant theme from the mid-1930s on. Skiing, which had once been for rugged outdoor collegians, then a sport for the cognoscenti, was becoming something of a business. Winter culture was becoming civilized.

A major part of the civilizing of the sport of skiing was economic. So important to New England was it that the economic power of the lumber industry gave way to winter tourism. Much of this can be traced by following two developments: the mechanization of skiing, and the advertising of all facets of skiing. A chapter is devoted to each of these and constitutes a period of skiing that ended with the outbreak of World War II, when the number of skiers was estimated anywhere from one to three million across the United States. All needed equipment, clothing, and suggestions on where to ski. All this was put on public display at the Boston Garden— the first of America's ski shows.

In Boston, two ski shops were favored: Asa Osborne's on High Street and Oscar Hambro's on Carver Street. "Shop" is the correct word, but they were much more. Rockwell Stephens, AMC member, author, ski train organizer, and later to be a ski shop partner, explained that when he was out of a job, "I'd go in and chew the rag with Asa and Charley [Proctor] and the rest of the skiers who were there. It was a sort of gathering point." Osborne's clientele, reported the *Herald*, "has always regarded the shop more as a club than a store." This was where snow train destinations were decided, material for the *Ski Bulletin* looked over, fine points of technique and style discussed, and race results admired. Oscar Hambro had moved to the United States in 1925; in the 1930s his business boomed. In 1937, the year that Osborne enlarged his quarters with a special clothing section and opened a satellite store in Cambridge, Hambro opened a branch in New York City and a ski factory just across the New Hampshire border.

These two were not the only Boston stores selling ski equipment. Wright and Ditson, Jordan Marsh, Kennedy's, Filene's, Bjarne Johannsen's Ski Import, James W. Byrn, Spalding, and Sears began to appeal to different economic levels, with skis ranging in price from $18 down to $1. One new store that was immediately popular was run by Rockwell Stephens and Charley Proctor, a Dartmouth Olympian of 1928 and a mentor to most of New England's better skiers. The 1930s were difficult economic times, but these two had no trouble finding capital. "We had perhaps eight or ten stockholders, all of them skiers," recalled Stephens, "who apparently decided to take a fling more or less for the hell of it. The nature of our stockholders was such that one of them told us to go to a certain bank and we could probably get a little credit there. He apparently swung a big enough stick so that anything he told his friends to do, they did and the bank did."

The skier dressed from earmuff to sock in both imported and U.S.-made materials. Skis, boots, poles, and such essential extras as wax, ski spreaders (to keep the tips bent when not in use), boot straighteners (to keep the boot soles flat), and ski racks for automobiles were all advertised and sold by the growing number of Boston ski stores. Filene's featured Swiss pro Wendelin Hilty, Jordan Marsh relied on Fred Nachbaur, and Hambro employed Norwegians and Germans. A Sun Valley agent showed films to attract the upscale clientele to Averell Harriman's new destination resort in the Sawtooth Mountains of Idaho. Smartly modern snow togs and accessories were advertised, and live models presented style shows at Jordan Marsh, Kennedy's, Whites, and Filene's. Costume was most important for the snow train fan, and advice was tendered that it should be warm, adjustable, lightweight, and colorful. Some stores had snow train departments. Armstrong actually ran a shop on the regularly scheduled snow trains.

This economic activity was put on exhibit for the first time at a three-day Winter Sports Show in Boston Garden in December 1935. Along with over twenty manufacturing companies from the United States and Canada, hotels, winter sports clubs, and travel bureaus exhibited, including Garmisch-Partenkirchen, host of the 1936 Olympic Winter Games in Bavaria. Hambro displayed his new laminated skis, Proctor and Stephens their handy ski pack, and well-known skiers were on hand to answer queries as well as perform in an elaborate ski extravaganza. A hill that doubled as a jump had been constructed in the Garden. Ice chips covered the slope and the landing so that Norwegian, Austrian, and homegrown stars could do their tricks. Sig Buchmayr's "famous pin wheel in which he goes into a reverse spin over the top of his poles" drew nightly applause from a crowd of ten thousand. Triple jumping was an attraction, and on the last night a five-man jump preceded the somersault-and-flaming-torch routine. On the final night, thirteen thousand showed up, and another 3,500 had to be turned away.

"Purists may shudder," commented one journalist. "These amusing extravaganzas," wrote another, were "more and more of a spectacle." In 1936, the show was extended to four days, and in 1937 and 1938 it was spread over five days, with about sixty thousand in attendance. There were two exhibitions daily; in 1936, these included "the whole Sun Valley crew of Austrians," in addition to some Swiss, some Norwegians, and a Finn. In 1937, two girl jumpers appeared; the renowned Ella Gulbranson, a Norwegian, was on the program the next year. By 1938, there was little equipment on view, just more and more advertising for hotels, along with regional and national displays. One European country publicized its railways without bothering to mention skiing. The French advertised their mountains and their skiing method. The ever-increasing number of skiers became so great that there was little need to persuade them to buy equipment. The competition was to attract them to a particular venue.

The showbiz aspect wore off. "As to the grand finale of torches and hoops of fire," the *Ski Bulletin* reported on the 1938 Garden show, "we noted a general movement towards the exits, rather than the expected bated breath." Between 1935 and 1939 the untutored, who had been amazed at the tricks on snow, had become skiers. "Skeptics will say it's only a circus," commented the bulletin, "but they *do* introduce thousands of skiers."

These new thousands had also had the wearying part of skiing removed for them. The rope tow, J-bar, T-bar, chairlift, and aerial tram were all in evidence before 1940. Most of these contraptions were in New Hampshire and Vermont. In Massachusetts, Bousquet's rope tow in Pittsfield was prominent in 1936: 1,400 feet long with a 275-foot vertical drop, it served two open slopes and two novice trails, could carry thirty to forty skiers at a time, and once had a record seventy-four on it. Another tow one thousand feet long above this one was projected for the next season. "The ski tow at Bousquet's pulled well over fifty at one time last Sunday. A sprocket chain broke, so it then had to be run more slowly," reported the *Ski Bulletin*. But "those who had tickets Sunday, it is said, will be given half price next time they visit Pittsfield."

Early tows were put up by tinkerer-owners. In 1938, the Underwood Company of South Boston advertised a tow that traveled eight miles per hour at a minimum; four years later Underwood titillated its users with the prospect of traveling up to 100 miles an hour on the level ground! The New Bedford Maritime Manila Company and Plymouth Cordage saw a new market for their ropes in 1938. That year also saw

Bousquet's introduction of a rope-tow gripper. "Rest while you Ride," skiers read, and save "in gloves and linament [sic]." The expression "ski area" was a post–World War II nomenclature. Bousquet's, just out of Pittsfield, was the first ski center in the state. Pittsfield had seen plenty of ski activity after World War I. In 1917, the town fathers had strongly supported a Winter Sports Club. Their three-day winter carnival included ski trips, ski races, and ski jumping competitions. They followed this up with two junior jumps and arranged to have instructors at Clapp Park every Saturday afternoon. Pathé News was brought in to film the Dartmouth men as well as a Swede who missed being on the U.S. Olympic team because of residency status. It was a star-studded show, and the film was expected to be shown in hundreds of theaters all over the country. Pittsfield was on the ski map. Members of the Mount Greylock Ski Club skied on Clarence Bousquet's pastures in 1932–33, and he turned his garage into a warming hut and built a couple of outhouses. The following season he visited Woodstock to inspect their new uphill contraption, and by the 1935–36 season he had his own rope tow ready. Bousquet's saw its first snow train clientele arrive from New York on February 10, 1935. It is said that over ten thousand people thronged the station to watch the 477 skiers! With success and innovation, including the first incandescent lights for night skiing, Bousquet's immediately doubled its facilities for the next season. That same season the town of Pittsfield ran a "Snow Bus" to take skiers to the Williams Winter Carnival and later to the state downhill championships on the Thunderbolt. This section of the Berkshires was leading the way to modern skiing.

Ski venue development increased as depressed communities capitalized on winter economic possibilities. Farnhams-in-the-Berkshires, eight miles from Pittsfield, offered competition. Great Barrington's G-Bar-S Ranch had trail skiing on only three inches of snow. The state government involved itself in the state forests at Eastern Mountain and Beartown, in South Lee. The Mount Greylock Ski Club quickly sought out Civilian Conservation Corps (CCC) labor to clear the Thunderbolt. This trail immediately became the only first-class racing trail in the state. When a journalist, by way of praise, called it "almost as difficult as the Taft" in New Hampshire, the president of the Mount Greylock Ski Club bridled at that description; he considered it "a good deal more difficult." The Massachusetts State Championships were run there in February 1936. The speed with which the club countered the journalist's opinion of the Taft and Thunderbolt Trails suggests just how important racing—and expert racing—had become. As in earlier times, jumping had been the crowd-drawing spectacle, so in the mid-1930s the reckless downhill aces—*Kanonen* they were called—meant not merely prestige but an economic lift to the region on race day and kudos for the hosting club as well.

Other notable areas were Pioneer Valley, especially the Chickley Alp development in Charlemont boasting a "two-directional horizontal tow from skiing area and refreshment hut," and the Black Panther Ski Center at Huntington, north of Northampton. At Holyoke, Mount Tom had six novice trails. The Worcester Speedway boasted day and night skiing in 1939, a long way in time and attitude from Sverre Lund, immigrant from Drammen, Norway, setting up the New England Ski Club in the city that held its first race in 1904.

Near Boston, devotees could ski at the floodlit Commonwealth Country Club in Newton; Marlboro's Jericho Hill was also favored. There was a trail and an open slope at Shrewsbury. Melrose and Woburn drew local enthusiasts, as did the Blue Hills, already noted by Dr. Andreas Christian in 1910. Amesbury's Lock Hill, with two parallel rope tows and floodlighting, was one of the few places you could ski and look over the ocean. The *New England Downhill Ski Travelers Log* took up an entire page of the *Boston Herald* at the start of the 1935–36 season. Massachusetts had sixteen listings in all, of which eleven were designated novice. Vermont, by comparison, had fifteen, and New Hampshire, fifty-five.

So much for description. The Pittsfield Chamber of Commerce had a free booklet and map of local trails ready for the 1934–35 season. This was replaced the next year by the Mount Greylock Ski Club's Berkshire Ski Map of thirty-three trails. The first complete guide to "all forty-six Massachusetts winter sport locations" was available by Christmas 1938. Much of the reason the "skiing bug had bitten hard," to use *Appalachia*'s expression, was based on the Thunderbolt racing trail. The AMC, the Hochgebirge, and other clubs had conducted a "constant search for new skiing regions of promise" ever since 1928. That was the year that the Arlberg downhill and slalom became the passion. A "sporty run," meaning in 1929, "a series of problems none of which can be solved," was by 1936 a race trail through the Needle's Eye, timed with the use of two short-wave radio sets. As racing became increasingly attractive, more and more competitors were involved, so much so that Otto Schniebs felt it necessary to call for "Sanity in Competition," opposing the "Win or Die" attitude and calling for "no-fall" downhill races. In 1939, the Mount Greylock Ski Club Race was run as a no-fall race, and the following year, it was run as a giant slalom.

If you wanted to race—almost if you wished to ski—you had to become a member of a club. The United States Eastern Amateur Ski Association was founded in 1922. In 1934, fifteen of the fifty-five member clubs were from Massachusetts; by 1941 the number had grown to forty-five out of a total of one hundred. Seventy-seven different clubs from the state comprised about 25 percent of Eastern's membership throughout the 1930s.

These clubs were varied. There were the powerful moneyed organizations such as the Appalachian Mountain Club and the Hochgebirge that were joined by many town, college, and school clubs. Locals capitalized on their exotic past (the Innitou Ski Runners of Woburn) or presented a devil-may-care attitude (Lowell's Black and Blue Trail Smashers), and even the prestigious Mount Greylock Ski Club's official publication was called *Bruises and Blisters*.

In 1935, the Western Massachusetts Winter Sports Committee that had laid out the Thunderbolt Trail, interested the state, the United States Department of the Interior, and the CCC to help with the construction of skiing trails. The committee's second annual conference that year promised "to touch on almost every phase of winter sports activity." The speech by state commissioner of conservation Samuel A. York's, "Winter Sports in the State Forests," was well received. Indeed, it was a state forester who suggested that Mount Grace be developed "to provide work for the men of the Warwick Transient Camp as well as better recreational facilities in western Massachusetts." In 1938, the Industrial and Development Commission first portrayed the state as "Nature's Gift to Skiers" in a drab full-page advertisement that gave equal space to skiing, skating, tobogganing, and snowshoeing. It was quite different the next year when "Millions of Flakes of Fun in Massachusetts" promised—from the look of things—fast and handsome *Geländespringer* (terrain jumpers) and chic *Skihaserle* (ski bunnies) for "Hills and Valleyfuls of glorious sporting snow." That year the national *Ski Annual* ran two pages promoting skiing in Oregon and at Mont Tremblant in the Laurentians of Quebec, along with one full page each for Sun Valley, Idaho, the Canadian Rockies, and Vermont. Later issues would advertise Alta in Utah and the skiing joys of Colorado. Patently there was an effort by the state's Industrial and Development Commission to give a boost to what we now call the ski industry.

The commission's brochure for 1938 listed forty-seven ski sites, including New Ashford's Night Hill, "easily illuminated by auto headlights," and Bousquet's "tremendous sweeping run" of 835 yards. By 1940, fifty-seven runs were detailed, and the brochure was published in cooperation with the Massachusetts State Planning Board, the New England Council, the Western Massachusetts Winter Sports Committee, and the Department of Conservation.

Skiing as a necessary means of locomotion in the 1870s had fifty years later become a social sport, with the attendant modern features. Nowhere was this more obvious than in the role played by the urban center of Boston. When Dr. Andreas Christian was interviewed in 1910, although there were no successful ski factories in the eastern United States, skis could be brought in by rail from the Scandinavian immigrant-founded factories in Minnesota and Wisconsin as well as imported from Europe. Iver Johnson, Wright and Ditson, and Spalding carried skis for their Boston population. With the rush to Alpine enjoyment in the 1930s, a number of specialty shops catered to the discerning sportsman, while large department stores advertised a wide range of skis, boots, poles, and fashion items. The 1930s snow train era—first from Boston and then, because of its success, from New York—socialized skiing; the city's middling classes enjoyed their amusements in snow and sun. The Boston-centered clubs provided the leadership in discovering skiing venues, in popularizing the sport, and in building trails, tows, and even the country's only aerial tram in Franconia Notch, a 150 miles north in the White Mountains of New Hampshire.

Geography turned Boston's interest toward New Hampshire. Western Massachusetts relied more on the north-south corridor of the Connecticut and Hudson Rivers as access routes to its snowy delights. As winter tourism brought revenue to the Berkshires, the Western Massachusetts Winter Sports Committee capitalized on Depression-spawned agencies to upgrade the region's ski centers.

State government, in the form of the Industrial and Development Commission, understandably saw vast revenue possibilities as winter business became highly competitive in the years before World War II. Now there was, after all, a vast pool of skiers. A transportation network existed whereby entrepreneurs of bus, rail, and plane—not to speak of the growth in the number of automobile owners—could capitalize on a skiing population in Boston and New York.

Equipment was available in the city centers as well as in the suburbs and other towns throughout the state. And mechanical lifts, parking lots, inns, and resting houses all now existed. Sherwood Anderson in his 1940 *Home Town* described winter as "waiting time," but even he noted that "the boys have taken up the new sport of skiing." The necessary infrastructure was in place for the spectacular ski boom of the postwar era.

CHAPTER 2

IMMIGRANTS AND THEIR SKIS
FOR A MAINE WINTER

While the main stages of skiing history lie elsewhere, Maine nevertheless provided two unique contributions. One is the first documented account of people on skis in the northeastern United States, from William Widgery Thomas's community of New Sweden in 1871. This presents an opportunity to look at the transfer of skiing culture from the old country to the new land. The second is the production of America's first "How to Skee" book. Published in 1905 by the Theo. Johnsen Company of Portland, *The Winter Sport of Skeeing* primarily appealed to a wealthy clientele who enjoyed sporting on skis, something quite different from the utilitarian activities of Maine's immigrant Swedes.

To give some perspective on Maine's contributions, it is appropriate to make some generalizations about what constituted the sport of skiing in the United States. Skiing itself is at least seven or eight thousand years old, and presently the Chinese are claiming an earlier vintage. Associated with nomadic hunting, some Norse gods and at least one goddess, folklore, and myth, in the nineteenth century skiing became a Scandinavian, and particularly Norwegian, preserve. When those northern folk took to skiing, they thought of it in terms of *idræt* (Norwegian) and *idrott* (Swedish), words that were always translated into English as "sport" but mean so much more; they carried a cultural heritage that nineteenth-century Norse savants had molded into a nationalistic morality brought about by muscular effort in God's great outdoors. Oversimplifying, a skier, for this bookish elite, was a secularized muscular Christian. These attitudes were brought to the United States by Scandinavian immigrants who arrived in increasing numbers in the latter half of the nineteenth century. We should not make too much of this, since in 1880 out of a total of 18,822 foreign-born in Maine, 99 were Norwegians and 988 were Swedish. By 1900 there were 509 Norwegians and 1,945 Swedes. However, it is significant that at the Maine State Fair, held at Lewiston in September 1885, "a novel and entertaining feature . . . was the exhibit of the Swedish colony" that included "sno-shoes (*sno—skidor*) ten feet in length." One ski pole was pictured among the various items on exhibit.

The larger groups of immigrant Scandinavians settled mostly in what was called the Northwest, now the Midwest, and, indeed, a Norwegian-language journal provides the first known record of a person on skis in the United States near Beloit, Wisconsin, in 1841. In the Midwest and in the Californian gold mining camps of the Sierra Nevada, individuals on skis hunted, collected taxes, delivered mail, and were married. Skis were essentially utilitarian equipment used as they had been in the old country. But as winter closed mining activities, the Californians developed a unique form of down-mountain racing on short courses of one to two thousand feet. Camp rivalry provided the impulse, and liquor and prize money added a festive ingredient to the fun and frolics of a carnival race meeting. These races depended for speed on what they called "dope," secret wax formulae of such ingredients as balsam, paraffin, camphor, resin, and spermaceti. Frank Stewart from Skowhegan was one of the best-known makers; his secret mix went with him to the grave. In the Midwest, immigrant communities took to ski jumping as a way of promoting their club and town. By 1905—the year that Theo. Johnsen published his booklet in Portland—events in Michigan were sufficiently organized to effect a National Ski Association to regulate the sport.

It was different in Maine. In the post–Civil War decades, the rural population was declining, and vast areas of northern and western Maine were open lands. In March 1869 the state resolved "to promote the settlement of the public and other lands" by appointing three commissioners of settlement. One of them, William Widgery Thomas, Jr., had extensive diplomatic experience as U.S. ambassador to Sweden for Presidents Arthur and Harrison. Thomas had lived among the Swedes for years and was impressed with their hardy quality. He was held in high esteem by them. He returned to the United States convinced that Swedes would make just the right sort of settlers for Maine. When he was appointed consul in Goteborg (Gothenburg), he made immediate plans for encouraging Swedes to emigrate to America. Undeterred by the failure of a group of Maine gentlemen to procure Swedish labor in 1864, he raised money from private sources to send veterans from the 1864 war in Denmark to fight in America. Then he had a larger vision. He proposed to find "twenty-five stalwart young men with thrifty wives and families" to settle in Aroostook County. He recruited the colonists and brought them over to Halifax, Nova Scotia. Twenty-two men, eleven women, and eighteen children arrived in New Sweden on July 23, 1870.

The first two public buildings of the community were the church and the school, the latter opening on November 13, 1871. That first winter some parents with two children in school came for examination day on skis, pulling their baby on a sled. Thomas took pains to show the legislature how highly education was prized by the immigrants. Some children, as he pointed out, came five miles to school, "slipping over the snow on *skidor*, Swedish snow-shoes." Other immigrants may have been on skis in New England before these new-to-Maine folk, but Thomas's description stands as the earliest unequivocal record of the use of skis in the Northeast. He repeated this story as he chronicled New Sweden's success on the tenth and twenty-fifth anniversaries. Elsewhere, he remembered a row of skis lining the outside wall, "a strange sight in a Yankee school house." In Clarence Pullen's *In Fair Aroostook*, published in 1902, there is exactly this picture of the teacher with his class and three pairs of homemade skis standing against the wall. For these immigrants, skis were nothing but utilitarian, to get the kids to school and the family to church. What had been good for *Gamle Sverige* was good for New Sweden. But there were other uses, too. In 1899, a new sort of ski stick was seen at Houlton, Fort Fairfield, and in other villages along the Canadian line. They were made of metal. And, says a newspaper report, "it was also noticed that as they became more plentiful, the price of whisky grew less." There was plenty for sale, and yet the revenue did not increase in proportion to sales. That alerted the customs officers, who quickly learned of this new device. The metal sticks were hollow, the report explained, and the inside of the larger ones could hold nearly a gallon. These poles became extremely popular, and parties of half a dozen men made trips over the line in the morning, then "stopping at a saloon to quench their thirst," they filled up their sticks and came home "much refreshed from their healthy exercise in the fresh air."

Meantime, the price of liquor had gone down . . . and so an investigation took place. When the first snow came the following year, the revenue men were on hand to confiscate the sticks, "since which time the ski parties have not been so frequent." No doubt about it, the reporter was siding with those Mainers taking their fresh dose of *idrott*-air.

As Swedish immigrants settled in other parts of Maine, about a thousand by 1873, they had found the native Indian snowshoe the only method for snow travel. Downeast hunters on snowshoes found themselves in a bind when Swedish immigrant Frederick Jorgensen arrived as game warden in the Wilson Mills area in 1902. In that part of the state, no one had seen a pair of skis before, and Jorgensen was ridiculed while the merits of snowshoe and ski were debated. Inevitably there had to be a race. Jorgensen was home before the snowshoer had reached the halfway mark. Poachers particularly took notice. In fact, Jorgensen's skis became an "everlasting trademark," and from time to time he removed them, he said, "because if I got off the highway on skis it would have been a dead giveaway. . . . When people saw my tracks it was as if a loud speaker had announced over the countryside, The Warden Is Coming!"

Jorgensen's ability to move through the woods—over fifty miles a day in good going—was not lost on other state wildlife employees. Chief Warden H. O. Templeton took to a motorcycle in the summer and skis in the winter, traveling "a pile of country in a day" and caught "the up river gentry snowshoed and red handed." The *Machias Republican* in 1910 was impressed enough to print a reader's admiration in ten verses, one of which read,

> But when the winter came around
> What did the farmers see?
> But Warden H. O. Templeton
> A going on a skee.

The verse ended by suggesting that poaching would be possible only if Templeton, with his motorcycle and skis, moved on:

> And now the farmers' only hope is
> That some day he will move,
> And in another section,
> With his skees and cycle rove.

Although the skis that Warden Templeton and the immigrants used could have been made in Scandinavia, immigrants tended to make their own from local wood. A pair of very rough ash skis has turned up near Damariscotta, the sort of skis a farmer might tramp around on. The longest known skis in New England, 11 feet and 8 inches, and 11 feet and 8¾ inches, are on view in a lodge in Bethel. Unfortunately, very little is known of their provenance, but they are probably from the Norway–South Paris region. In New Sweden, birch was popular. Extant skis made in New Sweden around 1900–1910 have one aspect unique in the history of American skiing: they are of unequal length. Such skis were common in Scandinavia, the short ski with pelt-covered bottom was for pushing, and the other one, often longer by as much as four feet, for gliding. "I started out," Henry Anderson of New Sweden told an interviewer, "by making the regular Jemtland ski which we call long skis, one short, one long," in 1926. Others he made were known for their width; they were "two inchers." Turn-of-the-century New Sweden skis, however, show only a very small difference in length. Lars Stadig's skis, for example, differed by eight inches. One pushing ski from Madawaska with no skin underneath was nine feet and eleven inches, the gliding ski eleven feet and nine inches, both with similar grooves.

By that time, skiing had outgrown its utilitarian emphasis and had moved into the realm of the "skisport," a direct translation of the Norwegian ideal of *ski-idræt*. There had been indications of skiing as a leisure activity as early as 1895, when members of the snowshoe section of the Appalachian Mountain Club headquartered themselves at the Oxford Hotel in Fryeburg and recorded their success on the summit of Pleasant Mountain. An impressive display of webbing dominates the photograph in front of the Fryeburg Hotel, even though there was one "skee-man" on the trip. In other places in the Northeast the thrill of the "skeeist's" speed, as opposed to the "swish-and-walk-a-mile" of the snowshoer, was gaining attention.

If the AMC's 1895 excursion to Fryeburg had a social and organized quality to it, those who emulated the summer hike to mountaintops in winter displayed a more rugged individualism. The idea of mountaineering on skis was influenced by upper-class English sportsmen who enjoyed conquering yet another part of the world. This was a personal engagement between man and nature, and, once accomplished, one believed oneself to be more manly and more moral. Not all who climbed mountains on skis had such Victorian and Edwardian conceptions, of course, but remarkable was the strong sense of disciplined fitness experienced by those who took to ski ascents. Some even tried to influence others with this Americanized *idræt*. They were a select few, however, and many knew each other, or of each other.

For instance, in Maine, Norman Libby from Bridgton was attracted to Mount Washington, where for some years he had a hand in editing the summer news sheet *Among the Clouds*. We will hear of him again later. While he was enjoying skiing in the Bridgton area, college men had taken it up in New Hampshire and in the Midwest. Martin Strand's ski factory in Minnesota had eleven years of production behind it in 1907. The National Ski Association, headquartered at Ishpeming in the Upper Peninsula of Michigan, oversaw tournament activity from 1905. That year, the anti-Semitic and patrician Lake Placid Club remained open for the winter for the first time. On the more popular level, back in 1886, Pennsylvania readers of the *Wilkes-Barre Times Leader* were told that "'skeeing', a new fun in Maine, is sliding down hill on shoes five feet long." A few years later, in 1894, folk in the Midwest could read that the "Scandinavian and Finnish sport of skeeing has struck Maine this winter." It was "imported a few weeks ago by a gentleman just returned from Finland and has spread rapidly." Those well-crafted 11-feet-and-8-inch skis mentioned earlier may well be of Finnish origin. And, as we shall see, Theo. Johnsen planned on advertising to the Finn communities in their own language. This news snippet of 1894 found its way into eleven Kansas papers and one each in Oklahoma and Indiana. *Leslie's* got it exactly right in 1893 when it pronounced that "skiing is one of our foreign importations which is absolutely unobjectionable." By the turn of the century, there was a sense that America, left breathless by the ever-increasing pace of industrialism, could find a healthy release from its nervousness in this splendid outdoor sport. "Many people were out snowshoeing and skiing Sunday," reported the *Bangor Daily News* in 1900; specially noted was the otherworldliness of trips "in the bright starlight Saturday night."

In 1905, the Theo. Johnsen Company of Portland tried to capitalize on this growing interest by producing finely made skis and accessories under their own Tajco label. *The Winter Sport of Skeeing*, a quality catalog, half marketing tool, half instructional manual, spread the word. Although there had been a number of articles in the popular press on making skis and how and where to ski, the Johnsen catalog was the first publication in the United States to cover most aspects of the sport. Finding it impressive, the editor of the *Ishpeming Iron Ore*, the home of the National Ski Association and the center of the many immigrant skiing communities in the Upper Peninsula of Michigan, reprinted part of the manual in his newspaper.

A close look at the catalog's design and production reveals considerable information, including the fact that "skees" were available for youths at five and six feet, for ladies at seven feet, and for men at eight feet. These were the "popular models," worked on "true lines," which meant straight-grained and no knots. The five-footers were $2.25, and eight-footers, $3.50. Then came three varieties of "special-type" "skees," one for "coasting and all around skee sport," and two of "selected stock" suitable for any kind of snow. Jumping models had finishes of light natural wood, dark natural wood, black, and black with white grooves; the selection was staggering. Prices ranged from $2.25 to $18 for a ten-foot "special high grade skee of extra quality, specially prepared stock." Bindings ranged from loose leather wrapping lines at $1.00 to bamboo encased in leather at $2.50 to an expert binding with a rubber mat under the shoe, an aluminum plate, toe irons, and an adjustable leather heel strap for $4.00.

"No *skidor* [using the Swedish word] is well equipped unless he has at least one pair of push sticks and one long stick to use as occasion may require." Bamboo sticks, four-and-a-half feet long, started at $1.50 a pair; a six-foot single ash stick was also $1.50. A locking pair, which could double as a single pole, was $3.00. The single pole, a strong staff of five to six feet, was the usual equipment. Scandinavians did not necessarily use poles, but those who were learning needed them to balance and brake. The use of two poles—common in Finland—became normal only around 1920.

Low moccasins and high moccasins were the cheaper footwear, at $3.25 and $4.50. For those who could afford the best, Johnsen offered a "special Norwegian skee shoe, grain leather, hand sewed, made particularly for skee sport" at $12.00 a pair. Socks, heavy woolen leggings, a toque, and two pairs of gloves completed the outfit. The skier's investment ranged from $15.00 to $45.00, not to speak of the possibility of knickerbockers and a double-breasted jacket that Johnsen suggested was most suitable. It was advisable to buy different skis, not just because one pair was for coasting, one for jumping, and the third for all-around skisport, but also because different types of skis ran better on different types of snow, which could be "downy, fluffy, powdery, sandy, dusty, flowery, crystalline, brittle, gelatinous, salt-like, slithery, and watery." Is it any wonder that Johnsen advertised so many selections? Even then, it was expensive to ski unless you made your own equipment.

However much Johnsen wished to sell special skis for different events, the East did not offer the competitive network of clubs and tournaments. There were no college outing clubs, and little enthusiasm for winter out of doors that could be found in the organized skisport in the Midwest. The only competition in Maine was a by-product of the utilitarian aspect of skiing: Was the ski faster than the snowshoe? Would a warden on skis catch more poachers than one on snowshoes? Johnsen—an immigrant from Britain—had changed his name from the British Johnson to the Swedish Johnsen when he married a Swede and became enthusiastic about skiing. He appealed to communities of Finns in West Paris and South Thomaston by advertising in their language. But even those did not produce any of the cross-country races they were used to in the old country. Ten years later, in April 1917, the Finnish Ski Company of South Paris advertised its "High Grade Finland and Swedish Skis and Ski Poles" in the *Chamber of Commerce Journal of Maine*.

If towns in the Midwest brought in top jumpers to secure an economic lift, in Maine locals jumped off little "thankee ma'ams" to add to the thrill of a meadow glide. The Johnsen company did not attempt to control the development of the skisport for economic advantage but simply to engender interest in what immigrants perceived as a glorious activity, and if money could be made out of it, so much the better. Johnsen marketed his skis widely by advertising in many of the middling classes' papers, such as *Youths Companion* and the *National Sportsman*. Records show he spent $1,921 promoting skiing for the 1905–6 season. In today's value that is close on $44,000. His sales force reached as far west as Salt Lake City, traveling with exactly made scale models rather than sending out skis by bulk on consignment. Out in Wisconsin, Norwegian immigrant Martin Strand, who had been manufacturing skis since 1896, admired the quality of the Johnsen skis but knew exactly why they failed to sell: they were priced too high. "The average young American is a sort of hot house plant, who does not care to spend much time out of doors, as the cheap show houses and pool rooms seem to be more attractive. They do not want to spend enough money on a pair of skis so that cheap skis are the only ones that have sold in any quantity in this country up to the present time." The market was simply not there for the high-quality products of the Portland company and, indeed, Johnsen was forced to stop production after two seasons.

Johnsen's *Winter Sport of Skeeing* holds great interest because it portrays aspects of skiing that combined the cultural traditions from Scandinavia and the foundations of modern sport—aspects that were becoming increasingly apparent, particularly in towns. Johnsen was aware of the enthusiasm for skiing in the Midwest and of the isolated interest in New England but was prepared to instruct the wealthier sections of society and to show the appeal of skiing's outdoor enjoyment, its sporting allure, even while retaining vestiges of the heritage associated with *idræt*.

From the instructional section, Mainers could learn to stand properly, herringbone up a hill, do a kick turn, climb sideways, stem, and stop by stick riding "but only in cases of extreme need." The Telemark swing was given pride of place. "The excitement reaches its climax when the skidor, speeding down a sharp slope, strikes some inequality of ground or artificial rise and bounds through the air for a distance." A jump of a yard or two would whet the appetite for more.

Johnsen's catalog portrayed the *ski-idræt* as something in which "a man—or a woman for that matter"—could "breathe in the clear crisp air and feasting the eyes on the passing landscape, enjoy its myriad panoramic charms." The catalog thus promoted the sport as a source of health and morality in a natural outdoor setting, exercising "wits as well as muscles," as one of his advertisements put it. Skiers were privileged, in a pantheistic sense, to experience "the enchantment of a picturesque country in a snowy shroud." These carefully worked descriptions acquainted those who knew little or nothing of *idræt* with the concept of skiing as a means to achieving a natural experience in God's winter countryside. Many if not most sports have their origins in religious rites. Skiing, although it arose out of necessity, had similar roots; Ullr, one of the most powerful of the Norse gods, was its protector, and for women, there was the goddess Skade. This secular religious tradition, still attached to nineteenth-century skiing, was not lost on Johnsen as he attempted to pass on the Scandinavian winter heritage to Maine's better sort.

But out of business he was in 1907. Perhaps he should have persevered; for a decade later isolated hostelries began to sense that those who enjoyed Maine-woods hospitality in the summer might be tapped for winter business too. As early as 1913, one of the owners of the Poland Springs Hotel spent the winter in Switzerland "taking notes with a view to developing winter sports on a large scale." Before the Great War, Switzerland was invaded by the English upper classes, who appropriated both the art of skiing and the ritual of après-ski. They formed clubs, instituted tests, required instruction, reserved hotels exclusively for themselves, insisted on tea, pressured local railways for reduced fares, and imported English society holiday culture to a number of Swiss villages. The Poland Springs Hotel, like many of the grand hotels in the woods and mountains of New England, aped what the English wealthy considered proper, and skiing became one of the attractions. In 1915 the Bethel Inn advertised its snow delights, too, along with all the "real sports of winter," in which "snowshoeing over wonderful trails through pine and balsam forests" was obviously the most "real." But along with tobogganing, skating, and sleigh riding, skiing also found a niche in the inn's advertisement in the Portland *Eastern Argus*. In 1917, the Portland Country Club's "biggest carnival yet" included a skiing exhibition for the first time. It apparently did not impress; only the hockey match was reported in the following day's paper.

It is significant that the hoteliers took to advertising their winter delights in the newspapers. There was evidently a city clientele to be encouraged to spend leisure time and money in the pure air of Bethel and Poland Springs. The refreshing aspect of a winter sojourn was an appeal to the wealthy urbanite. And then perhaps even middle-class men and women might be attracted to skiing if they encountered its appeal. The Portland carnival provided such an incentive.

These modern trends, along with the formation of clubs, competitions, and manufacturing enterprises that would emerge in the 1920s, were built on the first fifty years of ski activity in the state, during which the utilitarian use of skis gave over to recreational development. Johnsen's promotion of "skeeing" and the inns' promise of winter delights provide an insight into cultural transference when skiing was becoming a sport and a business—harbingers of things to come.

This transference of cultural values continued into the 1930s. Take, for example, the "marathons." Although there had been a "100 Miles of Hell" race from Portland to Berlin, New Hampshire, in 1926, it was a publicity stunt between two Berlin boys, Bob Reid and Oscar Oakerlund, rather than a race. The wicked weather had forced postponements, required medical attention for the racers, and should have been a forewarning never to try such a race again. But the idea of distance racing was kept alive by immigrant Swedes and Norwegians. In New Sweden, they were sitting around discussing the last five-mile race, and according to Harold Bondeson, the "idea developed of a real long race." Bondeson knew what he was talking about, for he was one of the six New Sweden runners (of twelve competitors) in the 1935 Fort Fairfield 100-miler, and third in the 1937 Bangor-to-Caribou 179-mile race. It is not difficult to understand the proposal of such tests; Sweden's *Vassaloppet*, a ninety-kilometer (fifty-six miles) run from Salen to Mora, was inaugurated in 1922, and Norway's *Birkebeinerrennet*, from Rena to Lillehammer, fifty-four kilometers (thirty-four miles), in 1932. Both were almost instantly part of the nationalistic cannon of the countries and remain so to this day. Here, then, was one major impetus for the Maine proposal. But they also transformed it by carrying Marathon Mail—treasured by those interested in historical philately—in the Bangor-to-Caribou run. That was the last of those runs. Another that Mainers took part in was the Rivière-du-Loup marathon up in Quebec. If those town-to-town marathons in Maine (and New Hampshire) are no more, the present-day Canadian marathon has a growing clientele up in Quebec and finds many Americans going north for that annual extravaganza.

In a different vein altogether, yet indicative of the continued interest in support for the culture of the Northlands, a musical evening was a great success for Houlton's 1934 concert lovers. Miss Mary Burpee, soloist, Marjorie Turner, accompanist, and violinist Harold Inman put on a formidable evening, starting with Stradella's *Pieta Signore*. Then Miss Turner gave a solo piano rendition of an adagio from Beethoven's *Moonlight Sonata*. Three French pieces followed, by Chaminade, Massenet, and Saint-Saëns. Tchaikovsky, Schubert, Fibich, Brahms, Grieg, and Dvorak were also performed. It was a true "musicale," as the *Bangor Daily News* enthused. And then the violinist struck up with a piece by Henry Clough-Leighter—I had never heard of him—"My Lover He Comes on the Skee," sung by Miss Burpee. This anonymous Norwegian folk song was translated into English by Hjalmar Hjorth Boyesen, who was well known in America:

> My lover, he comes on the skee
> And his staff o'er his head he is swinging
> The hawk in the air is not fleeter than he
> As he scuds o'er the snow on the skee, on the skee,
> And the wind in his wake is singing
> The wind in his wake is singing.

The Boston Music Company, printing the work in 1901, explained that a "skee" was a "Norwegian Snow Shoe." The 1934 audience would instantly hark back to tales of Ullr and Skade, to mythical Trysil Knud, even perhaps to the Lapp (Sami today) lover recorded by Schefferus in the seventeenth century. This lover coming on skee had two centuries behind him and was vibrant enough to add support to the Houlton cultural mix in the mid-1930s. Norse heritage was alive and well in Maine.

Figure 1. The artist may have got it all wrong; single poles were out of fashion a good ten years before this attractive girl, incorrectly dressed, skied into family homes in February 1931. *Comfort,* whose circulation had been over a million, was advocating what it imagined was possible for rural women. Author archive.

At the same time, Maine was "edging into the winter sports picture" in 1936 with the state's ski capital at Fryeburg, where an active winter sports committee created one of the biggest open slopes in New England and a novice trail, both served by a ski tow. Fryeburg benefitted from the booming Mt. Washington Valley ski developments in neighboring New Hampshire, and was one of twelve ski-minded towns to join the Western Maine Winter Sports Association in 1936: Andover, Bethel, Bridgton, Casco, Fryeburg, Harrison, Norway, South Paris, Rumford,

Sebago, Sweden (not to be confused with New Sweden), and Waterford. By 1938, for the Maine State Championships, Rumford could bring in Dartmouth star John Litchfield (later to double for Jimmy Stewart in the film *Mortal Storm*); Warren Chivers, 1937 National Champion also from Dartmouth; and Birger Torrissen, one of the Connecticut contenders for the Olympic team. This was the heart of Maine skiing as war became reality in Europe. What happened in Maine at the end of the 1930s and into the 1940s was that different hills in various parts of the state began to be developed. There was little coordination. "For years, Eastern and Northern Maine have wanted to bring the public's attention to their sport," wrote the *Bangor Daily News* toward the end of the 1939–40 season, "to make known the ski opportunities in their various communities." To this end a news-laden publication geared for those sections of Maine was launched: *Ski Heil*. The title was important; this was an appeal to the German *Schuss*, the world of alpine skiing, not to Maine's reputable cross-country history. Mount Desert tows were featured, and the Caribou Northmen's club trail was a broad, fast run, "one of the best in Maine." Millinocket planned a new trail that "takes the sportsman right down to the door of the newly built lodge." There was skiing at the Arlberg Ski Club of Belfast, and Bangor's 1940 new ski school was run by William Eldredge, "a product of the world-famous Hannes Schneider Eastern Slope Ski School." Certainly, Maine was doing more than merely edging into winter sports as the war became increasingly likely. Still, there remained something of the experimental nature of skiing when the University of Maine's Orono campus held a carnival in February 1944: three of the sixteen events were the ski dash for men and women, and a "novelty ski climb up the ski slope." Dashes, obstacle races, skijoring—initiated at Camden in January 1941—all date back to the early days of skiing.

In the post–World War II decades, Maine has provided formidable alpine ski areas, such as Sugarloaf, while continuing a cross-country tradition based in Rumford. That community's success in taking over the events from a weather-plagued Lake Placid in 1950 provided a firm foundation, including world events sponsored by the Fédération internationale de ski (FIS) and various U.S. National Championships, including the first North American Women's Ski Jumping Championship in 1996. Rumford has also hosted biathlon championships, and the center at Fort Kent on the Canadian border hosted the 2011 FIS World Championships, bringing 250 competitors from thirty countries to northern Maine. As all over the skiing world, the COVID pandemic put events on hold. However, the 2021–22 season showed that Maine's place in the New England alpine and cross-country competitive and recreational pleasure economy seems as secure as any of the other New England states.

CHAPTER 3

BERLIN AND THE BIG NANSEN

Five miles north of Berlin, New Hampshire, on Route 16, you will find a mighty wooden structure at the Nansen Wayside Park. In 1938, this was the most famous of America's ski jumps. For years there was a hope that it would be put on the historic register, but because of lack of funds and political will, that did not happen. It is an impressive memorial to Norwegian explorer Fridtjof Nansen and to Berlin's Nansen Ski Club. In 1938, the year the jump opened, it was selected for Olympic tryouts; jumpers leaped from "the world's largest ski tower," as advertised in the souvenir program, and the meet was broadcast from coast to coast.

Berlin had already been on America's ski map for fifty years. The founding of the Nansen Ski Club is shrouded in mystery; the older records have disappeared, one account book has the first fifty pages cut out, and club fact sheets list no sources. The early years of the *Berlin Reporter* (late 1890s) contain nothing on local skiing. It is claimed that a ski club was founded by and for Scandinavians and their descendants in 1872. The late Alf Halvorson—for years the mainstay of the club—on an oral history tape in 1972 told why 1872 was the founding date: the figures "1-8-7-2" were up on the old chimney of the Brown Company sawmill. I have been unable to find any photo of the sawmill chimney with those figures on it, but I have found one with the figures "1-8-9-0." Forty years before that taped interview, at a 1932 meeting of the United States Eastern Amateur Ski Association (USEASA), Alf Halvorson urged that the following year its convention should be held in Berlin, it "being the 50th anniversary of the founding of the Nansen Ski Club so it would stimulate activities in the club and also in the surrounding towns." Further, in 1936, Harold Grinden, the historian of the National Ski Association, in a discussion of the oldest ski club in America, writes that he had received a letter from Halvorson saying that the Nansen Club "was founded by a group of Scandinavians on January 15, 1882, and was known as 'The Ski Club.'" This thirst for firsts is bound up with pride of positioning in the bragging rights for ski history. When Halvorson was writing, Berlin was in competition with, particularly, Brattleboro in Vermont. In Berlin, however, immigrant Norwegians who came to work for a logging concern first took to skiing as they had done in the old country. In the early 1870s, about thirty families were located in Norway Village in the northern section of Berlin (today's Norway Street). Here is where Halvorson's claims of the 1872 Skiklubben (using the Norwegian word) originate. Members, we are told, paid no dues but agreed to clear trails summer and winter, and to build a hut and so on. The Skiklubben became known as the Berlin Mills Ski Club, and in the early years of the twentieth century as the Fridtjof Nansen Ski Club in honor of the Norwegian explorer. As more French-speaking Quebec laborers arrived, the name Fridtjof was dropped, and so in 1912 it became the Nansen Ski Club, a name it proudly bears to this day. Until 1912, only Scandinavians could join; minutes of meetings were written in Norwegian. Even in the late 1920s, one excellent young skier, Sel Hannah, who went on to captain Dartmouth College's ski team and who would have competed for the 1940 Olympic team, recalled that "before big meets, you'd go hoping to be picked. Half the time, meetings would be conducted in Norwegian. Sometimes if you hadn't close ties to Norwegians then you wouldn't be chosen."

Fridtjof Nansen was very important not just to his compatriots in Berlin but also as a world figure. In a recent analysis, I claim that he was one of three men (Englishman Arnold Lunn and Austrian Hannes Schneider are the other two) who provided the foundation for modern skiing. Nansen crossed the lower third of Greenland with five others in 1888. In 1890, his book *Paa Ski over Grønland* was immediately translated into German and English and became what I can best describe as an outdoorsman's bestseller. What held so much appeal was, as shown in the introduction, the manly physicalness of skiing and its tie to Norwegian nationalism; "skiing was of greater national importance than is generally supposed."

Nansen was, of course, talking of Norwegian nationalism. Norway became free from Sweden in 1905. Nansen was immediately sent to Great Britain as the country's ambassador, and later he became a world figure, receiving the Nobel Peace Prize in 1922 for his humanitarian relief work after World War I. That was only seven years before he came to Berlin (and Maine) on one of his lecture tours. There was local apprehension in town "lest his actual presence should dim the luster of his fame." In 1980, I asked Otto Mason, who had been in charge of the upkeep of the Nansen jump for over forty years, if he had ever met Nansen:

MASON: Yes. Back in 1930. I didn't meet him really; there were too many important people around him.
ALLEN: So you didn't talk to him?
MASON: No.
ALLEN: Did he really mean something to you then?
MASON: [*vehemently*] Why wouldn't he? Didn't George Washington mean something to you? He was bigger to us than the president. He was an honorable member of our club.

Ski jumping in Berlin began in Norway Village and moved to Paine's Meadow, where Carnival jumps were held starting in 1906. In 1921 a major structure was erected, with a run-out of about 170 feet. There was a hope that this would develop local talent to the extent that one or two jumpers could go to Holmenkollen in Norway in 1924. This did not happen.

The jump was enlarged in 1927. The best-remembered ski jumper in Berlin is Ingvald "Bing" Anderson, who has become legendary. Locals will allow little talk of stories of his forging checks, being jailed for auto theft, obtaining loans under false pretenses, or having committed murder in New Brunswick, Canada, for which he paid with his life. Otto Mason, for example, and many of the jumping fraternity in town when I talked to them in the early 1980s, tended to give Bing a clean record. They would enthuse over his exploits on the jumping hills: in 1922 six firsts, including two hill records at Berlin and at Brattleboro, along with one second and a third; three firsts in 1923, including a hill record at Bristol, and a second out in Revelstoke, British Columbia, with a mighty leap of 172 feet.

Ski jumping by "sky riders" making "daring bounds" was considered by most folk as the most thrilling event of the skisport. "At best," judged the *Literary Digest* in 1934, "all other forms of ski-sport remain a dull and uninteresting rival for the gagging thrill of the ski jumpers' soaring flight from the take-off to a wild, sliding landing, and a sudden, slithering stop in a shower of flying snowflakes on the flat at the very feet of the spectators." That is, by the 1930s, ski jumping held such a place in the skiing world that skiing almost became a spectator sport. The city of Berlin decided to play a major role. In 1936 it bought just over eight acres of land from the Brown Company for $75 ($1,400 today), and with $1,100 ($20,500) coming from the Nansen Ski Club, and a further $1,400 ($26,000) from the city, the National Youth Administration started construction of the jump. It was very convenient that "Old Man Winter Himself," Alf Halvorson, was the local director of the NYA as well as president of the Nansen Ski Club. When the big jump was ready two years later, there was a parking lot for seven hundred cars. The design was based on the jump at Steamboat Springs, Colorado. The steel trestle rose 171½ feet into the air. The distance from the takeoff platform to the foot of the hill was 312 feet.

The great question of the day was who was going to inaugurate the jump? Birger Ruud, the world champion, was proposed, as was his brother, Sigmund. Johanne Kolstad, who had made such a splash on her American tour, was, however, rejected, largely because she was a woman. Eventually the idea of a local hero gained momentum, and thirty-five thousand watched Clarence Spike Oleson clear 180 feet. If anyone queried the large amounts of money spent, they were told that the Olympic Jump at Garmisch-Partenkirchen cost $1 million (c. $18 million today), Lake Placid's was almost the same cost, and locally, the new jump at Laconia/Guilford, not so large as Berlin's, cost about $500,000 ($9 million today).

After World War II, the record was held by Norwegian Ernst Knutsen, at 255 feet, then by Charles Tremblay of Lebanon, New Hampshire, at 256 feet, followed by Arnsten Samuelsten of Steamboat Springs, at 262 feet. Although the Berlin jump was modernized, it was condemned in 1961. The state of New Hampshire then budgeted $45,000 to restore it and raise the height to 181 feet. The city of Berlin added $25,000. There were two annual meets after that: the first in 1963, and then in 1965 Duluth, Minnesota's two-time Olympian, Jay Martin, cleared 263 feet. The final record belonged to Christian Bergrav in 1976, at 271 feet. But then Robert Brown had a tragic accident and filed a $2.5 million lawsuit against USSA, USEASA, and twelve (some say eighteen) members of the Nansen Ski Club. This put paid to jumping in Berlin, and the center in the East moved to Lake Placid, where a ninety-meter jump had been constructed.

These jumping occasions were certainly special, and spectators flocked to them, but what brought out locals and those from the towns nearby were the annual carnivals. It is not clear when Berlin's winter carnivals began. With frequent connections to Montreal, known as a carnival town, and with accounts of the Saint Paul, Minnesota, carnivals from the 1880s on, it is surprising that we don't know the beginning of the fun and games that Berlin enjoyed. In those early days, carnivals often lasted for a week or ten days. By the 1920s, Berlin was coordinating a two-day "Celebration of Winter" with, for example, the 1926 USEASA Ski Championship. The program opened on the YMCA grounds at 9 a.m. with the mayor and Miss Berlin presiding. Immediately there were woodsmen's contests "by picked woodsmen" in tree chopping, wood sawing, and fire lighting. These work themes were followed by junior ski events; two of the most popular were the obstacle and the barrel races. There was also a "ski dash." Even as late as the mid-1920s there remained some competitions that harked back to the rules of track, hence "the dash" competition. Sterner stuff followed with a cross-country run and the USEASA Championship. The high school band performed, and E. P. Clark's dog teams from West Milan were featured.

At 1 p.m. the parade led from Green Square to Paine's Hill, where the jump had been built, and the USEASA Senior Class A and Class B Ski Championships got underway at 1:30. Men competed for the Governor Winant Trophy. Jumping through a hoop of fire was a hit in the carnival of 1930. Scandinavian folk dances were on the program, as were "novelties," and Clark's dog teams were back again. The Burgess Band wound up the afternoon. At 8 p.m. the Carnival Ball began at the city hall. In the meantime, one of Alf Halvorson's publicity stunts came to fruition.

According to Sherman Adams, later right-hand man of president Dwight Eisenhower and owner/builder of Loon Mountain in Lincoln, New Hampshire, once described Halvorson "teamed with P. T. Barnum as one of the greatest showmen and promoters of the world." He dreamed up the idea of having a ski racer carry a letter from the mayor of Portland, Maine, to the mayor of Berlin by way of celebrating the opening of the city's winter carnival. Bob Reid, then twenty-four years old, and Helmer Oakerlund, a thirty-eight-year-old Swede, both members of the Nansen Ski Club, were the only contestants. They were hardly contestants, or even racers; they were to see if such a hundred-mile run could become a traditional event to start the carnival. Reid was well known as a cross-country man. He had impressive placings in major tournaments in Montreal, all throughout New England, and at Lake Placid, and a third in the Canadian National Cross-Country Championships. He had won the Weeks Trophy, the Mount Washington race, and Lake Placid's twenty-five-mile run, and was the U.S. National Cross-Country title holder. Oakerlund, "a top-notcher on the hickory staves," had won the Canadian Championship in 1922 and had come first in the previous four local carnival cross-country meets. Halvorson promoted this, but the weather took a hand.

The weather in early February was terrible in 1926. Reid and Oakerlund set off from Portland at 9 a.m. on February 11 in the face of a blistering north wind that blew the storm out but left terrible skiing conditions. Thirty miles away was the destination, Poland Spring, Maine. At Gray they decided to stop after a seven-hour struggle. Meanwhile, Alf Halvorson was having trouble getting any skiing story at all; the papers were full of storm-related deaths. Never at a loss for ideas, Halvorson got his newsmen aboard a makeshift snowmobile, a car rigged up with short, wide skis. But it broke down—perhaps fortuitously—near Gray. He skied into town, borrowed a couple of horses, and pulled the newsmen to where Oakerlund and Reid were holed up, so he did get his publicity alright! The two skiers were persuaded to continue their trip after food, medicine, and rest and arrived at Poland Spring soon after midnight, where their frostbites were treated before they went to bed.

The next day the weather continued to storm and blow. They delayed departure until 2 p.m., and in very difficult going against the continuing north wind, they skied the twenty miles to Norway, where they arrived at 6 p.m. Oakerlund was having real difficulty in staying the course; the blowing gale had almost blinded him, but a doctor was on hand to treat his eyes. It is also well to remember than these men were on wide nine-foot skis with fairly loose bindings. Thankfully, on Friday the thirteenth the weather cleared. Reid led Oakerlund the twenty-five miles on to Bethel, where they bedded down for the night. The next day the "race" began "amid the cheers of a large party of ski enthusiasts," and at 3:37 p.m. Bob Reid crossed the line in front of the Berlin city hall to the plaudits of the crowd and delight of the newspapermen. Oakerlund, fourteen years older than Reid, was only eight minutes behind. "The blizzard conquerors" received two gold watches for their epic run. Halvorson got more publicity than he bargained for, and the Berlin Carnival was a grand success, but the overwhelming difficulties of the race made it clear that it should not be an annual fixture. Although Bob Reid won many other skiing honors and went on to represent the United States in Olympic competition at the 1932 Lake Placid Winter Games, his "100 Miles of Hell" remained his trademark.

If this experimental race was not the success that had been hoped for, jumping remained ever the attraction. As we have seen, after World War II, the competitions continued to draw top jumpers and huge crowds. However, the last jump attracted only ten competitors, and to keep the crowd happy, each made the leap five times. Gone were the old days; it appeared to one of the organizers that was "The Day Ski Jumping Died." The year was 1985.

For almost thirty years the Big Nansen lay dormant, becoming older, in increasing disrepair each passing winter, an out-of-the-way trash dump, too. Some locals—remembering the glory days—formed the Friends of the Big Nansen in order to put the jump on the National Historic Register. To do that, the state's Department of Natural and Cultural Resources put $25,000 aside to haul away the trash, clear trees, and make a wayside park. Some now wanted to bring jumping back too. $400,000 would be needed to bring the jump into compliance with required standards. The Northern Borders Commission contributed $250,000, with the Nansen Club coming up with a 20 percent match. Then enter Red Bull, an Austrian energy drink company sponsoring sports—often the more extreme ones—which came up with a $75,000 contribution to stabilize the jump sufficiently for their star U.S. women's ski jumper, Sarah Hendrickson (with local ties to New Hampshire), to put on a show for the cameras. A friend, Anna Hofmann, pre-jumped "to see if we had the correct amount of speed." She did, and Sarah leaped fifty-five feet on March 17, 2017 (her record is 486 feet at Oberstdorf, Germany), thereby not only giving a boost to getting the Big Nansen on the Historical Registry but also sending a jolt through the ski-jumping community to fix the Big Nansen so Berlin could, perhaps, become a part of the twelve-jump circuit for junior competitors across the country. After much negotiation, Governor Sununu and the executive council granted the Nansen Ski Club a license to operate the state's property for ten years, renewable for another ten years. Construction was underway in the summer of 2020 . . . but then the COVID-19 pandemic put everything on hold, and the first event scheduled for February 2021, the Nansen's share of a Northeast series of competitions held in Connecticut, New York, and Vermont, was put on indefinite hold. As a side issue, in the hope of making Berlin Nordic-minded again, a bump jump will be made for youngsters, and the high school's jump will require landing modifications. We will see how it all turns out.

CHAPTER 4

FRED HARRIS OF DARTMOUTH COLLEGE

When Fred H. Harris of Brattleboro, Vermont, first began skiing as a young man in the winter of 1903–4, very few in the region had ever strapped on skis, either for travel across the snow or for sport. Norwegian immigrants in the Midwest brought their skiing knowledge with them, founded clubs, held competitions. In the Far West, in gold rush California, miners and their ladies sported in mining camp rivalry in the Sierra. As we have seen in New Sweden, Maine, immigrant families sent their children to school on skis in the 1870s, about the same time as folk in Norway Village, another immigrant community just north of Berlin, New Hampshire, founded a Skiklubben. Before the turn of the century a few other individuals used skis out of necessity and enjoyed them for sport. John Perry's journal entries in the mid-1880s, for example, reveal how he made his own skis, and he referred to other skiing activities, including traveling to school and to the dentist in Ipswich, New Hampshire. We have heard, too, that the snowshoe section of the Appalachian Mountain Club included one or two skiers in the 1890s. One of them, near the summit of Killington, Vermont, in 1897, "thrust his arm at the end of the ski pole far down into the snow recording a depth of seven feet." That party found quarters at the Woodstock Inn, which occasionally hosted skiers in the 1890s. A hearty group in Saint Johnsbury formed a club in 1890 that sponsored overnight trips on skis and, for thrills, skied the ruts of the toboggan chute.

Fred Harris, though not the first to ski for recreation, yet turned out to be a pioneer of skiing in America. He founded the Dartmouth Outing Club in 1909 and the Brattleboro

Outing Club in 1922. He served as president of the United States Eastern Amateur Ski Association from its beginning in 1922 until 1926, and he frequently represented Eastern ski interests to the Midwestern-dominated National Ski Association that he served as vice president in 1929. The next year he represented the United States at the Fédération internationale de ski (FIS) Congress in Oslo, Norway. At the Lake Placid Winter Olympic Games in 1932, Fred Harris served on the ski jury. In his later years he spent much of his energy with youngsters, an interest he had kept up since his college days. Harris Hill, the Brattleboro jumping hill laid out by him, witnessed the first national championship of the United States held in the East in 1924. It was named for Harris in February 1951. In an early entry in his journal, Harris noted that he had "skeeing on the brain evidently." His journals from the years 1903 to 1911 are the most detailed accounts we have of all matters dealing with skiing and are by far the most valuable of sources for understanding the early years of skiing in northern New England. Over his life-time, Fred H. Harris helped turn his version of brain fever into a major sport and business in his native Vermont, his college at Hanover, and the state of New Hampshire, and, indeed, helped to bring the ski world to Lake Placid for the 1932 Winter Olympics.

In a 1922 article aptly titled "How I Learned to Ski," Harris related meeting a Dr. Lawton while skating. The doctor invited him to try skiing. Although Harris does not mention the actual date, he drafted the article as early as 1903, and the January 1904 entries in his journal mention going skiing with Lawton and bending skis with the doctor. Throughout his early skiing years, the older Lawton remained Harris's companion both on cross-country trips and on the more exciting "slides," as he called his downhill thrills. Harris's mentor was Dr. Shailer Emery Lawton, the superintendent of the Brattleboro Retreat (a psychiatric and addiction hospital) and notable personage in town. After finishing his medical degree, Lawton had joined the staff of the retreat in 1881 and was given a sabbatical leave in 1889. He spent six months at the Post Graduate Medical School in New York, and six months in Europe. It must have been during that half year abroad that he took up skiing. Of the few skiing photographs that we have of him, none are pictures from Europe, none have come from the *Brattleboro Reformer*, so what I propose is educated conjecture. No matter what, he obviously passed on his expertise to Fred Harris. "My white-haired friend's enthusiasm was contagious," he said of the man who took him up and down some tough hills on 9½ foot-long and 5-inch-wide skis.

Figure 2. Fred Harris learning how to ski from Dr. Shailer Lawton in the Brattleboro area in about 1905. He would take his enthusiasm to Dartmouth and to the rest of New England in the 1920s. New England Ski Museum photo 1982L.016.003. Used by permission.

Harris, through the formation of the Dartmouth Outing Club, transferred his personal love of skiing into an organized, collegiate ethos that contained something of the legacy of the nineteenth-century type of muscular Christianity best personified by Greenland explorer Norwegian Fridtjof Nansen, who thought of skiing as keeping civilization at bay.

"One's whole being is wrapped in one's ski and the surrounding nature," he enthused. Skiing developed the soul and not the body alone. The general urge to be youthful, masculine, and adventurous permeated much of middle-class American life after the 1890s. In that view skiing was not an aimless urge; it had a clear goal. Sport, especially organized sport, deserved serious attention as part of the business of life. This attitude equated character with virility; moral fiber was proved by physical qualities. Work and discipline were virtuous, and their opposite, leisure, was considered idle. Idleness bred immorality and lacked any spiritual value, possibly even being dangerous. These were the old Puritan beliefs making a new case for themselves in the industrial world.

There was also much concern about health. That classical ideal of *mens sana in corpore sano* adopted by the late Victorians found its American outlet in magazines such as *Physical Culture,* with the slogan "Weakness Is a Crime." This ideal played on the senses of young men of Harris's age. The outdoors—the great outdoors—provided spaciousness and cleanliness for the virility that young Americans found compelling as they confronted the urban sprawl, factory towns, and malaise of automated society. Skiing satisfied both the values of muscularity and admiration for the natural world. It took a Fred Harris to organize the values and have the drive to keep it all going, and the hills and woods of New England provided a receptive environment for skiing activities. Was not New Hampshire the Granite State?

> Have the still North in their hearts,
> The hill winds in their veins;
> And the granite of New Hampshire
> In their muscles and their brains.

Harris transformed skiing from an individual enthusiasm to a structured sport. The modernization of sport, following Allen Guttmann's memorable analysis, includes the creation of bureaucratic organizations, quantification, the quest for records, and general rationalization of sport. In the organization of the Dartmouth Outing Club in 1909, Harris blazed a trail for others to follow. The *Boston Globe* took note of the DOC's formation. Other colleges followed: McGill University joined in an intercollegiate meet with Dartmouth in 1914, the University of New Hampshire in 1915, Colgate University the next year, and very soon afterward the University of Vermont, Williams, and Middlebury Colleges also became involved, and Yale "seemed interested." As skiers graduated from these eastern colleges, they continued their love for the winter life in other clubs, and nearly all of them had a distinctly collegiate and "outing club" atmosphere, one even calling itself "the Dartmouth Outing Club of Boston."

Even before he headed to Dartmouth as an undergraduate, Harris had learned to make his own equipment, as other early ski enthusiasts had to do. It is not clear where or how he obtained his first pair of skis. Ski manufacturing had begun in the Midwest, but many believed reliable skis could be obtained only from Norway. Harris made a contrivance for bending the boards' tips up, then finished them off by painting them with boiled oil. Bending skis became a major activity in his mother's kitchen, and he happily noted it in his diary when he got "a fine bend." Instructional articles with diagrams were available, and Harris had read an article in *Country Life in America* in February 1904. He may also have taken some of his ideas for bending the skis from his mentor, Dr. Lawton.

A good ski required the right wood with good grain, and Harris spent time looking over "some fine ash wood" as well as having Smith's in Brattleboro rough-cut skis for him. The shop once produced six pairs for him according to his pattern. Most of these shop-produced skis needed finishing: bending, sandpapering, and coating with oil and shellac. He frequently added "dandy brass tips." After a season he washed the skis down, applied a new coat of shellac, and stowed them for the summer. One time at Dartmouth he had the college paint shop "strip and varnish" his skis for him. He makes no mention of any rigging to keep camber in the skis or the tips bent sufficiently, something necessary during summer storage.

Bindings—harnesses, fasteners, or footgear, as Harris alternatively referred to them—were primitive. Leather workers and harness makers with a ready clientele in the hill country farms easily adjusted to making "ski straps." In Brattleboro, Brown's was the place. Harris fixed the straps onto the skis with screws. His frequent falls often resulted in tearing off a strap and the need for repair. Many diary entries concerning straps end with "worked on my skis." Harris also purchased buckles designed to tighten up the straps. In February 1907, he experimented with "a new skee fastener" that he tried out on his sister's skis the next day, much to his satisfaction. The journal entry does not reveal what innovation he had attempted, nor if he continued to use it on other skis. However, by 1909 a real change occurred with his bindings. On February 19 he "had [a] blacksmith make me some irons"; on March 6, "got irons made," and after that the notations for failure of binding straps became minimal.

Harris makes only two references to ski boots. In December 1906, a pair needed patching. The next year, Harris did buy a pair of "skee boots at Dunham's," but again he made no comment about them in his journal. There were ski boots available commercially, but skiers mostly used farmers' rubbers, and the usual working winter boot did almost as well as those advertised for skiing, bindings were so loose in those days.

Harris also experimented with poles. After breaking his nine-foot hickory pole on February 1, 1904, he cut an iron-wood pole. But he found it "awful heavy. Not much good." Four days later he "made a new pole [of] hard pine." But a pole was not just a strong shaft. On January 22, 1905, he "fixed the ferrule on Bingham's pole." Two years later he "worked in shop trying to get a round hoop ... for [a] pole," and on the day he wrote "I have been overdoing lately and decided to lay off one day" (only two days in February 1907 contain no entry on skiing) he fixed up his own ski pole.

The six pairs of skis at a time that Harris ordered were for others. They arrived raw. Harris bent, sandpapered, and shellacked them, installed the foot harness, and made enough money to support his own skiing. On December 3, 1904, he paid three dollars for two pairs of those raw skis. At the end of the month, he ordered six more pairs, as he fashioned skis for young and old. "Merrill Whitney brought his skees down for me to bend," he wrote. "Pa said that Charlie Crosby wanted me to make him a pair of skees. Took the contract for $4.50." He sold two pairs to John Tasker for $9.70. "J. A. Austin came over before breakfast and wanted a pair of skees." And so on. He disparaged a pair a friend had bought "for 50¢!!!!!!!!"

In his second skiing season, February 14, 1905, Harris summarized his thoughts about his equipment: "My idea of a skee now is between 8 and 9 ft. long, at least 5½ in. wide. As stiff as possible in back and still have it balance down. Wider at the front than at the back. Quite thin and bendy at the front. Grooved of course, nearly to the back end, am not so sure about the front one. I wonder," he concluded, "what my idea will be a year from now!?!" Harris certainly had an experimental turn of mind, a great flexibility in trying new things, and a stubbornness to see things through.

When Harris entered Dartmouth in the fall of 1907, he tried to get orders for skis, but he had no luck. By this time manufacturers had learned that skiing offered a market. During the 1905–6 season, ten thousand skis were distributed in Ashland, Wisconsin, and in New England we have noted the production figures for Theo Johnson's Tajco skis of Portland, Maine.

Fred Harris's interest in organizing the Dartmouth Outing Club (DOC) and crafting ski equipment all stemmed from his tremendous enthusiasm for skiing itself. As he taught himself to make equipment, he also learned to ski. First, he went through the usual neophyte efforts. On January 6, 1904, he wrote, "[I] put them on and tried skeeing. Liked it very well." The next day he reported, "I like skeeing so far." On the ninth, he was trying "the steepest hill in the PM." On the eleventh he "took a jump of about twenty feet and landed hard. Tore the strap off the buckle part of my footgear. Hurt my back some. My skee went away and left me on another dump. Dark when I came home . . . I am tired." He went skiing on the twelfth and the thirteenth, and on the fourteenth "before breakfast. Pretty good. Awful fast. Took some bad dumps." And split his skis. That day a friend "got his knee hurt and face cut up some. He said he would sell his skees." The pace continued as he went skiing every day, often with Dr. Lawton, who took him up some tough hills for the increasing thrill of the downhill rush. On January 20, Harris took "a number of bad falls," and on the next day "took one fall on Bradley's and two on the Asylum bank." To his journal he confided, "It is better to ride on your pole," his first reference to this technique—a maneuver having already created stiff debate in Europe for a decade.

On January 11, 1904, Harris had managed to jump. At the end of the month he made "a jumping place on Bradley's and jumped quite aways." Bradley's became the place to jump, and a variety of jumps were contrived, modest affairs without superstructure and only about thirty feet long. But the thrill of the flight was quite apparent, and Harris regularly recorded his lengthening efforts:

17 Feb '04	Could clear 15 feet
8 Feb '05	30 feet
1 Feb '06	45 ft. 9 in.
21 Feb '07	50 ft.
28 Feb '07	Spent the day jumping 40–50 feet. Merrill [Whitney] jumped for the first time and made 40 feet with skis Harris had made
5 Feb '08	Spent an hour making a jump . . . jumped 40 feet [at Dartmouth]
11 Feb '08	Made a new jump . . . jumped 50 ft.
20 Feb '08	Made jump higher. Made about 40 ft.
13 Feb '09	Watched winner of Montreal jump doing 82 ft. 6 in. I tried it and made the hill after a fashion.
13 Dec '09	Approached Mr. Davison about building ski jump on his land for DOC.
15 Dec '09	I constructed framework of ski jump.
7 Jan '10	Got ski-jump framework pretty well finished.
8 Jan '10	Broke my skiis all to pieces on second jump. Rebuilt jump.
15 Jan '10	Fell twice.
16 Jan '10	Tried jump several times, and at last made it. Hurrah! Twice Oh! Ye! Gods!

Harris listed his failures and successes while Scandinavian communities in the Midwest had already warmly embraced jumping for decades. The jumping fraternities were popularized as "the Winged Vikings" or "Knights of the Air," and tens of thousands of spectators turned out to watch at the larger meets. Cross-country racing was replaced by the spectacle of the high-flying jumpers, and the ski jump became the centerpiece of carnivals great and small. Ski jumping played an important dual role in the growth of skiing, as it popularized skiing while making it into a spectator sport. Fred Harris helped to bring this excitement to the Dartmouth Winter Carnival, where it has remained a centerpiece of the weekend to this day.

Harris also opened up cross-country skiing as an activity for as many as cared to get out into the New England winter. Harris traced the development of his cross-country touring. In the beginning he was content to accompany two friends on snowshoes. Then on February 20, 1904, he took his first cross-country ski trip. He "started to skee to the Lake. Went through Bradley's, down to the three bridges, on to the river and up to Chickering. From Chickering's I branched off up the hill and went over toward the place where grandfather was born. From the top of that hill I went down by John Harvey's old farm to Wilder Harris's and up the first part of the mile hill, where I branched off to the left and went up the hill to Amidon's about noon." At Amidon's Harris stopped for dinner, and within an hour "started off then but the snow stuck to my skees and it went hard. I started off above the old mill on a circuit to the left going up some steep hills and coming down a wood road which ended near Silverdale." The difficulty of snow sticking to the skis remained a problem. Harris and his friends seemed unaware that concoctions or existing waxes could alleviate that condition. On occasion the sticking snow stopped Harris from skiing at all. Until he entered Dartmouth, he made his cross-country excursions "skeeing alone, all, all alone; alone as a wide wide territorie."

When Harris enrolled at Dartmouth, few students or residents had seen many ski tracks, though there had been skiing off and on in the Hanover area for the previous thirty years. Hanover's renowned astronomer, Edwin Frost, recalled that "skiis did not come into use in Hanover until the end of the eighties. I inherited a pair from a classmate who shared them with C. S. Cook. The skiis were so long that a pair of old shoes had been attached to the rear for a second passenger. The situation got very painful for the man riding behind when the leader began to toe in and skiis spread at the rear."

The earliest photo of skiing at Dartmouth shows Herman Holt jumping over Rollins. Bill Jarvis found a pair of eleven-foot skis in his room when he arrived in 1889, and John Thomas brought his own skis with him from Maine. John Ash, with western experience, entered Dartmouth in the class of 1899 and "showed his partner how to make skis out of some boards used for fencing. We had a lot of fun around there, and a few of the boys got into the act, but most preferred to stay in their warm rooms."

The year after Ash left Dartmouth, a Swedish exchange student was seen going up hill and down dale on skis he had brought with him from his homeland. He attracted a small crowd. But no store in Hanover sold skis. Skiing enthusiasts at Dartmouth asked head carpenter Fred Gairey to make skis. Gairey wanted to use the steam heater of a local furniture factory, but the factory was too busy. Gairey steamed the tips over his own kitchen range with several assistants, including George Worcester, who received a pair of these skis as payment. These skis can still be seen in the Thetford Historical Society just across the river in Vermont. "A group of us," recalled another Dartmouth man, "skied in 1902 on skis made locally" and enjoyed the slopes and hillsides around Hanover. Before Harris had arrived, skiing at Dartmouth had been an on-again, off-again affair.

On November 30, 1909, Harris drafted a proposal to found a ski and snowshoe club and published it in the *Dartmouth*, the college newspaper. Harris's plan for the club was:

1) To stimulate interest in out-of-door winter sports.

2) To have short Cross-country runs weekly and one long excursion each session (say, to Mooselac).

3) To hold a meet or field day during February at which a program of events similar to the following may be contested. 100 yard dash on snowshoes, 100 yard dash on skis, Cross-country run on skis, ski jumping contest, and other events that may be suggested ... Dartmouth might well become the originator of a branch of college organized sport hitherto undeveloped by American colleges.

Harris's idea became reality. The first DOC expedition he recorded occurred on December 10, 1910. Harris and his friends "left on 1.50 train north. Stopped at Pompanoosuc and returned by ski or snowshoe. Found 3 good slides. Stopped by the side of a pond and cooked some coffee and bacon with doughnuts and so on. Got in before the snowshoe men even though we took several slides twice." A weekend later the gang made "a dandy trip. Cooked quantities of beefsteak for supper. Dandy skiing at moonlight. Slept in a farm house." The next year thirty Outing Club members took the train to Thetford, missed their return by way of Moose Mountain cabin, and came home through Hanover center and across Reservoir Pond.

The DOC also began the tradition of the winter carnival at Dartmouth. Harris did not invent the carnival. He knew of the big jumping meets in the Midwest. He had been taken to the Montreal Carnival by his father in 1908, where he had been thrilled by all the commotion of the jumping meet, with the "Boxes of Honor" overflowing with royalty, government officials, and judges. And the hill—if it had looked bad from below, "it was appalling from above." If he had been apprehensive before, he was paralyzed at the top. But it was either "death or disgrace," and he swooshed down the runway, misjudged the takeoff, landed and half fell, and kept on, now in traffic for some four city blocks before coming to a stop! Could he ever reproduce something like this in Hanover? He also knew James "Pop" Taylor, an energetic master whose "scheme to get the boys going" at Vermont Academy in Saxtons River had come to fruition on Lincoln's birthday in 1909. It included ski and snowshoe races both for sprints and distances, and downhill events that included stopping, called "gliding races." Obstacle races provided the most enjoyment, but the jump, with leaps from fifteen to thirty-five feet, was the most thrilling. Some boys skied on handmade skis, others had ordered some from Minnesota. Taylor found a response in the preparatory school boys, just as Harris's enthusiasm eventually found favor among the college crowd.

Harris received help from several Vermont Academy boys in organizing the first carnival at Dartmouth in 1910. Taylor himself was convinced that Harris got the idea for the Outing Club from him. Harris, however, had been mulling over some such organization for at least a year. There were types of outing clubs at St. Olaf's in Minnesota, at the Michigan School of Mines, and, nearer to home, at Plymouth Normal School in New Hampshire. But Harris authored the proposal in *The Dartmouth*. His journal on that day only records: "Went skiing up towards Balch Hill. Sent an article to *The Dartmouth* on the formation of an outing club." Sixty students appeared at the opening meeting, but "there was considerable scoffing at the idea and The Club had to justify its existence." At the January meeting, Harris registered fifty-five men. It took even longer to get the snowshoe men on skis. The DOC was copied by other colleges, and Outing Club members, used to winter on the snow, became the backbone of New England skiing in the 1920s and 1930s.

Fred Harris was a remarkable skiing pioneer. He transformed skiing from an individual, unstructured activity into an organized sport. The "outing" part of the DOC, the building of huts, and trailing a winter's day to a feast of bacon and beans with the camaraderie of like-minded souls, was a major attraction for those young men. Harris kept statistics on who did how many miles of cross-country per season. For the 1910–11 season, Harris did ninety-eight miles, Professor Goldthwaite ninety-two miles, and Dr. Licklider ninety miles. In 1917 it was announced that Dartmouth "will take on the Finns in a ski race." Until the end of World War II, the organization of race meetings and the overseeing of all the activities involved remained a strong influence among those who skied.

Harris also was an agent of the process of the modernization of the sport. The same year that Harris was first writing his journal, the National Ski Association was founded, with five affiliated Midwestern clubs. Before Harris went to Dartmouth, the number had risen to twenty-three, and increasing numbers began to enjoy the winter outdoors on skis. Fred Harris was such a one, but beyond that he had the energy and drive to challenge and organize the Hanover community to "take better advantage of the splendid opportunities which the admirable situation of our college offers." The college men took up Harris's challenge. Since then, many evidently have had "skeeing on the brain," and have enjoyed life better for it. In 1920, *National Geographic* published Harris's article on the DOC, illustrated and captioned with photos of students coming through the woods without caps or shirts. "Not only has the Outing Club improved the physical well-being of Dartmouth's student body but faculty statistics show that scholarship has profited by the weekend excursions of skiing parties." The trail was "a skyway leading though grandeurs of winter scenery wholly unknown to those who nestle beside steam radiators." It meandered "to seek solitude in the solemnity of Nature's cathedral trees."

Freshmen applications for admission rose 300 percent, from 824 to 2,675.

The Outing Club that Fred Harris built was kept going in the early years by committed students and by two or three faculty members. Professor Proctor of the Physics Department made himself the fulcrum around which Dartmouth skiing turned. As early as 1914, Proctor had taken a party of twelve students and faculty to compete in Montreal against McGill University, a typical move following Harris in promoting international sporting rivalry. He would go on, after the world war, to be a major proponent of the Intercollegiate Winter Sports Union, which came to fruition in 1924. The first meet comprising teams from eleven universities was held in Hanover on February 19 and 20, 1926.

The early 1920s were key years for skiing, not least 1924, when the annual French International Sporting Week, that year at Chamonix, was turned into the First Winter Olympic Games, although it was only a year later that the designation as the First Winter Olympics became official. Closer to home, it was the year that Dartmouth hired its first ski coach. Fred Harris had been lobbying for a coach for the Dartmouth team. Professor Proctor persuaded the administration that it would be worthwhile; it would keep Dartmouth in the forefront of skiing. In fact, Gus Paulsen from Berlin, New Hampshire—known for his somersaults off the jump in 1916—was helping out, but he was hardly a real coach of the ski team. No one was in charge of the growing number of recreational skiers. An experienced skier was required who could also teach newcomers to the sport. In a roundabout way, this coincided with the development of alpine skiing (as opposed to Norwegian skiing). Here, a connection was made between Dartmouth's best skier, John Carleton, now a Rhodes scholar at Oxford University, and this new alpine skiing. Carleton had met and would ski with the most important promoter of alpine skiing, Arnold Lunn. Lunn had set the first slalom in 1922. Through Carleton,

Professor Proctor connected with Lunn, and the first slalom in the United States was set in 1925, the first downhill in 1927.

For the 1923–24 season, after, it is said, some persuasion by Proctor, the college hired Anton Diettrich, onetime colonel in the Austro-Hungarian Army, as Dartmouth's instructor in fencing and skiing; he was a better fencer than skier, having won the national sabre championship. He had been a skiing student of Mathias Zdarsky, the man who had impressed the military brass by stressing safe skiing in the mountains. His dogmatic, disciplinarian approach to the sport brought in thousands of students. Diettrich, then, came to Dartmouth with this reputation. According to the latest Dartmouth accounts in Steve Waterhouse's *Passion for Skiing*, Diettrich had also written about skiing. The only article I can find is a pedestrian account of where to find skiing in the neighborhood of Buda and Pest, hardly a persuasive plus on a ski vita. Later, Diettrich was photographed by the *Boston Herald* in his "celebrated splitting snow farce entitled 'Coming or Going'" but admits "does always his left foot know what his right doeth." Such was Diettrich at his publicity best, doing a standing kick turn. But Diettrich had served with the Austrian mountain troops and could tell tales of his own mountain descents. It was all very thrilling in tucked-away Hanover.

Diettrich had a serious side: the first lecture on skis and skiing was turned into a twenty-three-page booklet. The next two lectures were never published. Diettrich was fortunate to have Professor Proctor's son, Charley, as team leader. This was a period in skiing where what was beginning to be called alpine skiing was in its experimental stage. This was particularly obvious with the growth of racing. Courses were all down the mountain; the ones requiring many turns were being called slaloms, and the ones from the top of the course to the bottom were "down-mountain races." In 1925, Professor Proctor, with Arnold Lunn's rules at his side, and with the help of Diettrich, set a slalom on the golf course. This was the venue where he was also promoting recreational skiing not only among the students but also giving instruction to the ladies of Hanover, who, it was said, were taken by his accent—shades of things to come in the "benz ze kneez" era.

With the memory of those vast stretches of the Alps above timberline, Diettrich suggested a down-mountain race to be held on Mount Moosilauke two years later. Diettrich had recommended the German magazine *Der Winter* for the DOC clubhouse; even if, as one excited student wrote home, the boys could not read the text, they could imbibe the photographs of the Bavarian Alps, the Black Forest, the Harz, and the Riesengebirge. Skiing in Germany seemed so developed. Sophomore Harold Leich hoped that "this race will become a fixed tradition; it will go far to put skiing where it belongs." This, indeed, was what happened. Quite suddenly, "Everyone here is crazy over Moosilauke" as that first 1927 race drew near, and the tradition continued with the first National Alpine Downhill in 1931. It was, perhaps, fitting that Professor Proctor's son, Charley, won that first race, covering the approximately 4.5-mile course in twenty-one minutes. By that time, Diettrich had given up his skiing duties—war wounds made such physical activity painful. He was able to remain as fencing instructor.

A search was on for a new ski coach. In 1927, Sig Steinwall, a recognized jumper from Sweden, had won the prestigious Fiskatorpet Cup in 1915 and represented Sweden at Holmenkollen in 1913–15 and again in 1917. In 1919, he held the U.S. national record of 176 feet off the jump at Dillon, Colorado. When Dartmouth came calling, he was a member of Chicago's Norge Ski Club. His team did not do well, partly because Charley Proctor was away at the Saint Moritz Winter Olympics. But there were other factors coming into play with the increasing emphasis on alpine skiing. Steinwall's contract was not renewed. In his place came the Munich university student, and very popular, German (Gerry) Raab. Raab had some success, the Dartmouth team winning the coveted

President Harding Trophy—for university competition—at Lake Placid in 1930 by half a point over the University of New Hampshire's team. After the 1929–30 season, he returned to Germany to finish his medical studies.

Enter the inimitable Otto Schniebs. Schniebs came from the Schwarzwald (Black Forest), an early center of German skiing. In the Schwabian championship of 1927, he had come second in the *Altersklasse*. More importantly, he had passed Hannes Schneider's examination for ski professionals in the Arlberg system of skiing and, once in America, had made a reputation with Harvard University. AMC skiers, too, delighted in his instruction at the Braeburn Country Club, always accompanied by a blitz on the English language. Professor Proctor hired him to work part-time in his physics lab (Schniebs was working in a watch factory in Massachusetts) and the rest of the time as a ski coach. Very quickly, it was plain that the physics lab would not be part of Otto's contribution; it was "skiing as a way of life" that he advocated in the DOC, in Hanover, and at surrounding colleges. As his notoriety grew, Schniebs began entering into the ski business as well . . . and that brought on conflicts. There was an "Otto problem." Fred Harris, who kept his eye on all things skiing at Dartmouth, suggested that he become a full-time employee of the DOC, but Schniebs turned that offer aside as he became a ski equipment supplier. He had had great success: four of his students skied on America's Olympic team, led by German-schooled Dick Durrance, for the 1936 Nazi Games at Garmisch-Partenkirchen. And it was Durrance who was asked to scout around Europe—he was already there skiing—for a possible coach. Thus it was that Switzerland's Walter Prager arrived in Hanover and served until the war. He entered the U.S. 10th Mountain Division, where he was among the European instructors. He starred in a recruiting film, too. Prager returned to Dartmouth after demobilization.

Professor Proctor also had a staunch ally in Dartmouth's librarian, Nathaniel Goodrich, who took the post in 1912. He was mountaineer, an enthusiastic snowshoer, and was taken by what he saw of the students and faculty skiing. "I tried the game in the winter of 1912–13," he wrote, and the following season "felt like tackling something more interesting than the pasture hills around Hanover." He aimed high: Mount Mansfield, out of Stowe, Vermont, had a toll road to the top at 4,395 feet. On February 1, 1914, Goodrich and his friend Charles Blood made it to the top—and down in safety. That, in itself, is of note, but it had virtually no effect.

Goodrich, though, played a major role not just in Dartmouth skiing but in American skiing as well when he became editor of the USEASA's *Ski Annual* in 1934. He saw Dartmouth as a leader in the growth of American skiing. Although this volume was Eastern's annual, it had a broad appeal, with articles on ski centers in the Alps, European equipment and fashion, and the coming Winter Olympic Games in Germany, but the bulk of the volume was written by men whose names would be recognized by New England skiers: Otto Schniebs, Jack McCrillis, Alec Bright, Charles Dudley, Park Carpenter, Greenough Abbe, Roger Langley, and Doc Elmer. Their topics also reflected a New England interest in the newly arrived Tempo turn, British tests, Lunn's *British Ski Year-Book*, and so on. The British influence was more than recognizable. The annual was published in Brattleboro. The Stephen Daye Press in town became New England's ski publisher, with important works such as McCrillis and Schniebs's *Modern Ski Technique* published in 1932, and in its eighth edition in 1937, and Max Barsis's humorous take on the developing ski world, *Bottoms Up!* Nansen, who had called for a history of skiing as early as 1890, finally found a taker in Charles Dudley's *60 Centuries of Skiing*, the first major effort at a historical overview in the United States, competed with Peter Lunn's up-to-date *High-Speed Skiing*, George Herring's social *Ski Gang*, and Fritz Heinrich's *Games to Play on Skis*—one of which was called "Collision"! Finally, in this 1934 annual, Goodrich allowed thirty-one pages for the results of races.

The national championships in jumping, cross-country, and downhill shared space with the Junior Intra-Club Meet of the Lebanon (NH) Outing Club. Roger Langley had been correct when he said that virtually all the clubs were also racing clubs; you had to be a club member in order to race.

The Dartmouth tradition, one might argue, of Olympic participation continued after the second of the world's wars. We will meet the mercurial Joe Dodge later on Mount Washington, where his son Brooks, Dartmouth class of 1951, learned to ski and went on to represent the United States at Oslo in 1952 and raced to fourth place in the slalom at Cortina in 1956. Exchange student from Japan Chick Igaya, class of 1957, was there in force, winning a silver in slalom, and a bronze medal at the World Championships in Bad Gastein, Austria, in 1958. Tom Corcoran's fourth in the downhill at Squaw was particularly memorable—his second Olympics. The recently retired CEO of the US Ski and Snowboard Association, Tiger Shaw, was a team member at the Sarajevo and Calgary games in 1984 and 1988. However, his greatest contribution has been in the way that top collegiate skiers, and not a few seniors in high school, can obtain a college degree with a flexible academic timetable. In 2020, fifteen universities and colleges in the United States (including Dartmouth) promote this flexible learning while continuing to train for the U.S. team. Shaw resigned after the Beijing Olympics, and Sophie Goldschmidt has been selected as the next CEO. Andrew Weibrecht, class of 2015, surprised America with a bronze in the Super-G at Vancouver, and a silver medal at Sochi in 2014.

As the various regulations governing skiing changed, most pertinent here was the official recognition of women's skiing at the top level—Olympic and World Cup. When the Paralympics were officially blessed, Dartmouth's Sarah Billmeier participated in four Olympics—at Albertville (1992), Lillehammer (1994), Nagano (1998), and Salt Lake City (2002)—winning an astonishing seven gold medals (three in downhill), five silver (three in Super-G), and one bronze (giant slalom). In free-style moguls, a new event in 1992, Elizabeth McIntyre competed that year, and in 1994 won the silver medal. Her last Olympics was in Nagano, Japan, in 1998. Surely this must have given inspiration to Hannah Kearney, class of 2011, who won Gold at Vancouver (2010). Cross-country racing also revived, in large part due to the Caldwell family, who has represented the country— John at Oslo in 1952, and the indefatigable Tim at Sapporo (1972), Innsbruck (1976), Lake Placid (1980), and Sarajevo (1984)—a remarkable Dartmouth contribution, surely something that Fred Harris could have hardly envisioned that day he sent in the proposal for the Dartmouth Outing Club.

CHAPTER 5

THE LURE AND LORE OF MOUNT WASHINGTON

The great attraction of Mount Washington, so named in 1784 by a geology party exploring the area (its Abenaki name was Agiocochook, Home of the Great Spirit), is in its extremes: highest mountain east of the Rockies and north of the Carolinas; the world's highest recorded wind gust; really cold temperatures; first climbed in 1642; its Carriage Road was the first man-made tourist attraction; first cog railway; and first region of New England—the White Mountains— that owes its tourism to art. Quite a pedigree. In the last 280 years Mount Washington has been seen and climbed with quite different attitudes. When itinerant Irishman Darby Field climbed to the top in 1642, it is said he was doing so to ensure that this mountain world would be American land, not Abenaki. The native Americans believed the summit was the home of the gods and they would not intrude. QED.

The fact that the mountain is six thousand feet high is not of particular interest when compared with the country's other mountains; there are many twice as high in the Rockies. Even Independence Pass, just outside of the skiers' mecca of Aspen, is over twelve thousand feet high! But before the West was opened up, having such a high mountain east of the Mississippi added distinction to New England. Already the center of the American world with its proximity to New York and Boston, New England boasted economic and intellectual leadership. Now it could put this natural superlative on display.

This natural leadership was enhanced by "the worst weather in the world" (first noted in 1940), but it had that reputation as early as 1885, when a temperature of minus fifty degrees was recorded, and almost fifty years later, on April 14, 1931, the wind was measured at 231 miles per hour. Discounting wind generated by tornadoes, this remains the highest wind speed ever measured by scientific instrumentation in a continually staffed meteorological observation station.

These extremes interest us in our scientific age; we seem to relish and fear these mathematical horrors. However, before the twentieth century, that other science, natural science, played the most important role in publicizing Mount Washington. The whole region was a naturalist's paradise. Well-known professorial types have left their marks all over the mountain, for instance on Boott Spur (on the map since 1859), named for physician and botanist Francis Boott, who in 1816 had been on the White Mountain exploration team of Jacob Bigelow, for whom Bigelow Lawn is named. William Oakes combined studies of plants and mosses with books extolling the art of the White Mountains. They earned him a great following, and he is now remembered in Oakes Gulf. And for skiers, most important of all was Harvard graduate and Amherst College professor of botany Edward Tuckerman. Tuckerman searched for lichens in the great cirque that now is memorialized with his name and is known countrywide, even worldwide among skiing cognoscenti, as Tuckerman Ravine with its famous Headwall.

Explorers tend to write books on their experiences and, indeed, there are a few notable ones extolling the pleasures they found on Mount Washington, such as Thomas Starr King's *The White Hills: Their Legends, Landscape, and Poetry*, published in Boston in 1865. The title tells all. Yet far more important were the artists who, following the Hudson River school, formed a White Mountain school of art. Two of these artists were Benjamin Champney (1817–1907), who worked in the Conway valley, and Frank Henry Shapleigh (1842–1906), who worked out of the Crawford House and had a studio in North Conway as well as in Jackson. However, it was two paintings that launched White Mountain tourism.

The first painting, by Thomas Cole (1801–48), depicted the tragedy in which nine died. It became public news across the country. Cole had read about the rockslide of August 28, 1826, that had taken the lives of the Willeys—all seven of them—and had visited the site on a tour with a friend. The house itself remained unharmed, but the family and their two hired hands had decided to ride out the storm in a stone shelter that was destroyed. "It was impossible," Cole wrote in his journal, "to give an adequate idea of this scene of desolation." But his painting conveyed the awe-inspiring force of nature by depicting the scarred landscape of stumps and boulders while at the same time showing admiration for the romantic aspects of mountain living. The house that remained untouched by the rock and the mud slide was not included in the painting. About two years later, Cole painted *Distant View of the Slide that Destroyed the Willey Family*. The original painting has disappeared, but we know the details from a lithograph made at the time. Here, again, like the enjoyment of weather extremes, the macabre scene appealed in its voyeuristic way: nature in the raw, untamed, uncontrollable, and part of the great natural world that used to be America but was now becoming industrialized. It was on Mount Washington where a man—and it was a man's world—could find challenges. Samuel Willey's brother, a reverend, began charging a fee for conducting a tour of the still-standing house. Nathaniel Hawthorne capitalized on its notoriety in *The Ambitious Guest*, published in 1835. Ten years later, Horace Fabyan would turn the Willey House into a fifty-room hotel. It burned down in 1898.

Tourism had arrived in the White Mountains thanks to the exploitation of a tragedy. But it was the second artist, John Frederick Kensett (1816–72), who in 1851 painted a large canvas titled *Mount Washington from the Valley of Conway* that epitomized this natural world. Thirteen thousand engravings were sent out, and Currier and Ives produced a lithograph in 1860. As these two paintings became admired and the artists.known, especially in Boston and New York, the slow trickle of visitors grew relatively quickly, with the result that accommodations, limited to primitive out-of-the-way inns, were inadequate. Big finance got involved in building many vast hotels that catered to a moneyed summer bourgeois crowd from the urban centers coming north to experience nature. Now it was no longer the horrifying nature of the Willey slide but the sublime mountain scenery that drew visitors. The word "sublime" is important, having its archaic origin in the matter of height, but in the latter half of the nineteenth century epitomizing something awe-inspiring, especially when associated with height, just what the wealthier adventurous city people were seeking. Having found it on high, they made a connection to God. What had once been the abode of native deities became an earthly paradise to be explored. As Thoreau put it, if life "were sublime, I wanted to know it by experience and to be able to give a true account of it." In fact, on a second trip to Mount Washington in 1858, a botanical outing (he had been up with his brother in 1839), Thoreau and his guide had a rather bad time on the mountain. Having let a campfire get out of control, they had to scramble for a new site! Then Thoreau sprained an ankle in Tuckerman Ravine . . . but he saw for the first time "the leaves of the *Arnica mollis*," so all was well! The name "soft arnica" or "hairy arnica" refers to the soft hairs on the leaves. It is native to Alaska and the West but also flourishes in isolated populations in the White Mountains—hence Thoreau had his find.

In the mid-nineteenth century, to get to the top of Mount Washington no longer required the physical strength of a Darby Field, for a carriage road was built. First came a rail connection. At milepost 91 of the St. Lawrence and Atlantic Railroad connecting Portland, Maine, to Montreal, Quebec, lay Gorham in New Hampshire. The rail line opened in 1851, thus ensuring easy access to the eastern side of the White Mountains. Private interests modernized the eight-mile stretch of road from Gorham to Pinkham Notch at the base of Mount Washington. The Alpine House in Gorham, described as "spacious" in 1861, became a central accommodation for mountain travel. The tourist infrastructure was in place. All it needed was a road to the top.

Leading Portland businessmen interested David O. Macomber in the project. With cost overruns, Macomber backed out and David Pingree's new company finished the road to the top. Work began in 1854, reached the halfway point in the autumn of 1856, and opened with a public gala on August 8, 1861. The Carriage Road (now called the Auto Road) claims to be America's oldest man-made attraction. The Summit House was waiting for the crowds. Built in 1852, it was immediately enlarged to accommodate sixty overnight guests. One hundred and fifty could dine. An annex, called the Tip Top House, was built the following year. A U.S. Army Signal Corp's observatory was manned in the 1870s and 1880s, then closed. The present Mount Washington Observatory has existed since 1932. All you have to do is drive up that Carriage Road. It was an immediate success . . . and has remained so. A Stanley Steamer climbed the road in 1889; by 1935, 3,100 private cars had paid the toll, and on the centenary anniversary, 12,800 vehicles made the trip. I am told that presently the annual total of bumper stickers boasting "This Car Climbed Mount Washington" is about forty-five thousand. What had once been a secular pilgrimage has become a site of mass tourism.

Notwithstanding the Carriage Road's success, by 1869 the industrial marvel of a rack-and-pinion, wood-burning locomotive surpassed the glory of the road. A charter for the Cog Railway was given to Sylvester Marsh (who had come up with the idea while climbing the mountain in 1852) before the Civil War, but the rail line did not reach the summit until July 1869. Marsh died in 1884, and the enterprise has been bought and sold many times since. The present owner is a New Hampshire business man, Wayne Presby. In all its years, the railway has taken about five million people to the top. There have been only two major accidents, one in 1929, and the other in 1967. Until 1910, wood was the fuel used, then coal was burned until 2008, when diesel was brought in. In the 2003–4 winter, ski trains ran up the mountain to about 3,800 feet and dropped skiers off after a fifteen-minute ride. The slopes were about fifty feet wide on either side of the rail track. On the whole this was not a success—due to the long wait for the train to return to the top, the fickle weather, and the low number of riders—and these special ski excursion rides were discontinued in 2006.

However, there would be skiing on Mount Washington. Very few of the White Mountain school painted the mountains in their winter hues. John Ross Key's *After the First Snow Storm: Mount Washington from Jefferson Highlands* was sold in Boston in 1877. The critic for the *Boston Evening Transcript* contrasted the shaggy browns and greens of Mount Jefferson with the "white crown and purple robes of the monarch of mountains," Mount Washington. Artists were giving "a new viewing to popular subjects." Winter was exciting . . . and challenging.

When artists such as Benjamin Champney, Thomas Hill, Franklin Stanwood, and John Ross Key were painting winter scenes, the only groups of skiers were immigrant Scandinavians in the Midwest and men who had made it out to gold rush California. There skiing was both a means of communication and a competition. Once the vast amounts of snow had closed down mining operations, razzmatazz was generated by inter-camp rivalry, fought out on straight downhill racing skis of twelve feet in length over courses that took twenty to twenty-five seconds. In the Midwest it was jumping—a cultural artifact brought from the home country and kept very much alive by the continuing immigration, from Norway in particular.

Skiing up—and down—Mount Washington came from neither of these origins. The attempt to reach the top on skis had two cultural sources and one practical one. In the latter nineteenth century, the growing bourgeois society seemed to be driven by the ever-increasing quest for superlatives. Or, to put it in terms of the Olympics (first held in 1896), *citius, altius, fortius*: faster, higher, stronger. This triumvirate of goals suited anyone attempting to climb Mount Washington admirably, summer or winter. The second cultural factor was the advent, in Europe, of winter mountaineering on skis. Mountaineers conquered their peaks one dogged step after another. They left their cold mountain huts in freezing predawn weather. Often coming from palace hotels, skiers struggled to slip-slide to the top, and if it all became too steep, well, they simply took off their skis and continued on foot. And then came the way down. Careful plod after plod for the mountaineer, sheer speed and delight for the (competent) skier. For the mountaineering fraternity skiing was acrobatic tomfoolery, while climbing was man's work.

These ideas emanated from Europe, and major mountaineering feats on skis began when a German, Wilhelm Paulcke, and three friends, crossed the Berner Oberland in Switzerland on skis in 1897. Meanwhile Norwegian immigrants settling in Berlin, New Hampshire, and Swedish and Finnish communities in Maine, still using their homeland modes of skiing, would not even think about ski mountaineering. It took a Dr. Wiskott from Breslau, Germany (now Wrocław, Poland), to have the idea to climb Mount Washington while he was in the United States on a visit. He made the attempt in either late 1899 or early 1900. For many years, all we knew came from a brief remark in a 1926 German book on sports around the world. No note of Wiskott's trip made it into the *Berlin Reporter* or the *North Conway Sun*, nor, indeed, into *Among the Clouds*, Mount Washington's own newspaper. In spite of the paper being printed only in summer, it contained ski interest pieces, at least from 1905 on. It is, therefore, surprising that an attempt like Wiskott's never received any mention.

A month or two before this book had its final copy editing, new material came to light in astonishingly quick succession.

First came information that a Dr. Max Wiskott from Breslau had arrived in New York City and was among prominent people booked into the Netherland Hotel in July 1899. A couple of months later, he registered his arrival at the top of Mount Washington on September 9. In December, in a season of plenty of game but few hunters in Maine, he bagged two deer and a moose on a hunting trip. And, finally, his story appeared in the *White Mountain Republic-Journal* of April 6, 1900, that turned out to be a reprint from the *Boston Sunday Herald* of March 11, 1900.

The article in the *White Mountain Republic-Journal* was headlined "Summit of Mt. Washington" and subtitled "Famous Alpine Climber Makes a Winter Ascent and Discovers a Phenomenon—Perilous Trip Safely Made." Those were editorial comments to Wiskott's own account that followed. The weather was against him. Still, we learn he had been ski mountaineering in Europe. Indeed, there is an article partially based on some of his skiing exploits in the German magazine, *Der Winter* of August 1928—another last minute find. His skis, Wiskott tells us, were Norwegian models. With one snow-shoed partner—never named but included in one illustration—he skied in to the few dwellings where they found Mr. Marcot (Eugene Marcotte, the caretaker of the cog railway), whom he enlisted to carry supplies for the ascent. Marcot was also on snowshoes. The going was difficult; it had rained a couple of days before, and then came frost. The two men left their snowshoes at the point where the trail steepens. Wiskott, with his skis, followed suit very soon after. This was also the place where the railway was mounted on trestles, thus keeping it above the snow. They got to the top all right by clambering up the trestle. At some stage, Marcot went down by himself. On top, Wiskott and his companion were duly amazed at the three-inch ice that layered everything; it was something that he had not seen in Europe and considered it a real discovery—the phenomenon mentioned in the subtitle. Wiskott and his partner spent some time admiring the panoramic views before bedding down for the night. In the morning, because of oncoming weather, they started slip-sliding down and found their equipment.

At this stage, Wiscott really enjoyed himself. Mr. Marcot came up to meet them, by which time Wiskott was on his skis and reported that Marcot had "never seen before the sight of a man on skis bearing down on him at full speed." Compared to his snowshoed companion, Wiskott then had a comparatively easy ski run out to the Mount Pleasant cottage, even as a darkening storm started to unleash rain. So ended the first attempt on skis for the summit of Mount Washington.

There are two outstanding aspects of Dr. Wiskott's endeavors. The first is that he was alone in having the idea of an attempted ski ascent on the highest of the White Mountains. Others were snowshoeing the Whites in winter but never before had there been the thought to try ski mountaineering. (One does wonder whether his visit to the top in September was a reconnaissance trip.) That this ski mountaineering came from his European experience is obvious. Not only was the example of Wilhelm Paulcke only two years old, but Wiskott himself had skied in the Riesengebirge (Giant Mountains) that are almost the same height as Mount Washington. It is not surprising that his attempt was not immediately followed; mountain skiing was simply unknown in New England. And he had obviously had—from a skiing point of view—a disappointing trip.

The second aspect is this: however much Wiskott might have impressed Mr. Marcot with such skiing never before witnessed, when the next attempts were made—by Libby and Chandler in 1905 and 1907—Marcot still used snowshoes, and there is no mention at all of his previous connection with Dr. Wiskott and his skis. Only when the Dartmouth men made their trips to the mountain, and especially into Tuckerman Ravine, did Mount Washington gain its ski fame. Still, there is no denying that Dr. Max Wiskott was out there testing those snows with the hope of reaching the top on skis, and it is worth recording.

Norman Libby, a well-respected insurance agent from Bridgton, Maine, had had a hand in editing the *Above the Clouds* summer news sheet for a couple of years, and in February 1905 he made a pleasure excursion to Mount Washington. You might expect when the *Gorham Mountaineer*'s column on Libby's trip was headlined "Skiing on Mount Washington" with the subheading "Norman Libby First to Try" that the article would be full of this feat. Besides being told that the point of the expedition was "to slide a portion of the down trip which he did without mishap," we learn details such as that part of the cabin roof had blown off, and the kitchen shutter too. The most important section of the column was devoted to Mr. Marcotte, the caretaker of the cog railway's property at the base station. Sometime before this trip, he had thrown a bottle into the Great Gulf to see how far he could throw it. Not far. So he tried again, slipped, and fell three hundred feet. "But for the bushes, this story might not be told." Mr. Libby left for his home "well pleased with his trip." That's all! The account in the *Portland Sunday Telegram* did strike a different note, editorializing that "skiing [is] destined to be a popular and fascinating sport in this country."

So much for first ascents, so much for the heroics of bottle throwing. Libby's second trip in 1907 was more ambitious. He convinced Bates College bookstore owner Algernon Chandler, "one of the most companionable fellows," to come along on the hundred-mile "walk," mostly on skis, from Bridgton to Gorham, taking in Pleasant Mountain on the way. It was not the original intent to go for the summit but only to the Halfway House, "for the ski ride down the Carriage Road" and a stay at the Glen House. Then the proprietor offered to obtain creepers, so they changed their minds.

While waiting for these creepers, described by Libby as moccasins, an early form of crampons, they decided to ski up to the Halfway House and slide down. Tying rope under their skis—this was an era before skins were widely known and available—they made good progress, often remarking on the superiority of their skis over snowshoes (a much-debated topic at the time). The way down was, as Libby put it, "rapid. With allowance for delays (mostly tumbles) . . . we made the four miles in a running time of twenty minutes."

They left the next day for the summit with the mountains "receiving the first rays of the rising sun." Up to the Halfway House, the trip followed the previous day's excursion, but after that "not even a twig offered a clutch in the event of a mishap." "We had a thrilling moment [when] we passed a declivity." A dead deer was inspected—so exhausted that it had simply frozen to death, which "abounds in suggestions." Near the five-mile post, for almost half an hour they went step by careful step, "daring to look neither right nor left, for fear of dizziness." This was excitement to say the least. And yet the summit was "the least enjoyable part of the trip," and they were unable to locate the Lake of the Clouds. The solitude they felt was depressing and cured only by the "rapid and comfortable down-going." They reached the Halfway House at five o'clock and skied the last four miles to the Glen House, where, "looking back to the mountain . . . the day had given rich rewards for our effort."

These first Mount Washington excursions by lone ski-ers demonstrate the appeal they had for a few middle-class outdoorsmen. The disciplined effort of the hundred-mile expedition was tempered by the fun of the down-mountain slides on Pleasant and Washington—just that combination of muscularity and merrymaking that a number of men were beginning to find so attractive in the years around the turn of the century. These individual ascents drew little notice. Libby's detailed accounts come just from the local papers, the *Gorham Mountaineer*, the *Bridgton News*, and the *Portland Sunday Telegram*, hardly papers having a wide distribution.

But larger things were brewing in Hanover, on the west-ern side of the state of New Hampshire. Fred Harris had enrolled in Dartmouth College in 1907, and two years later he sent a letter to the school paper suggesting an Outing Club.

On the possibility of a program for the DOC, he had included one major ski hike during the winter, "say to Mooselac," Dartmouth's own mountain. Mount Washington would be an even more attractive goal.

We get a real flavor of what it meant to go off on a ski trip from Fred Harris's journal entries starting Friday, March 3, 1911:

> Awful rush to get started on 1.53 train north. Twelve members of Outing Club started for the White Mountains. We arrived at the Ravine House, Randolf [sic] just in time for a fine supper. Planned out our trip for tomorrow.

> SATURDAY, MARCH 4, 1911:
> Breakfast at 6. Drove over to Glen House. Tipped over once. Skied the last 4 miles over. Started up the mountain about 10. Got up to Half Way House a half hour ahead of the snowshoe men. Men that had my bag of food turned back. I slipped once and only a bush saved me from death. Watts came along with picaroon and helped me. Finally got so hungry we decided to turn around. Had feed at Half Way House. Made 4 mile slide down mountain in 14 minutes without stopping. Tea at the Glen House. Left camera there by mistake. Drove back to Randolf [sic] through Gorham.

> SUNDAY, MARCH 5, 1911:
> Got up and had breakfast about 10. Took pictures of crowd as they started out. Licklider told me I would have no difficulty on skiis but he led me into some awful country where there was even no trail. Saw three deer. Got back before the snowshoe men arrived. Fine dinner about 5. Sat around fire and told stories afterwards.

> MONDAY, MARCH 6, 1911:
> Got up at 6. Had early breakfast and left for Hanover arriving at 11.19.

There is much to digest here. The importance of the train departures/arrivals was always a factor, whether for a day or even an afternoon hike, and more so on a four-day excursion such as this one to Mount Washington. The Ravine House in Randolph, located only eight miles from the Glen House, was often used as a center for day trips. Horses and "pungs"— simple sleighs—were available for hire. When Harris wrote "Drove to Glen House. Tipped over once," this was by horse and sleigh. The derring-do of near-death, of awful country (the word "awful" had more awe in it at the turn of the century than it does now), contrasts with photographing the crowd and taking tea. This social/nature split was part of the joys for young men at this time, imbued with romantic ideals bounded by masculinity. The mention of Licklider is important, too. Harris had continual and fervent support from a number of professors; Professors Goldthwaite and Licklider in particular had been in on the DOC from the start, Goldthwaite even admitting that skipping class for the great outdoors was not necessarily all bad!

In March 1913, Harris, Carl Shumway, and Joseph Cheney skied up the Carriage Road, and—roped together—down the eight miles to the bottom. This time, it was reported by the *Boston Evening Transcript* and the *Boston Evening Record*. There was more to it than just that.

The ultimate goal was to reach the top of the New England world on skis. *Altius* may have been foremost in their minds that March day, but the weather did not allow a summit expedition, so skiers Harris, Shumway, Cheney, and three others turned off on the Raymond Path—named for major Curtis Raymond, a regular Glen House summer guest for forty years who had cleared the path to the ravine—to Tuckerman Ravine. Serendipitous, then, and important for the future was the fact that Dartmouth men would be the first skiers into the Tuckerman Bowl. "It was," wrote Shumway for the *Boston Evening Transcript*, "one grand wild coast down through the ravine." A blizzard sent blinding "boiling snow flurries" while "frozen snow waves kept me rocking back and forth."

The next day, March 10, the weather turned fine and the three of them made it to the top. Notes by Carl E. Shumway, in his own hand, describe how they rode in pungs from Gorham to the Glen House. They skied "all the way to the top of Mount Washington and down again tied together with 150 feet of rope." Planks had been taken off some of the bridges to ease water flow, so they leaped over the open spaces.

Every winter from then on parties of DOC skiers (thirty signed up in 1914) journeyed to Mount Washington to test themselves against the mountain. And almost immediately others joined in, realizing that the DOC had the experience. Men such as 1932 Nobel prize–winning chemist Irving Langmuir and his conservationist friend, John S. Apperson of Schenectady, New York, were keen to join DOC parties on the mountain. Others, such as Williams College student Roland Palmedo, was part of a Dartmouth group in 1916, as was Wendel Paul, the secretary of the Montreal Ski Club, who had experienced ski touring in Switzerland and was looking for a new field and saw advantage in what Dartmouth was doing. The Outing Club extended a warm welcome to such men, and its influence spread.

It was only in 1926 that skiers came into the bowl regularly, and in 1927, the Appalachian Mountain Club (AMC) kept open their camp at Pinkham Notch at the base of the Mountain, Joe Dodge in charge. Dodge was a twenty-seven-year-old ex-naval radio submarine man of World War I, salty in spirit and words, and ran the huts until forced into retirement in 1959. He had to deal with increasing numbers of skiers who came to the Tuckerman Bowl in spring. As more and more people took to skiing, and as skiing became more mechanized, the great glacial cirque on Mount Washington drew the collegiate and club crowds. To ski up there took a climb of between two and three hours, and when combined with other like-minded hair-shirt youth it gave the adventure the status of a tribal rite of passage. The backdrop of the bowl is the headwall, fifty degrees steep, dropping nine hundred feet, that was first climbed and descended on skis in April 1931 by U.S. Olympians and Dartmouth men Charles Proctor and John Carleton. They had climbed up onto the cone when it started to snow and decided to get on down. "We had a nervous time up there, I think," recalled Charley Proctor in 1981. This was no *Schuss*. The first man to come straight over the Headwall and down was Sigmund Ruud, in May 1932. He had been in the United States for the Norwegian team at the Lake Placid Olympics and had to stay over to have his appendix removed. Describing the Ravine as "a great natural ice-box," up he climbed, just onto the cone, and then jumped into the fall line for a straight *Schuss*. So . . . fast skiing was possible, even desirable: *citius, altius, fortius* on display down the Headwall.

In 1926, Arthur Comey was the first up Mount Katahdin, Maine's highest peak. Comey was a man for all things and all seasons. Much respected as a town planner, he was an AMC stalwart in many capacities. Having climbed Katahdin on skis, he read an account of what the British were calling the "Inferno," a one-of-a-kind race with a 7,500-foot drop over about five miles above Mürren down to the Lauterbrunnen valley floor, a race "containing the most difficult ground that has ever been raced on": four hours to hike up, and about one and a quarter hours down. In *Mountain Magazine* of 1929 Comey quoted the account in full because "it beggars any abridgement," and went on to add that we in America were far behind but "have plenty of little 'infernos' ready not far away." Here was the challenge, and it was taken up four years later at Easter by the Ski Club Hochgebirge, one of the wealthy new downhill clubs out of Boston. A summit-to-base run, over the Tuckerman Headwall, was the test. All competitors had to sign saying they could ski reasonably well and absolving the Hochies of any responsibility.

Fourteen entered, eleven ran, one lost the way, and one broke a ski in this American Inferno, also called Suicide

Race. Hollis Phillips, a Northeastern University student, won in fourteen minutes and 41.3 seconds. One wonders if he had any advantage having taken a ski course with Hannes Schneider at Saint Anton. Alexander Bright—a leading light of the Hochgebirgers—was second, in seventeen minutes and

Figure 3. In the 1930s, the New Hampshire State Planning and Development Commission published ski posters by such well-known artists as Dwight Shepler and expert skier Ted Hunter. This late 1930s silkscreen of "Spring Skiing," designed by S. Underhill (artist unknown), caught the delight of a day's outing in the Tuckerman Bowl. New England Ski Museum poster 2017.045.033. Used by permission.

twenty seconds, and the club's John Lawrence, third, only eleven seconds behind. The last man down—from the Ski Smashers—took twenty minutes and 46.2 seconds. It was a grand success. None of the thirty Nansen Club patrol was needed for the three toboggans strategically placed by the course. All were extremely satisfied with the timing mechanism, a radio telephone borrowed from Harvard's Cruft laboratory and installed by Joe Dodge. Runners left at one-minute intervals, Dodge calling "Go!" from the bottom to be heard from the Observatory's reception at the top. So much better than a *Geschmozzel* start, where all competitors started together, as the British did. This was the first time in any ski race, it was believed, that the radio connection proved so efficient; it had been used in air races but never before for a ski race. With this success, naturally, there was going to be a repeat.

In April 1934's race Dartmouth ace Dick Durrance brought the record down to twelve minutes and thirty-five seconds. He had learned his skiing as a high schooler in Germany and was in school in Newport, New Hampshire, before enrolling at Dartmouth. He fell several times but still won handily. This year the course was slightly different, ending with a run down the Sherburne Trail to Pinkham. Bob Livermore of Harvard's Stem Like Hell Ski Club was second, in just over eighteen minutes after "the world's most terrific spill," and Lawrence was again third, in twenty minutes and 24.5 seconds.

Even after the first Inferno, Bob Monahan, stationed at the summit observatory, did not believe that the race could become a fixture; the winter snow conditions above the tree line made the skiing "decidedly unsatisfactory except during a very brief period, which the Hochs so fortunately struck." He was right. The next inferno would be held in 1939; of forty-four entrants, forty-two completed the course. "The fascinating thing about that race," recalled third-place man Dartmouth's Ed Wells, "was that as you came down the course there were occasional flags but it would be very easy to miss the place where you go over the headwall . . .

unless you had a good memory." He was right. "I remember we wore long, red avalanche strings in case of an avalanche that you'd be able to be dug out," added another contestant.

Coming off wins in Europe in 1938, nineteen-year-old Toni Matt from Saint Anton, Austria, had at least seen the Headwall. He decided to take the nine-hundred-foot precipitous descent with a couple of turns right at the top in order to run fast enough to keep his speed up over the slight rise leading on to the Little Headwall. He would then carry that speed down the Sherburne Trail to the finish. What he didn't know was that coming from the summit, you cannot really see where you actually go over the lip. The tale of what happened next has been told many times, including by Matt himself in a tape held by the New England Ski Museum in Franconia. He did his couple of turns all right, but on the relatively gentle approach to the headwall below the cone, then . . . the Headwall, over and down, where he picked up terrific speed and, as he said, it is impossible to "turn when you're going that fast"—it has been estimated he was going about ninety miles per hour. At the bottom of the nine-hundred-foot drop, the bowl's base was a washboard, enough to make "your knees fly up above your ears." But the speed carried him down the Sherburne to the finish in an astonishing six minutes and 29.2 seconds to beat Dick Durrance by over a minute, with compatriot Dartmouth competitor, Ed Wells, coming in third in seven minutes and 46.3 seconds.

Back in 1980, when documentary filmmaker Rick Moulton was putting *Legends of American Skiing* together, the New England Ski Museum had just received about ten home movies shot by Dr. Walter Crandell of Hanover. One showed part of Matt's run. Moulton's film was completed in 1982 and is shown on various New England Public Television stations from time to time, so you can still catch this one-of-a-kind "Meteor on Skis" who is now a major part of the lore of Tuckerman.

CHAPTER 6

CANNON MOUNTAIN

THE STATE OF NEW HAMPSHIRE IN ACTION

Interstate 93 runs directly north from Boston for 140 miles to Cannon Mountain in Franconia. Up in the Notch Parkway, the road has only one lane in each direction and the speed is limited to forty-five miles per hour: environmental compromises by the New Hampshire Highway Department and the Park Service.

It is right to start off by emphasizing the role of the state of New Hampshire in the matter of Cannon Mountain. When the Profile House—one of those Grand Hotels that dotted the north country in the nineteenth and early twentieth centuries—burned down in August 1923, its land, comprising about six thousand acres, including all of Cannon Mountain, was for sale at $400,000. The State of New Hampshire, the Society for the Protection of New Hampshire Forests, and some fifteen thousand private contributors enabled the state to purchase the property. It created the Franconia Forest Reservation and Memorial Park, thereby inheriting the guardianship of the Old Man of the Mountain, the famous profile immortalized by Daniel Webster: "God Almighty has hung out a sign that there He makes men." Nathaniel Hawthorn wrote a story; presidents Ulysses S. Grant and Dwight D. Eisenhower visited. It was the most potent of New Hampshire's symbols and, indeed, the official symbol of the state since 1945. Once the state had bought the land, it was realized very early on that the forehead of the Great Stone Face was cracking. Crews attached chains to hold the fissures together. In the late 1950s, the state legislature passed a $25,000 bill for weatherproofing that included cement, steel rods, and a concrete gutter for taking the runoff. In spite of annual repairs, in the early hours of May 3, 2003, the Great Stone Face collapsed. I have heard that local revenues fell 30 percent.

When the Franconia Forest Reservation was created in 1928 (by 1933 it had become the Franconia Notch State Park), the Parks Department had a managerial role in its summer and winter development. As far as skiing was concerned, though, just about every suggestion, innovation, and actual proposal—and much of the bureaucratic work—was by people outside the state apparatus. Today, Cannon Mountain is the state's only ski area (Mount Sunapee, opening for skiing in 1948, was leased to Okemo, then the ski operation was leased to the conglomerate of Vail Resorts) and as such is beholden to the state legislature. But it did not start like that at all.

In the summer of 1900, Robert and Katharine Peckett opened up their farmhouse on Sugar Hill to guests. This was not unusual, and given the attraction of nature in the raw at Franconia Notch, it seemed a perfect spot: the views across the valley took in the vast high country bounded by Cannon Mountain on one side of the Notch, and Mount Lafayette on the other. Better viewing, for sure, than from the Profile House down at Echo Lake. Ten years later, Peckett's opened for the winter season; they were not by any means the only north country hostelry offering skiing. Bretton Woods advertised skiing in the *Boston Globe* in 1912, and there were "exciting runs" in Dixville Notch in 1917. In February 1911, the Pecketts entertained a party of twenty from Providence, followed by seventeen from Boston, and the moment they left, another party of twelve was booked in. They tramped around on snowshoes and skis to the Profile House and to Peckett's own log camp or just over hill and dale to while the midwinter days away, as the *Littleton Courier* reported on its front page of February 16, 1911.

It is unclear how Peckett's attracted guests: it was too small to be part of the Grand Hotel clientele, and certainly many cuts above any local inn. Robert and Katharine Peckett provided—eventually—enough room for some sixty guests who were waited upon by sixty-five employees, working in a homelike atmosphere to serve an extraordinary client list: two presidents of the United States (Coolidge and Hoover), two chief justices of the Supreme Court (Hughes and Stone), Eleanor Roosevelt and Wally Simpson (twice divorced and future wife of Britain's King Edward VII), and Bishop Manning—once asked if Salvation could be found outside the Episcopal church, he is supposed to have replied, "Perhaps so, but no gentleman would care to avail himself of it." A surprising number of Broadway and Hollywood names appear in the guest book: Leland Heywood, producer of *South Pacific* and *Sound of Music*, signed in. Perhaps it is no wonder that Mary Martin stayed too, and so did Bette Davis, Margaret Sullivan, Janet Gaynor, and ballerina Joan Fontaine, bringing glamour to Sugar Hill. Authors were prominent: Booth Tarkington, twice Pulitzer Prize winner for fiction; Dorothy Thompson, influential journalist; and acid-tongued *New Yorker* writer Alexander Woollcott stayed, as did Kenneth Roberts. Dr. Charles Mayo, one of the founders of the Mayo Clinic, and Helen Keller were among the number of guests that also included many extremely wealthy businessmen: Sir Edward Grenfell, a British banker and politician associated with J. P. Morgan; Laurance and other Rockefellers; and railroad tycoon Jerome Hill, as well as Wanamakers, Vanderbilts, and a Chrysler! And Lowell Thomas, of *Lawrence of Arabia* fame, broadcast all across ski-America, extolling each of the venues from which he was broadcasting. He did so from the base station at Cannon and on another occasion from the summit. And then there were the up-and-becoming-well-known skiers, many of whom have already been mentioned in previous chapters or will be in future chapters: John Carleton, Fred Harris, Charley Proctor, Roland Palmedo, Alec Bright, and Minnie Dole, to pick a representative half dozen.

After World War I and before the Depression, those with disposable wealth tried to get away from their city and professional lives to what was perceived as a more natural existence; it would make for a pure break of their normal routines. Winter in the 1920s made a stay away from home even more desirable. In the 1930s Depression years and beyond, winter was transformed into an economic vehicle to better the lives of those who lived in a ski land penetrated by industrialization. And Peckett's played a two-part role in the modernization of Cannon Mountain. The first role was ski instruction, the second the building of a downhill race trail on Cannon.

Those who took to skiing in the 1920s came from a college background and wanted to continue their winter joys, some even recreating their university activities in such organizations as the Dartmouth Outing Club of Boston. Others took to skiing in clubs already devoted to outdoor activities. In particular, the Appalachian Mountain Club (AMC) headquartered in Boston had huts already available in the White Mountains for summer hiking. These comparatively wealthy ski people had often tripped to Europe, where they tended to visit two particular venues: Mürren in Switzerland and Saint Anton in the Arlberg region of Austria. The British made a Rock of Gibraltar out of the small Swiss village across from the Eiger, Mönch, and Jungfrau where Arnold Lunn held forth. Saint Anton was home to Hannes Schneider, *Skimeister* to the world. When Americans returned home, they brought with them a British attitude to skiing and, from Saint Anton, Schneider's Arlberg technique. Both provided aspects to the sport different from the established Norwegian norms still present in the United States.

In 1928, daughter of the house Katharine Peckett took time away from her studies in Paris to visit Engelberg in Switzerland, about an hour south of Luzern. The village had a ski season going back to 1902–3 and was "one of the strongholds of Messrs. Thomas Cook & sons." Perhaps Kate Peckett was also interested in seeing how the Thomas Cook travel agency handled matters. With the grand mountain Titlis in the background of Engelberg, skiing was to the fore, and Kate hired two instructors for the next season at Peckett's, but only Hermann Glatfelder is remembered.

Glatfelder came for the winter of 1929–30 but has left no ski tracks for us to follow. This is curious, given that he was the first European brought over. You might imagine there would be some publicity attached, but that, evidently, was not the Peckett way. However, the following season an itinerant half-Russian, half-Bavarian duke related to Napoleon, Dimitri von Leuchtenberg, already known in Saint-Sauveur in the Laurentians north of Montreal, was hired by Peckett's. Brought up in Russia on the fringes of the Romanovs, Duke Dimitri enrolled in the Imperial Cavalry School at Saint Petersburg, and after Lenin's revolution joined the anti-Bolshevik Whites, eventually escaping to Schloss Seeon, a onetime abbey converted to a castle in 1892 that the family had inherited. It lay about an hour west of Munich.

Duke Dimitri emigrated to Canada to join yet another of his relatives, the Marquis Nicolo degli Albizzi, well-known as an adventuring skier at Lake Placid and in Canada east and west. At Saint-Sauveur in the Laurentians, the duke taught skiing, laid out trails, did survey work, and coached Alpine ski racing. He came south to Peckett's—with cousin Albizzi—for the 1930–31 season. Originally, Albizzi was to lay out and supervise the trails in the Franconia region, but he quit in July, and immediately his cousin, the duke, replaced him. Kate Peckett had an eye for mercurial skiers. She ran across Siegfried Buchmayr demonstrating at the Alex Taylor store in New York City and immediately invited him to Peckett's. He had passed the Hannes Schneider Ski School examination in the 1929–30 season. Buchmayr joined Peckett's ski school in the winter of 1931–32 as "trainer," nominally under the new director of winter sports, Otto Steinhauser from Munich. "Sig would take the class out in front of the hotel," remembered Roger Peabody, later to be in charge of the Cannon Tram, "for 30–45 minutes of exercise, some of the time you would be jumping in place into a snowplough position." Peckett's, advertising instruction as "training," was following a British tradition that somehow believed that as long as pleasure was made to look as if it were work, or even to consider it as work, then it was quite all right to enjoy yourself. Fun was looked on as proletarian, and, as we have seen, Peckett's did not make an appeal to the lower lights of society. A series of Austrians followed in Buchmayr's tracks.

Especially important was Kurt Thalhammer, who it was reckoned did 70 percent of the teaching while Buchmayr played impresario. He was popular with the guests. It was not known at the time but Thalhammer had joined the Nazi party in 1933, and he returned to Salzburg and was the successful applicant (out of twenty) for the "aryanization" of a well-known Jewish clothing store of Ornstein. For lying about his past, he was imprisoned for fifteen months after the war. Thalhammer recommended his friend Michael Feuersinger, who also came to Peckett's. Harald Paumgarten was another excellent Austrian racer, and we will hear more of him and his family in connection with the New England Ski Museum. In residence and teaching at Peckett's for the 1935–36 season was Otto Lang. He had been one of Hannes Schneider's leading instructors, but with the growing political unrest, Lang cast about for a ski school of his own. He had met up with the Hills—railroad magnets from Minneapolis, and their friend Kate Peckett—and thus it was arranged that he come to instruct in New Hampshire for that one winter. He went on to help Jerome Hill filming at Mount Rainier and as a result ran ski schools out in the West. We will meet Otto Lang again in the East at Snow Valley during World War II.

Kate Peckett knew how to arrange for top Arlberg instruction as well as provide terrain for increasingly advanced skiers. Realizing that the mild slope leading away from the lodge would no longer satisfy the better skier, especially one who had enjoyed skiing in the Alps, she started talking up a down-mountain trail on the north side of Cannon Mountain.

At this stage, the state stepped in and formed a Ski Trails Committee. The three leading people on the committee were, lo and behold, Kate Peckett herself, prominent Boston skier Alexander Bright (of whom more later), and Dartmouth Olympian John Carleton, now a lawyer in Manchester. Two other important and interested parties were on the committee: Arthur Comey, first to think of the Inferno Races, and David Austin, Waterville Valley hotelier. Assistant state forester Warren Hale was the only government official. Kate Peckett set up a fundraising organization and lobbied successfully to employ the Civilian Conservation Corps, that Depression-spawned agency for economic recovery and employer of young men. Good connections were forged with both the Franconia Notch State Park and the White Mountain National Forest. That is, yet again, the civilian—capitalistic—thrust to create a "broad but murderous Richard Taft Trail," as a *New Yorker* writer put it, was managed by private enterprise. Thanks to Kate Peckett, Duke Dimitri was to lay out the trail that led from the top of the mountain down to a short uphill before plummeting on the Franconia side. Started in the summer of 1932, the trail was completed by the following summer, although it was already in use in the winter of 1932–33 by Sig Buchmayr. Buchmayr had not only joined Peckett's roster of instructors but his antics and acrobatics on skis kept the clientele enthralled, including running the "whole course straight . . . and without a fall." He would be in charge of the ski school from the 1931–32 season until it closed in 1939. The Ski Club Hochgebirge, inspired by Alec Bright, held its Challenge Cup in March on the Taft Trail and continues to do so annually to this day. The Richard Taft—named for the first proprietor of the Profile House—immediately became the first-rate downhill racing trail in the Northeast; there was nothing like it in Massachusetts, nor in Vermont. It was now up to the state of New Hampshire to manage it.

Alec Bright had enjoyed funicular skiing in Switzerland in 1930. He was much impressed with the thousands of downhill skiing feet that riding the tramcar high into the mountains made possible. Back home, he listened to Harald Paumgarten, who had taken ten rides on the 1,070-foot section of the Hafelekar aerial tramway out of Innsbruck and got eleven thousand feet of downhill running that day—one of the many tales told while instructing at Peckett's. New England's mountains, however, are forested, so the cars would have to go above the trees to drop skiers off on downhill trails yet to be built. In 1933, Bright proposed such a tram to the New England Council, which had convened to discuss ways to promote the future sport of skiing, noting that it would be good not only for winter sportsmen but also for the summer tourist business. New Hampshire governor John Winant organized a Tramway Commission in 1934 to survey about twenty potential mountains. Alec Bright, a good friend of the governor, was on that commission.

In February 1935, Bright was in Europe again, this time with Tom Dabney, Sam Wakeman, and others—all from the Ski Club Hochgebirge—contemplating their day over tea with rum as they reran their day's three runs on the Nordabfahrt at Austria's Zell am See, in all 11,700 vertical feet. They computed that, since the Taft trail was 1,800 feet, very probably a skier would not climb it more than twice in a day, and it would take a skier three Sundays to equal what they had enjoyed in just one day. Putting it another way, "We've skied as much in one day here [in Zell am See] as we would in a quarter of the whole season in New England." This was yet another compelling argument for the building of a tram. By this time, there were a number of parties invested in the idea of an aerial tram, and the surveys started coming in. Particularly impressive were the surveys of the American Steel and Wire Company of Massachusetts. The two most prominent locations were Mount Blue, a slightly lower summit of Moosilauke, and Cannon Mountain. Mount Blue was dismissed in part because some Dartmouth men objected—Moosilauke was Dartmouth's mountain. But car traffic was also a limiting factor; only about 1,600 cars drove by Moosilauke in the season, whereas about two million drove through the Franconia Notch. So . . . Cannon it was, and governor John Winant was a friend of skiing.

Bright first got notable Franconia local Roland Peabody interested in the idea. With Governor Winant's support, a committee to look into financing a tram was formed. Peabody was joined by C. T. Bodwell, a well-known photographer and supporter for the Notch and its environment. Prominent Dartmouth alumni skiers John Carleton, 1924 Olympian and already on the Ski Trails Committee, and Edgar Hunter, standout racer and now an architect, were appointed. Committee meetings multiplied, inspections were made, and surveys carried out. The committee went before the legislature to present the proposal of such a tram. There were naysayers—even "yowls of protest" during the senate hearings. More than one member, Roland Peabody reported, "shook his fist at us in the gallery." Others objected to the many hotdog stands that would spring up. Facetiously, someone described how the Old Man could grasp the cable in his jaws and you could swing all the way to Mount Washington, stopping off at Mount Madison. "Those who love nature for nature's sake should spend their vacations in Canada." But the positive arguments held the high ground.

Two twenty-five-passenger cars were projected to carry 225 people per hour the 1,820 vertical feet to the top in five minutes. Preliminary studies showed the possibility of practice slopes near the summit station in addition to at least four trails terminating at the base of the tram. Other trails would lead off to the Kinsman Range. An impressive array of economic statistics from some of the European tramways was provided. Special emphasis was also placed on the ample tourist travel through the Notch during the summer and fall.

On January 22, 1935, House Bill 131 provided for the construction and operation of what almost immediately became known as "The Tram." Members of the Judiciary

Committee, to whom the bill had been referred, along with their confreres from the Senate and members from House and Senate Appropriations Committees, viewed the site in early February. No one spoke against the tram, although one man wanted to ensure the Old Man would not be trespassed upon. With some amendments in March and May, the bill took effect on June 20, 1935.

But it was going to be costly. The Tramway Bill appropriated $250,000 (about 55 percent of the total cost), and the Tramway Commission had been "reasonably assured" that the Federal Government would purchase revenue bonds for the remaining 45 percent. This did not happen immediately, and for the next month or two, there was a fear that the whole project might founder. But by September the American Steel and Wire Company set up a work camp and built a cable lift to haul men and matériel to the top of the mountain.

The American Steel and Wire Company represented the German-based Bleichert-Zeugg, whose various trams were well known to visiting American skiers: the Kreuzeckbahn at Garmisch had been erected in 1926; at Engelberg, the Trübsee lift was in service the season before Kate Peckett's visit; the Patscherkofel out of Innsbruck was built in 1928; and, most obviously, the Galzigbahn at Saint Anton was ready for the 1937–38 season. Work at Cannon started with excavating the base station and creating the foundations for the three towers. The base station was to have a spacious waiting room, a ticket office, toilets, an open fireplace, a first aid room, and offices for management. Adjoining the same structure were the counterweight pits, landing platform, control room, generator room, heating plant, water system, storage room, and the operating room. Parking for seven hundred cars was leveled by the CCC. Work continued throughout the winter, and the official opening was set for June 17, 1938, for the five-minute ride to the summit. Uniformed guides took visitors to the observation deck, where chairs were available. A number of short trails to scenic points were marked.

The tram, at twenty-five maximum capacity, was an instant summer success at forty cents to go up, thirty cents to go down, sixty cents round-trip, and children at half price. A total of 97,457 were thrilled as they rode "forty feet above the tree tops." In winter, the "Sky Route to Ski Fun" cost slightly more: sixty cents to go up, fifty cents to go down, one dollar round-trip, and children half price. A ten-ride book of tickets cost five dollars, and an unlimited weekly ticket was ten dollars. Thirty-seven thousand skiers took advantage of the "aerial tramway to end skiing drudgery," as the *New York Times* had urged in 1934.

From June 17, 1938, to May 24, 1980, when Tram I was pulled from service, 6,581,338 people had been carried uphill. No question that it had been a profitable venture. No surprise that waiting in the wings was a $4.6 million replacement by the Italian firm of Nuova Agudio. Tram II, with a maximum of eighty people aboard, has an hourly capacity of 770 and still takes about five minutes to reach the top. But this new tram was proposed, organized, and funded by the state of New Hampshire. The commissioner of the Department of Resources and Economic Development, George Gilman, had realized that although Tram I was still operating successfully, it was becoming increasingly difficult and expensive to find replacement parts. The state legislature hired a consulting engineer from Heron Lifts in 1977, and the following year Nuova Agudio, founded in 1861 and a leader in passenger lifts worldwide, received the contract, its first in North America. Construction began in the summer of 1978, and by February 1980, Tram II was approved for passenger traffic. There are discussions about rebuilding or replacing Tram II. To rebuild it will cost between $10 and $15 million, with an expected life of twenty years. To replace it will cost $20 to $30 million, with an expected life of between forty and fifty years.

The difference between the 1930s and 1970s is stark. Much of the development of skiing, whether in simply finding places to ski, instruction, manufacture of products and accessories or up-ski ideas, came from individuals who had taken to skiing for different reasons and had come up with ways to improve their experience. Cannon Tram is absolutely typical of this process. It simply would not have happened at that time if wealthy Bostonians had not had a European experience, had not had the personal connection with the state's governor, John Winant, to give impulse to an investigation not by state officials but by interested individual skiers.

Only two years after the tram was up and running, Winant would have one more ski card to play. Billy Fiske, holder of the Cresta record, gold medalist in the 1932 four-man Olympic bob, and one of the promoters of the Mount Hayden ski area in the ghost town of Ashcroft, outside Aspen, Colorado, was crippled in his Hurricane during the Battle of Britain. He managed to land the plane but died two days later. During World War II, Winant, the popular U.S. ambassador to England, oversaw and presented a plaque commemorating Fiske's sacrifice. You will find it if you visit St. Paul's cathedral in London.

It is important to include "Cannon's greatest day," in fact the three days of March 10, 11, and 12 in 1967, that shows the dual roles played by the state and its citizens. This was the first time the World Cup racers came to North America, a decision that allowed only four or five months of preparation after the Fédération internationale de ski had officially given their approval. The original idea of computing a number of races to see who was the best skier over the season was something like the bicycle race, the Tour de France. That race was supported by the French journal *L'Equipe*, whose main journalist was Serge Lange, and it was Lange who first broached the idea to the ski world, to Bob Beattie and Honoré Bonnet, the coaches of the American and French teams. Beattie, a New Hampshire native, knew Cannon well, indeed the U.S. National Championships had been run there in 1966. All that was needed—it was believed—was to widen and elongate the downhill course so it ran right from the top of the mountain to below the base of the tram.

The state of New Hampshire played major roles. Cannon management was in charge of the overall production of the race. The state provided a committee of advisers from various agencies and pledged nearly $42,000 (today's value $332,000). Other organizations contributed, such as Ski 93, a consortium of five ski areas off Interstate 93—Tenney, Loon, Waterville, Cannon, and Mittersill—as well as local businesses and the Eastern Inter-Club Ski League. This fifty-nine-member league not only pledged $20,000 ($158,000) that they hoped to be repaid via the sale of television rights but also supplied hundreds of man-hours for help in all the odd jobs vital to running such a large event: attending to parking, tying flags, arranging pole deliveries, gate keeping, and so on.

Cannon was not like most large resorts; there was no central ski village, no condo development in those days. There was Franconia village, and the teams were spread out to local hostelries and motels. The Austrians were the luckiest of all, since Austrian Baron von Pantz's Mittersill was within easy skiing distance of Cannon. But the Germans, for example, were put up at the Wayside Inn in Bethlehem, ten miles away. The U.S. team was quartered among local residents. The French team—a powerhouse that year—was at Lovett's, on the road from the mountain to Franconia village.

Leading the French team were the two stars, Jean-Claude Killy and Guy Périllat, and they did not disappoint, coming in first and second in the first of the races, the downhill. Killy was first, again, in the giant slalom, and when the two runs of the slalom were computed (he had come first in the first run, and seventh in the second), he came out on top again. The American hope was Jimmie Huega, the 1964 Olympic bronze medalist, and he did indeed come in second. Huega, from the Lake Tahoe area, was the son of French Basque immigrants, and he and Killy formed a friendship that lasted through his diagnosis of multiple sclerosis in 1970 until his passing in 2010.

In addition to the French King of the Hill, most impressive was the spectator turnout: over thirty thousand in the three days, "huge crowds," Killy remembered, "thousands more than had ever appeared at a U. S. alpine ski event." Here was something the state could brag about even if the governor's renaming the slopes the Killy Racing Trail never stuck. None the less, this was Cannon's day, and Jean-Claude's rise to supremacy was repeated in Vail and Jackson Hole ... not to speak of the following year at the Grenoble Olympics, where, again, he was the star of the downhill, the giant slalom, and the slalom. Cannon Mountain had shown him he could do it. "I keep a very warm memory of this epoch [the 1960s]," Killy e-mailed me, "and also because the Americans were much more welcoming than the Europeans." Take a bow, Cannon.

That was 1967, and the difference between those first races on the north side of the mountain, on the Taft trail of the 1930s, and the World Cup runs on the west side, down Vista Way and Avalanche, was immense, not least because of the role of the state. In 1967 its responsibility was managing the area, ensuring funding, and keeping tabs on nongovernmental groups, especially the Eastern Inter-Club Ski League, innkeepers, and even local homeowners, who were all on board in looking after the racers. The old tram whose idea, planning, and final construction was organized by citizens still took the runners up to the start at the top of the mountain.

How different it was for Tram II's planning, construction, opening, and managing, which was done entirely by state officials. It is true, therefore, that Cannon is the state of New Hampshire's ski resort, but however much the state may control all aspects of the ski experience, it remains Killy's mountain and, as it was at the beginning, "a skier's mountain."

CHAPTER 7

THE SCHNEIDER PHENOMENON

AUSTRIA—GERMANY—NEW HAMPSHIRE

Past the vast array of shopping malls, through the once typical New England small town of North Conway, now a tourist center for New Hampshire's White Mountains, turning east to the ski hill of Mount Cranmore, you drop your skis off right in front of a statue in full downhill form: Hannes Schneider arrived in bronze in 1988, fifty years after he and his family had been permitted by the Nazis to leave Austria. Commissioned by the Mount Cranmore Ski Company, Maine sculptor Ed Materson, who had already made bronze renditions of famed Maine and U.S. marathon runner Joan Benoit and even more famous Romanian gymnast Nadia Comaneci, presented Hannes Schneider to Mount Cranmore. This statue is, in fact, one of six of the *Skimeister* in the world. Two are in Austria: one at Schneider's birthplace village of Stuben, and one in stone at the Kandahar Haus in Saint Anton am Arlberg. In Japan, there are three: one in Nozawa Onsen and one in Shugadaira, both in Nagano prefecture, and one at Tamagawaga commemorating Schneider's trip to Japan in 1930. How did the world's foremost skier end up in North Conway?

AUSTRIA

The 1938 Nazi takeover of Austria had been fermenting for months, even years, although the military had no firm plans in place. However, there was little doubt, if the numerous plebiscites in the 1920s can be believed, that the idea of joining with Germany had a lot of support. As this appeared increasingly

possible in the 1930s, Austrian politics became embroiled in virulent strife and so desperate that chancellor Engelbert Dollfuss
was assassinated in 1934. In 1937, Hitler spoke menacingly if
not exactly about the possibility of the annexation of Austria.
Hermann Göring, now in charge of the Four-Year Economic
Plan, needed Austria's raw materials, and they could best be
acquired by *Zusammenschluss*, a merger with Germany. Hitler
had Dollfuss's successor as chancellor, Kurt von Schuschnigg,
brought to the Berchtesgaden to be railed at for hours on end,
and von Schuschnigg, browbeaten, finally signed an ambiguous
document. He returned home to announce on March 9 that
there would be a plebiscite on a possible merger, much to the
fury of Hitler. Using the Austrian national colors, it was quite
plain where Schuschnigg stood:

Rot, Weiss, Rot	Red, White, Red
Bis Wir Tot	Till we're dead

Considering this total treachery, Hitler gave orders to
have the military units ready to march, and at 5:30 a.m.
on March 12, the "friendly" visit of German troops began.
Hitler crossed the frontier at 4 p.m. that day, and the following day spoke to an adoring crowd estimated at a quarter
of a million in Vienna's Heldenplatz. The whole invasion
was nothing but a *Blumenkorso*, a "Carnival of Flowers,"
as Schuschnigg had instructed the Austrian military not
to respond to the Nazi soldiers.

While these world historical changes were taking place,
on a local level, bands of Austrian Nazis acting on their own
were causing chaos in village and town. So it was that Hannes
Schneider, practicing Catholic and forty-eight years old, was
ordered out of his home in Saint Anton am Arlberg in the
early hours of March 12, leaving his wife and two children
behind. With five others he was imprisoned in the school
before being transferred to the regular prison in Landeck. He
did not know for what he was charged. He was in prison for

twenty-five days before being permitted to go to Garmisch-Partenkirchen, just across the border in Germany, under a form of house arrest in the care of an old skiing competitor, friend, and lawyer Dr. Karl Rösen. Almost a year later, he was allowed to leave Germany. The family was reunited in Munich before taking the train to Paris and on to Le Havre, where they boarded the *Queen Mary* for the crossing to New York. The Schneiders arrived on February 9, 1939, and were taken by train to North Conway, New Hampshire, where the *Skimeister* remained until his death in 1955. Behind these bare facts lay a mix of politics and sport the likes of which were never seen before or since. Schneider was Alpine skiing's most respected instructor of the 1920s and 1930s. In his younger years he had been a keen competitor too, but he had made Saint Anton famous throughout the skiing world. "More than any other person, Schneider is responsible for skiing's world-wide boom," judged *Time*. How had he done this?

Schneider, born in 1890, had taken ski lessons with Viktor Sohm—an adherent of the Norwegian technique—in the winter of 1903–4. In 1907, he recounted, "I received my call to St. Anton am Arlberg . . . as a ski teacher." Teaching in those days was demonstrating. And that is what Schneider did, adding "*So macht man es*" (That's how you do it). Only Mathias Zdarsky had given thought to explaining the hows and whys of turns. Zdarsky commanded an enthusiastic following in Vienna and among army officers. Schneider found Zdarsky's skiing labored. Still, Zdarsky's Lilienfeld method, along with his strong personality, attracted over a thousand to his classes in 1904. Schneider had so few pupils when he started teaching, he spent his time in lonely experimentation of what emerged as the snow plough and the stem turn. When he could link one stem-Christiania to another, he could make a speedy, safe, and aesthetic descent of the fairly steep mountainsides around Saint Anton. He became known for the speed of his skiing. In fact, others were also questioning the Norwegian way of skiing. Even a Norwegian, Chapell Jakobsen over in Kitzbühel, was experimenting, and further east in Switzerland so was Eduard Capiti. Schneider had competed against Capiti, and automatically the two took stock of each other of those factors that enhanced their own techniques. Other instructors were also demonstrating only and made their mark locally, such as Reinhard Spielman in Semmering and Alois Skazel at Mürzzuschlag. But Schneider began to be noted abroad in the *Year-Book of the Ski Club of Great Britain* in 1910 and in Germany in 1913.

As Schneider put more emphasis on the stem-Christiania, he neglected the Telemark turn. Two factors indicated that this new technique was a success. Schneider now had so many pupils that he divided them up according to ability, taking beginners for two hours, intermediates for two hours, and advanced skiers for two hours. Students moved up only when they had mastered the particular instruction to a certain degree of perfection . . . and Schneider was a perfectionist. Soon he was unable to teach everybody who came, so he recruited and trained some local lads as instructors for the following winter. When Walter Bernays, a regular Saint Anton visitor, filled out his application to join the Ski Club of Great Britain in 1912, after listing his accomplishments of stem and stem-Christiania turns, he added, "Did my last Telemark in 1912. Hope I shall die before I do another." However gratuitous the remark, it shows just how effective Schneider's technique had become.

In World War I, Schneider was removed from the Eastern Front by an old ski student, now Leutnant Passini, who immediately arranged for him to be seconded to the Italian front. Passini and Schneider first took a hundred and twenty men between them and drilled them in cross-country techniques, snow ploughs, and swift and safe descents. Then they selected the best, turned them into instructors, and received a new batch of men for ski training every four weeks. Although there were Austrian military manuals available, and although Zdarsky's method was generally preferred by the top military command, and Hauptmann Bilgeri had a following too—both produced how-to ski books—Passini gave Schneider free rein. Since these were military courses, Schneider ordered and the men obeyed. He would carry this discipline into his civilian courses in the 1920s and 1930s. In this way, the Arlberg was both a way to instruct, a way to learn, and, finally, a way to ski.

In 1924 Schneider's method of teaching skiing was prescribed by the Land Tyrol for the entire region. Leading German instructors came to Saint Anton and returned home committed to the Arlberg technique. The Tyrolian Ski Association and the Association of Tyrolean Professional Ski Teachers conducted the first ski instructor's written examination in February 1925, and the Germans in the Allgäu and in Bavaria followed suit. They conferred on Schneider the title *Ehrenlehrwart* (honorary instructor) and made him *Ehrenförderer* (honorary patron) of the German Ski Association. The Austrian Ministry of Education made the Winterheim at St. Christof, on the way up from Saint Anton to the pass, the seminal teaching venue for children and then for teachers. In 1928, physical education teachers in the Tyrol were also required by law to be skiers as well as proficient teachers of skiing—all following Schneider's system, by this time known as the "Arlberg technique." It had become the European way to ski. The French sent instructors to the Arlberg. In London an Austrian School of Ski-ing opened in 1934. A year later, the London *Times* opined that Schneider's method "has come to be regarded as something with which it would be a sort of sacrilege to tamper." No wonder the Swiss objected to the "canonization of Hannes Schneider." Schneider, said an Austrian-American friend, had become "more papal than the pope."

The objections were partially theoretical ones of technique, but these were comparatively unimportant outside of Scandinavia. What mattered in the 1920s was that each country should "win the peace," as the French had termed the economic competition for tourists after the Great War. If Schneider's Arlberg method of skiing and teaching became the German way, too, the Swiss were determined to find their own economic freedom outside of the Arlberg. In a long chapter in Roland Palmedo's *Skiing: The International Sport*, published in 1937, Christian Rubi, head of the Wengen ski school, wrote of ski instruction in Switzerland without a mention of Schneider or the Arlberg technique. Arosa skiers found Schneider's method "ugly and unnecessarily strenuous." The French, who lagged behind the other Alpine countries, once they realized that the folk sport of cross-country running so well exhibited by the Norwegians at the 1924 Chamonix Week was not appealing to the moneyed crowd, simply imported Arlbergers to teach them how to *Schuss* down their own alps.

One reason Schneider's system was so thoroughly approved after the war lay in the success he had in displaying skiing on film. Films depicting skiing had been made before the war, in Europe, Japan, and the United States. Dr. Arnold Fanck, generally acknowledged as the father of mountain-genre films, got his start just prior to World War I with a short film made on the Monte Rosa. Fanck was fortunate in having Sepp Allgeier do much of the early filming. Allgeier had three excellent qualifications: he was an accomplished Schwarzwald (Black Forest) skier, he had a knowledge of filmmaking (having worked for Express Films of Freiburg), and he had made the 1913 Monte Rosa film in which Fanck and two others had taken part. Fanck trained other cameramen; Hans Schneeberger became prominent. He found the perfect star in Hannes Schneider, and the men of his ski school made powder skiing in the Alps look fascinating, entrancing, dare-devilish, and heroic. One excellent skier was Luis Trenker, a South Tyrolian champion who went on to make his own films. Another was Otto Lang, who later made films in Hollywood. Schneider starred in twelve of Fanck's films. The reception of *Wunder des Schneeschuhs*, premiering in the Paulussaal (Paulus Hall) in Freiburg im Breisgau in the autumn of 1920 to enormous enthusiasm, propelled Schneider to the fore. The next winter *Eine Fuchsjagd im Engadin* (A fox chase in the Engadine) was a marvelous success. Fanck had found a new genre for his mountain films, and he found in Schneider the perfect skier who could turn, spray snow, and speed by at exactly the right place for the cameraman, and with a style that showed the world what his ski technique could do. "Without him," Fanck wrote generously in his autobiography, "all my photographic knowledge would not have come to much." And Schneider was equally enthusiastic about Fanck's work, writing that "the huge success of these films carried my technique out into the world." There were twelve films. Besides the two already mentioned, the best-known are *Der weisse Rausch* (White ecstasy), *Die weisse Hölle von Piz Palü* (The white hell of Piz Palü), and *Stürme über dem Mont Blanc* (Storm over Mont Blanc). *Wunder des Schneeschuhs* (Wonders of skiing) became the most important instructional book of the 1920s, as masses of photos from the film visually explained the text. It was translated into English and French, and there was a Japanese version too.

This was not just Schneider skiing. He had his Saint Anton ski school behind him as he played "the fox" and the ski school gave chase. In a high-mountain world, yet unspoiled by mechanical lifts, audiences thrilled to see the best skiers of the world chasing the *Meister* in the most glorious of Alpine winter grandeur. Fanck was fully aware that a female star would add to the excitement. That star turned out to be Leni Riefenstahl, later infamous as Hitler's directrice. Although in 1925 she did not know how to ski (she was a gymnast, dancer, and outdoor sport lover), she persuaded Luis Trenker, South Tyrolean ski champion, mountain guide, and all-round good-looking sportsman, to show her how to ski. She improved under Swiss champion Walter Prager's instruction, and was even considered for training for the German 1936 Olympic team—something she did not take seriously. Movie patrons recognized a wild spirit in Leni, and Fanck capitalized on this, starring her in a further five films. In *Der weisse Rausch* she not only played the female lead opposite Hannes Schneider but also meddled in the shooting of some of the scenes. This annoyed Schneider and led to a severe falling out between the two, so much so that after the Anschluss, she made it clear that she thought Schneider had been milking his instructors for years (this was a common theme in anti-Schneider newspaper reports). "Aren't you happy now," she later asked one of Schneider's instructors, "that they've put that *Schweinehund* in jail after he cheated you all these years?" Before those evil days, the films brought worldwide acclaim, except in Norway, where they were boycotted. In Sweden, the first was shown in 1922, and fourteen years later *The Ski Chase* was advertised in a Boston paper as "90 minutes of breath-taking skiing." The magic still held good, and skiers were drawn into trying to perfect their Arlberg technique.

The films were superb propaganda for Schneider's ski school. During the Great War, slow-motion filming had been developed to help in the understanding of the curve and mass of a projectile. "The memory," wrote Fanck later, "of a shell as if it were floating in the air . . . boring itself before my eyes through the thick armor-plating never left me." He bought one of these new "wonder instruments" weighing some five hundred kilograms (1,100 pounds), lugged it up to three thousand meters, and had instant success with the results. The slo-mo shots still captivate today. At the time, one perceptive critic wrote that Fanck's films "have cultural values of the greatest importance." But what sort of culture? Was it that he made the natural world of rock, ice, and avalanche into living characters, as Béla Balázs wondered about *Stürme über Montblanc*? (Storm over Mont Blanc). Or was it forceful propaganda for the culture of the noble, white, human elite, as Axel Eggebrecht warned in 1927? The films also had a heroic quality to them, something that film historian Siegfried Kracauer believed was symptomatic of the toughened folk, men who struggled with rock, glacier, and snow, the sort of manhood upon which the Nazis could depend. Susan Sontag, writing more of mountaineering than of skiing, saw Fanck's work as "beautiful and terrifying," an unlimited effort toward some mystical goal, in the same way that later was to be made both visible and actual in the worship of the Führer. Some of these analyses come, of course, with hindsight. Schneider, who was invariably pictured as an unspoiled villager, who ate simple meals, worked hard, and who skied magnificently, had none of these thoughts.

While all this was going on, Rudolf Gomperz had a founding hand in the DAKS, the Deutsche Arlberg Kurs Schneider, a week's instruction for about two thousand German kids held annually from 1927 to 1932, described in 1939 as "a kind of pre-*Anschluss*." Rudolf Gomperz, an apostate Jew, came to mountainous Saint Anton in 1905 as partial cure for malaria. He quickly became a major mover in the development of tourism in Saint Anton, helping to pay for the first jump, the skating rink, and a toboggan run. He worked extensively with Schneider for many years, including a guide for the Arlberg region and ghostwriting Schneider's account of his 1930 trip to Japan. The infamous *Arierparagraf* (Aryan paragraph) of 1921 had been accepted by the Austrian Ski Federation, and the Ski Club Arlberg left the Association in 1924 . . . the year that Hitler (born in Austria) was on trial for his Beer Hall Putsch. Politics was becoming increasingly volatile.

Hitler took power in January 1933. In June of that year, the Nazi regime in Germany placed a thousand-reichsmark border tax on Germans entering Austria. Originally intended to reduce support for the Mozart Festival in Salzburg, that winter it caused disruption in the ski business, something made up only by increasing numbers of French and English visitors, the high point being the Prince of Wales's visit to

Kitzbühel. In reality, as onetime chancellor of Germany Franz von Papen put it at his Nuremberg trial, the border tax was the first step "toward preparation for *Anschluss*."

That same winter, Kitzbühel's already well-known Hahnenkamm Race was cancelled because of poor snow and lack of financial support. In 1934, it was cancelled again, this time because there had been what was described euphemistically as political "incidents," "prohibited actions" of competitors and spectators in favor of the national socialists. At Hall, a small town twenty minutes downriver from Innsbruck, just before the last event of the Land Tyrol championships, "Deutschland über alles" took over the proceedings, and competitors and spectators sang the Nazis' "Horst Wessel" with Hitler salutes. Austria had to abandon many races that season because of Nazi disruption, and there was no Fédération internationale de ski (FIS) representative to whom they could complain. Nazi Germany had supplied their Austrian confreres with weapons and explosives for use against railway installations, power plants, and government buildings. The assassination of Chancellor Dollfuss—he had once offered Schneider the position of "sports consul," which Schneider had refused—included the takeover of the chancellery. Kurt von Schuschnigg, now chancellor, had the progovernment forces seize the rebels, and the coup fizzled out. In happier times Schuschnigg and his family had skied with Schneider at Saint Anton, and it was well-known that he was a good friend of Austrian skiing. But all was not well in Saint Anton in 1934. Karl Moser, one of Schneider's instructors, tried his own coup to get rid of the *Skimeister*, a "Marmeluke of the business spirit," "a clever dick," and "*Nazifresser*"—devourer of Nazis. Moser supported the opinion of the National Socialist paper *Der Rote Adler* of February 2, 1934, "this helot, this hireling of the Austrian Jewish system," but Schneider's other instructors supported him, and Moser was forced to flee to the safety of the German Nazis. He vowed to return.

The political uncertainties were made increasingly obvious with the show success of the Olympic Winter and Summer Games of 1936, with Mussolini's capture of Abyssinia,
and especially with Hitler's astonishing move into the Ver-
sailles Treaty–forbidden Rhineland. France and England,
both mistrusting each other, appeared the sole guarantors
of a free Austria.

In 1934, too, Austrian ski officials had told Arnold Lunn,
the central figure of British skiing and cofounder with
Hannes Schneider of the Arlberg-Kandahar race in 1928,
that the A-K simply should not be run. Right from the start,
the A-K had proved extremely popular; the first A-K turned
out to be an international meet with forty-five entries and
three hundred spectators. Two years later, 140 men and
twenty-eight women entered, and the crowd swelled to two
thousand. In fact, Schneider was not even present at this
third running of the A-K; he was instructing in Japan. This
A-K produced such a field of experts that it had obviously
become the premier Alpine event of the world. 1930 was the
same year that the FIS accepted downhill and—with much
misgiving—slalom for international competitions. Both disciplines would make their Olympic debut in the 1936 Winter
Games at Garmisch-Partenkirchen. The A-K continued to
prosper, and results were weighed against other races. The
Swiss, whose prestige had somewhat suffered as a result of
the FIS races, were more than pleased when their man, Willy
Steuri, won both the "straight race," as downhill was called,
and the slalom in 1935. It was the Arlbergers' turn in 1936,
with Friedl Pfeifer winning the slalom and taking a third in
the downhill to get the combined. All seemed well, certainly
as long as the Austrian military guarded the course day and
night and was on hand during the races. The Arlbergers were
spreading the doctrine all over the world. The Skardarasy
brothers were in Australia and New Zealand, and, very importantly, there were some of Hannes Schneider's instructors

in the United States. Schneider himself was invited to Japan in 1930 and had performed at the Boston and New York ski shows in 1936. The A-K of 1937, its tenth anniversary, voted by the leading *Kanonen* as "the best and most exacting downhill course in the Alps," provided "sensational upsets," as two world champions were beaten. Arlberger Willy Walch beat Emil Allais by six-tenths of a second, and, most unexpected of all, the unbeatable Christl Cranz lost to Erna Steuri of Switzerland. Politics seemed not to enter this British-run sporting event on the neutral ground of Mürren. What excitements would next year's A-K produce at Saint Anton?

From the mid-1920s on, Schneider's ski school had been immensely successful, both in attracting tourists to Saint Anton as well as spreading the Arlberg technique. The world—an upper-class and wealthy bourgeois world—came to the Arlberg to learn the master's technique. Kings of Rumania and Belgium shared classes with actors and actresses from Hollywood and Berlin, industrialists from England stemmed with financial men from Boston. Thousands of the more well-to-do of Europe, especially the Germans, were there "not so much to ski as with the set purpose of *learning* to ski." In January 1930, Schneider had eighteen salaried instructors and fourteen probationers on his staff. It was said, "One almost expects to hear a military bugle call" as classes were divided and promotions took place. The determination to learn was intense; "it oozes at every pore." This sort of teaching is difficult for us to understand today. It found its critics when imported to the United States, but Schneider came from a world where discipline produced results, and that was the way it worked.

But in 1938, in the night and morning of March 11 and 12, Hitler's Anschluss began. When Schneider and five others were taken in the early hours first to the local school and then to Landeck jail, Alice Wolfe, a wealthy American who had made Saint Anton a second home since the late 1920s, and who had become an organizer, sponsor, coach, and confidante of American women skiers and women's teams, called Arnold Lunn, who happened to be in Rome. Lunn, who had already received the news, immediately caught the train north to Saint Anton and convened a meeting of the Kandahar Club. It was a foregone conclusion that the A-K race, scheduled for the following week, would be canceled. Four members made up a subcommittee and drafted a letter to the SC Arlberg explaining how impossible it would be to run the A-K without Hannes, since "he enjoys the affectionate respect of all those who have helped to organize or who have competed in this event." It would be, the letter went on, "an unthinkable dereliction if we were to hold the race under these tragic circumstances."

Lunn then tackled Karl Moser, the Schneider instructor who refused to disavow the 1934 *Rote Adler* article and who had now returned as Nazi mayor of Saint Anton. He told him that the traditional A-K simply would not be held. The name Kandahar was not to be used. Moser became flustered and decided to go to a higher authority. Dr. Martin in Vienna, onetime Austrian FIS representative, discovered that he too could make no decision. Lunn telegraphed the onetime *Sturmabteilung* lynch-gang leader, now *Reichssportführer*, Hans von Tschammer und Osten, who immediately saw a way out. Well and good, if it was not going to be the Arlberg-Kandahar, let it be the first Arlberg race. Lunn returned to England as quickly as he could and immediately went to see the Duke of Kent (the king's brother), patron of Lunn's Kandahar Club. The duke's wife's sister was married to a German *Graf* (count), Toerring-Jettenbach, a known anti-Nazi, and a good enough skier to compete with Dr. Karl Rösen in happier days of the 1920s. He had also skied against Leni Riefenstahl's cameraman, Hans Schneeberger. There was an old-boy network of social aristocracy and skiing athletocracy that Lunn could immediately latch on to for support in the release of Schneider. But nothing came of it all. The Germans were not about to bow to pressure from a bunch of Anglo-Saxon ski racers led by an irascible old

Englishman who did not even ski particularly well. Though boycotted by the British, Americans, French, and Swiss, the race did take place. Baron Peter le Fort from the German *Skifachamt* (Department of Skiing) praised the sixty men and fifteen women for making the First Arlberg Race such a success.

GERMANY

Meanwhile, Alice Damrosch Wolfe was doing something eminently practical for Schneider and his fellow prisoners. By bribing the jailers, she had regular meals brought to the prisoners on a daily basis. Wolfe, a member of the patrician Amateur Ski Club of New York, had been a regular at Saint Anton for many years. Her apartment in Haus Angelika was a home away from home for American women's teams in 1935 and for the Olympic squad in 1936. Wolfe was an enthusiastic hunter, and a good skier, and had won the ladies visitors class in the Parsenn Derby in 1930, and placed second in the *Altersklasse* the next year. She knew everyone. She started casting around for influential help. Austrian state secretary Guido Schmidt was contacted, and her local hunting guide alerted Germany's state minister, Hermann Esser, of Schneider's difficulties. He promised help if needed. Pressure came from other quarters. The Colorado Arlberg Ski Club, headquartered in Denver, "all Aryans, incidentally," telegraphed Hitler, unanimously protesting the recent persecution and incarceration of Schneider and urged Hitler "to use influence, if any, to obtain his amnesty." The club threatened a boycott of German ski resorts and competitions. The owner of Landhugel, a pasture in Vermont, across the river from Hanover, with a 240-foot rope tow, wrote to U.S. secretary of state Cordell Hull, saying that because the Nazis were persecuting Schneider, who, as he said incorrectly, was a Jew, he would offer transportation from Austria, and a permanent position if Schneider were released. Would he so inform the German government? The more influential Amateur Ski Club of New York sent wires, the Orange Mountain Ski Club of New Jersey wondered how it could entertain a visiting German team for an upcoming race. At Dartmouth, there was great uneasiness as the Nazi flag was flown at one meet. But more than telegrams and threats were needed.

Help came from two very different men. And here the tale takes a further political turn. Attorney Dr. Karl Rösen of Garmisch-Partenkirchen, longtime friend of downhill and slalom, had been appointed by the Bavarian High Court as legal counsel for Hitler in his defense at the Beer Hall Putsch trial in February and March 1924. Although Hitler conducted his own defense, the Nazis appear not to have forgotten Rösen's service. There is, however, not a word about Rösen as public defender in the three books of documents I have looked at, and Hanns Hubert Hofmann's *Der Hitlerputsch, Krisenjahre deutscher Geschichte, 1920–1924*, generally acknowledged the best book on the Putsch, makes no mention of Rösen. The documentary evidence, then, is entirely lacking. In fact, the only piece of written evidence is that Alice Wolfe wrote that she met secretly in Innsbruck with a lawyer who had done work for the Nazis. All indications are that this was Rösen. Otto Lang, one of Schneider's close associates and a man to whom he wrote fairly regularly when he first arrived in the United States, said that it was common knowledge that Hitler owed Rösen a favor. Rösen, a man who had refused to be bribed with an important party position, was never a member of the NSDAP (Nationalsozialistische Deutsche Arbeitspartei); however, he was able to make connections through a regular Saint Anton visitor, Oberleutnant Betzold, who worked in Göring's adjutant's office in the Reichsluftfahrtministerium under Ministerialrat Drabe and made it possible for Rösen to speak to Drabe. He must have been effective; Drabe, apparently on his own initiative, then brought the Schneider case to Hermann Göring's notice. A Rösen memorandum detailing

Schneider's importance for Arlberg tourism also impressed the Nazis. Göring had already been lobbied by Edith, Lady Londonderry, one of a coterie of English aristocrats who felt that the way to deal with Hitler was to befriend him. Her husband had been the minister for air. She was particularly exercised by the fact that Schneider and Obergurgl ski school director Hans Falkner (she spelled them "Sneider" and "Falconer") were supposed to have taken a part in the third annual Londonderry Snow Eagle race for which she had presented a cup. Falkner was also arrested but released after five days, and found his way, with the Londonderry cup, arriving in December 1938 in Canada, where he instructed at Gray Rocks and Tremblant in the Laurentians.

Lady Londonderry and her husband had also entertained the Ribbentrops and had been entertained by the Görings. They were on such intimate terms that she liked to think of the *Reichsmarschall* as "my Siegfried." Göring had replied that he would look into the Schneider matter. Rösen was given powers to manage the Schneider case, thus bypassing the local Innsbruck Gestapo office.

Dr. Fritz Todt, among Hitler's inner circle, had also made occasional visits to Saint Anton, and he knew Schneider superficially, so here Rösen contacted his friend Wörner, who had once employed Dr. Todt, to argue for Schneider's release. In 1928 Rösen and Wörner had organized the first German slalom run by the Bavarian Ski Association. Wörner also informed Hermann Esser, state secretary in the tourist department of the Reich's Propaganda Ministry, who promised to help if needed. Todt, Esser, Göring, and others were not the most savory people to deal with, but Rösen and Wolfe were going to get help wherever they could.

After twenty-five days in Landeck prison, Schneider was permitted to take the train to Garmisch-Partenkirchen to be under Karl Rösen's eye. He actually stayed in Rösen's house for some time; later he lodged at the Gasthof Melber, while Rösen's house remained his mailing address. Schneider had no idea of how long this comparatively liberal form of house arrest in Garmisch-Partenkirchen would last. He felt hopeful; he was offered the directorship of the ski school there, but this was later rescinded; obviously the German Nazis tried to capitalize on the *Skimeister's* fame. The Austrian Nazis remained antagonistic, and even hatched a plan to capture Schneider from Garmisch, and they took out their spite on his family back in Saint Anton.

With Rösen, Schneider went to see Ministerialrat Drabe, who immediately wanted to know if Rösen was acting as Schneider's lawyer. No, merely a friend, he was told. Schneider stated his case factually, with no nastiness or vengeful attitude. He left an excellent impression. Although Rösen maintained his "friend" status, it was observed that the "handling of all the negotiations does not lack the know-how which any savvy lawyer would use in such affairs." Rösen had opened a Schneider file and it was full of documents.

In mid-November 1938, Schneider sent a typed, six-page, single-spaced letter with much accompanying documentation to the *Reichsführer* of the SS, Heinrich Himmler. It was an item-by-item evaluation, rejection, and commentary on the many accusations of Schneider's conduct brought up over the previous four years. The careful organization, the logical and clear responses, and the not-quite-legalese of the document give the impression that behind the writer was a legal mind. Hannes Schneider had, after all, left formal schooling at fourteen. Rösen must have outlined the arguments and talked them over with Schneider before finalizing the request; there isn't a spelling mistake in the six pages. The letter was supported by many other documents and presented an excellent case for permitting Schneider to leave Germany. It ended by requesting a "personal interview with a specialist from the *Reichsführer's* office." The letter has a dual quality: it is obviously a personal refutation that Schneider is making, and yet the manner in which it is written is almost abrupt. It pulls few punches: "Moser gave orders that I was not to be greeted"; "I was visited in Garmisch-Partenkirchen by people from St. Anton, even Nazis"; "My situation was demolished by influences from St. Anton, maybe Innsbruck"; "I am pure Aryan"; "I was never in a concentration camp"; and so on. One of the supporting documents, and there were five of them, was "My Behavior towards *Herr Bürgermeister* Moser," six pages long (one page is missing), written in nonlegalese, with occasional spelling mistakes. It is the personal details that give it authenticity—very different from Schneider's letter to Himmler.

It appears, then, that Rösen sent Schneider to Berlin when it was probable that Austrian Nazis might kidnap him, and he was very cordially received there. Himmler had signed the papers. Hannes's later refusal to explain any of these things played against him from time to time, but one of the things he had agreed on for his release was that he would not talk at all of the relationship he had with the Nazis, and he stuck to that.

Besides the offer of heading up the ski schools at Garmisch-Partenkirchen, Schneider had received offers from Saint Moritz, from Lake Placid, site of the 1932 Olympic Games, and from Canada; but the most attractive was from a Harvey Gibson of North Conway, in ski country New Hampshire, whence the real help emerged. Gibson proposed a five-year contract for room and board in a fully furnished house with a cook, plus $1,500 for each four-month-long winter season. As long as nothing interfered with the development of North Conway as a ski center, Hannes could consult, fish, hunt, and travel. How and why was this man, relatively unknown to the ski world, willing to present such an offer?

Benno Rybizka, one of Schneider's Saint Anton instructors, had been hired to run "The American Branch of the Hannes Schneider Ski School" at North Conway. Rybizka had the ear of Harvey Dow Gibson, a native of the town, part owner of the ski development, and on the boards of many local institutions. Gibson was well known as the president of the Manufacturers Trust Company of New York, a large merchant bank. In this matter, however, he was far more influential as the chairman of the American Committee for the Short-Term Creditors of Germany. Gibson had already had many dealings with Hjalmar Schacht, the Special Currency Commissioner of the newly opened Rentenbank in 1924. Schacht had received his appointment only a week after Hitler's abortive Beer Hall Putsch of November 8–11, 1923. His was a herculean task: to convert the worthless paper into a currency based on the value of land and industry in Germany. Schacht, Hitler's "financial wizard," to use William Shirer's memorable characterization, had been sent to Washington immediately after Franklin Roosevelt's election in 1933. In 1938, Schacht, as president of the Reichsbank and minister without portfolio in Hitler's cabinet, addressed Austrian bank officials in Vienna and extolled the Anschluss, now a week old, as "a communion of German will and German thought." Patently, Schneider was not part of this communion. In Gibson's autobiography, he only hints at what went on in the year of negotiation. Schacht, he wrote, was "anxious to do me favors, and very kindly interested himself in the matter" of Schneider's release. Schacht had taken ski lessons at Saint Anton, and one cannot help wondering whether memories of those Arlberg days in the snow played a role. Probably not; money was what counted. How much money was passed over by Gibson's representative or what changes in the German debt structure were negotiated in exchange one cannot say based on the available evidence. On his side, Schneider would be free to leave Germany with his family on one condition: he was never to talk about his experience.

It was through H. W. Auburn, Manufacturers Trust representative in London, that Gibson worked to obtain Schneider for the ski school directorship at Cranmore Mountain, North Conway. Auburn had contacts throughout Europe. In Berlin, Mania Zborowska acted as a postbox and go-between in Auburn's arrangements with Schneider while he was at Garmisch-Partenkirchen. At the same time, Auburn was negotiating with officials of the Nazi party, Rösen was approaching Himmler's office. Auburn was in touch with Himmler's personal adjutant, *Obergruppenführer* Karl Wolff, a man who oversaw correspondence and investments at the highest level of the Nazi party and the state. Auburn had a direct line to Himmler, as did Karl Rösen. And it was through Himmler that Schneider finally received permission to leave Germany.

The official line was that Schneider was leaving for contracted employment, but the details of his contract with Harvey Gibson were not public knowledge. In fact, Gibson had trouble with his board of directors in North Conway, since some of them did not wish to give Schneider a five-year contract. Gibson had to buy them out. It was a disadvantage that Schneider was not to talk of his troubles; he was accused of harboring Nazi sympathies. To exchange prison for the comforts of Rösen's home and then of the Gasthof Melber could easily be misinterpreted.

Gibson's representatives met the family in Paris and saw them through to Cherbourg and aboard the *Queen Mary* for the Atlantic crossing to New York. Only a few people knew of Schneider's expected arrival, which was publicly announced two days before the *Queen Mary* docked. There was immediate jubilation in New England's ski community. Expectations soared: Schneider would repeat the phenomenal success of his Saint Anton ski school in North Conway. When a small group of people met Schneider, it included a few reporters. He was immediately asked about his difficulties with the Nazis. He "had nothing to say about it," and that was that because Schneider had given his word that he would not say anything, and the newspaper reporters had agreed not to press the question.

What do we make of this mix of politics and sport in the late 1930s?

Figure 4. The smiles of freedom: Hannes Schneider and his wife, Ludwina, flanked by Benno Rybizka and Harvey Dow Gibson, welcomed under an arcade of ski poles on arrival at the station in North Conway, February 11, 1939. New England Ski Museum photo 2021.098.002. Used by permission.

Schneider's removal was accomplished by Austrian Nazis acting out, vendetta fashion, to settle old grievances. Karl Moser had left the ski school in 1934 after the abortive Nazi coup, vowing vengeance on his return. Having removed Schneider, the Austrian Nazis discovered that their masters, the German Nazis, had an international problem on their hands. The very fact that Schneider was offered the job of coordinating the ski schools at Garmisch-Partenkirchen, tantalizingly close to Saint Anton, must have been as much of a temptation to him as it would have been a sporting and propaganda coup for the German Nazis. But Schneider was the sort of Austrian who would not go along with the post-Anschluss hurrahs of "Two souls with one mind."

That Schneider ended up in the United States is not so surprising; not a few of his instructors—and other Austrians too—were already there and in charge of ski schools. There were four from Saint Anton in North Conway alone. Benno Rybizka, the director of the ski school, knew that he would lose his job the moment Schneider arrived. He did, in fact, become assistant director.

The financial finagling between the representatives of Gibson and Schacht was crucial in bringing Schneider to the United States, and more particularly to North Conway. Pressure came from many skiers, men of the stature of Roland Palmedo and Lunn. Rösen said that he had found the letters and petitions, particularly from foreigners of help in making his case. After the success of the Anschluss and the comparatively minor political fallout it engendered, the canceling of the A-K was awkward for the Nazis, but that was about it.

Besides, all this soon faded. When Schneider arrived in the United States on February 9, 1939, World War II was less than seven months away.

NEW HAMPSHIRE, USA

"One of the most outstanding events in the history of American skiing," the *Boston Herald* announced on February 7, 1939, "broke like a bolt from the blue." Harvey Gibson, president of the Manufacturers Trust Company, announced that Hannes Schneider, "idol of skiers the world over," is coming to America, "to reestablish his famous ski school here in New England," to be more precise, in North Conway, New Hampshire. Gibson's idea was to make of North Conway an eastern Sun Valley, already marked as the Saint Moritz of America, and he invited his friend and owner of this Idaho destination resort, Averell Harriman, to give him advice. Gibson had in place available slopes for skiing, an Arlberg ski school already staffed with Austrian leadership and top instructors, and the knowledge of how to run a ski school. Rybizka was a disciplinarian of the old school and felt responsible for keeping the Arlberg technique simon-pure. Gibson bought the Eastern Slope Inn, North Conway's equivalent of Saint Anton's Hotel Post. All he needed was the *Skimeister* himself. Rybizka remained in charge until the next season, when he became assistant director.

Immediately on arrival, Schneider was in great demand both socially and professionally. Lowell Thomas interviewed him from the Eastern Slope Inn in March. In spite of his marginal English, Schneider spoke to the Penguin Ski Club in Portland, Maine, in April 1939. He was invited to a ski exposition at Saks Fifth Avenue in December 1939, and was formally welcomed at the New York World's Fair. *Ski Week* caught the excitement on its cover of December 1939, and later the *Boston Post* shouted, "Track! Here Comes Hannes!" On Schneider's first trip outside New England, he stayed in Minneapolis with C. A. Lund, the manufacturer of Northland skis, and became an adviser for Lund's eastern plant in Laconia, New Hampshire. He edited the 1940 edition of Northland's *Ski Manual*, which was advertising Schneider waxes. From his stay with Lund, he drove to the ski areas of the Northwest, where folks in Tacoma, Washington, were told that he spoke perfect English, which was patently untrue, but that didn't matter at all: the *Skimeister* was among them. Then it was on to California to the Sugar Bowl, where another Austrian, Hannes Schroll, was in charge. And—good tourist that he was—he visited Hollywood. Over the years, a number of opportunities were offered to him to preside over larger and more alpine ski areas than Mount Cranmore, but Schneider remained content at North Conway and ever grateful to Harvey Dow Gibson. Schneider's school "will grow at the same proportion as it did abroad," noted the *Boston Globe*. An increasing number of licensed instructors were on the rolls, and Schneider's son Herbert passed the exam in March 1940. Under Rybizka, the ski school had given 6,450 lessons in the 1936–37 season. The figure increased to 10,150 the following season as a second ski school opened under Saint Anton instructor Franz Koessler. Under Schneider's guidance, narrow trails were widened, which made for more open-slope skiing. He experimented with seeding grasses for the best possible base when there was little snow, as indeed happened: Schneider's first full season of running the ski school had a difficult beginning on account of the fickle weather. "I pushed to get the ski school open on December 29 with 43 skiers," he wrote to a friend, "I could only have ski instruction on the golf course." Even so, about twenty thousand lessons were given that season. From then on the number seems to have been ever on the increase. Herbert Schneider remembered that eight hundred lessons had been given in one day, and claimed that the ski school saw growth every year from 1939 to 1955, that is, until his father died. An auxiliary tow was installed from time to time to handle "rush hour." Urban problems had reached the White Mountains of New Hampshire. Prices for half-day tickets were $1.50; a full day was $2.00. A weekly ticket of six days cost ten dollars, and a private lesson outside ski school hours was five dollars. It meant that Schneider was handsomely rewarded. While he lived, according to his son, he received 50 percent of the profit, which amounted to between $7,500 and $10,000 for the four winter months.

There were other wondrous ski goings-on at Cranmore, not least of which was the Skimobile. Gibson hired George Martin, who had been instrumental in an overhead cable lift at nearby Jackson. This time, though, he designed and built a trestle, had sixty car seats on a rail hauled up by a cable to halfway up the mountain. When Schneider arrived, he immediately wanted the lift to reach the summit, so you changed cars—which led to a number of humorous episodes chronicled on film. Four hundred had been on hand for the lift's initial trip, and five thousand celebrated its third anniversary in the winter of 1939–40. It was taken out in 1982. One of these car-chairs sits outside the New England Ski Museum at the base of the Cannon Mountain Tram. More important, though, was Schneider's participation in all things skiing. Gibson had bought the Eastern Slope Inn not only as the centerpiece of hospitality in North Conway (the town claimed accommodation for eight thousand) but also as Schneider's headquarters. He had his office there, and in the same manner as at the Hotel Post in Saint Anton, Schneider received visitors at a small table during après-ski hours. Written into his contract was a requirement of a daily lunch in the hotel. "We would come down from the mountain, dining at 12:30 p.m. Father would go into the lounge and have a martini. Then he'd go back for lessons in the afternoon," recalled son Herbert. This personal appearance at lunch and during the après-ski hours shows just how much North Conway and Cranmore's ski ambience turned around the person of Schneider. Gibson had his re-creation of the world of Saint Anton in the wooded hillsides of Mt. Washington Valley in New Hampshire.

North Conway was easy to reach by snow train. The Boston and Maine Railroad had first run out of Boston, to Warner, New Hampshire, on January 11, 1931, with 197 people on board. The first snow train into North Conway brought 1,631 people on board on February 22, 1932. In the 1934–35 season, a total of 5,883 came by train. Special trains from New York started in 1936. The names of the "Eastern Slope Express" and "Skimeister" trains gave a flair for skiers coming from the urban centers. Snow trains remained popular after the war, but as the automobile became more easily available, snow train traffic dwindled, and the last season they ran to North Conway was 1951–52.

When Pearl Harbor brought the United States into the war on December 7, 1941, Mount Cranmore was favorably positioned; not only did it have one of the very few open slopes available (Sepp Ruschp, another Austrian, whom we will meet in Stowe, in neighboring Vermont, had also insisted on open slopes, especially for teaching), but in this era of gasoline rationing, the fact that these slopes were within walking distance of the railroad station was the real plus.

Even though snow trains were cancelled in 1943 and 1944, skiers came on regularly scheduled trains, and it was only fifteen minutes to the mountain. By contrast, Stowe's skiers left the train at Waterbury, some ten miles away, and then it was another six miles to Mount Mansfield. No wonder GIs on furlough chose North Conway. Meanwhile, some of the local Austrian instructors, Herbert Schneider among them, joined what would become America's ski troop unit, the 10th Mountain Division, stationed in Colorado. Schneider himself advised the U.S. military on equipment matters.

There remains one personal aspect to consider. "One cannot help but to be grateful and happy to be a human being again," Schneider wrote to his onetime Saint Anton instructor, now in the America Northwest, Otto Lang, "and to be offered the opportunity to earn a living." He felt the loss deeply on learning that "three of my instructors have fallen in Russia and three others I know of have fallen." He regretted that letters "from home" were becoming shorter, and there was "almost nothing in them." Still, he hoped for peace and his return. "Then when it is possible to earn my bread in my own country I will no longer be in the USA," he wrote. The letter was dated December 1, 1941. Yet only a year later, when asked by a writer from the *New Yorker* if he would return to Saint Anton after the war, he replied, "Perhaps I go back just to visit. . . . I am a little afraid of the changes that there may be in the place and the people. So, likely for good I settle here." When he did return after the war, in the autumn of 1947, the Austrian government offered him a substantial amount of money to return. "My wonderful little Austria," he is remembered as saying, "you will need it more." But he was always mindful of his Austria; he sent over some new Northland skis for the Austrian Olympic team of 1948 that were much appreciated. Patently Schneider belonged to America now; he even became a New York Yankees baseball fan, having met Babe Ruth. He was on the board of the Eastern Slope Ski Club, and he taught skiing to students of the local Fryeburg Academy, Harvey Gibson's alma mater. He was head usher at the church of Our Lady of the Mountains, and, once Harvey Gibson passed on in 1950, he was North Conway's most prominent citizen. Sadly, he lived only another five years and died at the age of sixty-five, survived by his son, Herbert, and daughter, Herta, and by the legacy he left at Mount Cranmore and North Conway. There is a lot of history behind that statue welcoming all to the ski slopes.

CHAPTER 8

AMERICA'S HOLMENKOLLEN?

SKI JUMPING AT BRATTLEBORO

In the collections of the New England Ski Museum, I found a postcard of a grainy black-and-white 1920s photograph of the massive Norwegian jump outside Oslo: Holmenkollen. On the back a Mr. Oscar W. Opsann of Mamaroneck, New York, wrote, "Brattleboro could be made America's Holmenkollen." This expectation—hope anyway—was most likely voiced in 1922, the year that Vermont's first major jump was completed in time for the initial meet on February 8.

After the Great War was over in 1918, competitive skiing returned to snow country USA, with the Midwest dominating the sport. The Scandinavian immigrant communities had made many a small town quite well known, Ishpeming in Michigan, and across the state line Ashland, Wisconsin, and so on. The immigrants, especially the Norwegians, had brought not only the practice of skiing with them from the old country but also the competition specialty of ski jumping. By this time, ski jumping in Norway, and in Sweden too, had become a major part of ski meets, and since the mark of excellence was an all-round ability on skis, a man had to both run in the cross-country race and take part in the jumping competition. Cross-country racing was, indeed, just that; you raced over field and dale, through wood and by lake, up and down hills, and most of the time the competitor was out of sight of the spectators. But the place where a jump was specially sited became a popular viewing spot and then an actual venue. Sometimes the takeoff platform was changed a little according to snow conditions, jumpers' preferences and so on, but the actual place of the jump was not only the hill, the track of the jump, the landing slope, and the outrun but also a vast spectator area. If the cross-country run was won by training, endurance, and sweat, and winners were accordingly honored at prize giving, the jump provided heroics for all to see. It really did seem that a man could fly. Here is an early description from 1893 of a Norwegian immigrant in the Midwest:

> Standing with one foot slightly advanced, his skis close together, and leaning forward, he sped down the hill. At the jump he gathered himself for the leap, and with a mighty bound sailed into the air. Twice he gathered himself together and leaped while in mid-air, raising himself as a bird would rise. It was a revelation to the vast concourse of people whose eyes were focused on him, and the cheers that arose when he came safe to the ground seemed to rend the firmament.

Torjus Hemmetsveit had jumped seventy-eight feet. The first Brattleboro record was held by John Carleton of the Dartmouth Outing Club with 150 feet in 1922 but was swiftly broken by Bing Anderson of Berlin's Nansen Club with 158 feet. Today's world record stands at 831 feet, achieved at Norway's Vikersund Ski Flying Hill by Austria's Stefan Kraft in 2017.

The Norwegians had held their jumping competitions on Huseby Hill on the outskirts of Christiania (the name was changed to Oslo in 1925), but its low elevation and lack of snow forced the authorities to cart in snow and sometimes even cancel the event. Up to 1881, the competition had tested climbing up, skiing down, jumping, and going along the flat. Here was the all-around skier in action. Two years later, the jump became a separate part of the competition, but all the same competitors had to enroll in both events. Only in 1933 was it possible to enter for just the jump or just the cross-country; the all-around ideal had given way to specialization.

By 1890 the jumping competition had been moved higher up to Ullbakken, and two years later it found its home at Holmenkollen, with the jump as the center of attraction—as it still is today. Thus the permanence of the jump, the exhibiting of skill on a prepared structure, made exact measurement of performance possible—it all smacked of athletic specialization acclaimed by the spectator crowds. Norwegians, for whom jumping had originally been one part of their cultural skiing experience, now found that their jumping success turned them into civilized stars of the skisport; the modernization of ski jumping had turned into grand theater, and Holmenkollen became sacred soil. That all this was taking place as Norway was trying to free herself from Sweden's political control made of skiing a national sport (the Norwegians regularly beat the Swedes) and, furthermore, made of Holmenkollen a national shrine.

Now consider how the immigrants from Norway felt about the skisport in their new country. They came to the United States in increasing numbers in the late nineteenth century. No wonder that ski jumping was *the* event on the winter sporting calendar. No wonder that every little town, sensing a lift to its morale along with economic benefit, would contemplate building a jump, enlarging it, and hoping to be successful enough to host local, regional, and even national tourneys. Could Brattleboro really become, as Mr. Opsann had hoped, America's Holmenkollen?

By December 1921, a site for the ski jump had been investigated. This was to be no ordinary town jump. It was to have advantages over the Dartmouth Hill that the *Vermont Phoenix* set out in statistical array:

Dartmouth's jump required a steel trestle, the Brattleboro jump was in a natural setting
Dartmouth's jump cost $7,000, Brattleboro's cost $2,000
Dartmouth's jump had a running space of 210 feet, Brattleboro's was 290 to 300 feet

> Dartmouth's jump dropped 120 feet, Lake
>> Placid's 200 feet, and Brattleboro's 268
>> feet
> Dartmouth's total length was 375 feet, Lake
>> Placid's 450 feet, Brattleboro's 750 feet

Arrangements were in progress with landowners of the Brattleboro Retreat, founded in 1834 for the care of the mentally disturbed. The retreat occupied about a thousand acres and would be listed on the National Register of Historic Places in 1984. It was a perfect venue; 90 percent of the jump was part of a natural hill. At the top a wood trestle was added to ensure jumper speeds up to sixty miles per hour on the takeoff. The structure requiired 350 steps to reach the top. A very important and unique feature was the "flexible takeoff" made of four three-foot "lips." When the snow was sticky, the takeoff platform, called "the brink" by the newspapermen, and *sats* by the Norwegian ski communities, could be moved forward. On a fast day, with the three-foot lip moved back, it was estimated that about forty feet could be added to the length of a jump. The five-man jump committee concluded negotiations to lease the land for ten years with an option to buy at any time. The committee included Fred Harris, already renowned not just in skiing circles of Dartmouth and New England but as "the major prophet of about all that has happened in the saga of winter sport in New England," according to a friendly neighbor.

There was much work to be done: cutting trees and blasting rocks, and the excavating and grading was put out to bid and won by the Falkill Construction Company for about $2,000, half of which had already been collected in cash, and the rest pledged. Patently, Brattleboro business realized the economic possibilities. Skiing was a "Swiftly Growing Sport," proclaimed the *Boston Evening Transcript*, and a year later the *Atlantic Coast Merchant* reported that winter tourism, basically starting in 1921, was bringing in one and a half million dollars. Brattleboro was going to latch on to its share.

It is difficult to realize a hundred years later just how thrilling each piece of news concerning the first major ski jumping meet in Vermont was to the Brattleboro community. First came the discussions about organization: Who to alert? Which jumpers to invite to the Vermont State Ski Jumping Championship, as they decided to title the event? Who was going to organize the cars? The spectators? And the VIPs? The governor was of course invited, but unfortunately he was sick. To the relief of the organizing committee, lieutenant governor Abram W. Foote replaced him. Would there be enough room in Brattleboro hotels and rooming houses? And—always a concern—what of the quantity and quality of snow?

Invitations went out to the Dartmouth Outing Club. Happily, John P. Carleton, Dartmouth's intercollegiate champion and star holder of the New England record leap of 103 feet, promised to compete, so there would be at least one well-known competitor. Carleton was regarded by Dartmouth students, reported the *Berkshire Evening Eagle*, as "the individual who has put "ski into skiing." He was also a man who "turned somersaults in the air on skis"—so this was not going to be simon-pure sport. Invitations were also sent to other college clubs: the University of Vermont, of course; Williams College, just across the Massachusetts border to the south; Colgate and Middlebury; and also the Sno Birds of Lake Placid (using the simplified spelling of Melvil Dewey). The Saranac Lake Ski Club would send their sixteen-year-old Adirondack champion. The Nansen Ski Club of Berlin would certainly come in force. North of the border, the Montreal Ski Club was invited, and a special request went out to Canada's champion, Frank McKinnon. To spice up the program, Anthony A. Maurer, winner of the Engadine Cup in Switzerland, would put on a show. It was known that he had jumped 207 feet in 1920. However, it was reported that "he will not compete, as the contest will be strictly an amateur affair." Amateurism versus professionalism was a hot topic in sport at this time. In fact, Maurer missed his train connections and never made it!

Some individuals were also invited: young Gunnar Michelson was one, only seventeen years old but already an international winner in Canada and the United States; Carl Paulsen, the first to accomplish the somersault on skis in the East; and two Norwegians. One of these was forty-six-year-old Ivar Dahl, who, readers were told, had been ranked third and fourth in Norway for some years. In fact, his best was a fourth in Class A at Holmenkollen in 1905, but when he reached the senior class, he had a first (1916), third (1917), second (1918), and fourteenth (1919). His thirty-six-year-old compatriot, Larsen, was also a prizewinner (which I have not been able to ascertain because there were three different Larsens at Holmenkollen meetings) would also be coming. These two were important. Up until the 1930s, Norwegians were the ski authorities of the world, and certainly of the ski jumping world, and they provided authenticity to any event at which they were present.

An effort to attract spectators was by invitation to the chambers of commerce of Boston, Springfield, Northampton, Holyoke, North Adams, and Greenfield. It paid off; the Holyoke Kiwanis had their own Pullman car attached to a regular train coming for the event. Particularly positive was that Fox Films of Boston had asked for the privilege of taking moving pictures of the jumping. And one should not forget the attraction of the prizes: a sterling silver pitcher, a three-piece sterling silver coffee set on a tray, and twelve-inch sterling silver bread tray were for first, second, and third in the jump in 1924.

Fred Harris called on his old geology professor from Dartmouth to judge the jumping. Professor Goldthwaite had been among the most enthusiastic supporters of the Dartmouth Outing Club (DOC) from 1911 on. The distance a man jumped was, of course, a major component of the competition, but so was form. Stemming from the Norwegian tradition, form was a vital part in recognizing the best jumper, and the essential elements for the purpose of scoring were "grace and control." So that spectators had some idea of its importance and what it meant, the printed score sheet for the meet included this explanation:

> In general, the word "form" is best described by the words gracefulness and confidence. The jumper is judged from the top to the foot of the hill. The judges watch the jumper carefully as he approaches the take-off and give credit for courage and easy manner. Points are given for [the] courage with which the jumper launches himself into the air. The flight through the air is especially emphasized, attention being paid to the position of the jumper's body and the position of his skis. The body should be erect and leaning well forward and the skis should be close together and parallel. Points are given for the way a jumper makes his landing, how he continues on down the hill and the way he completes his run at the bottom.

The details of how the points were actually calculated were not explained. Over the years there had been different rules. In 1890, for example, touching the ground with one hand was to be judged a fall. By 1905 touching with both hands was a fall. All competitors knew what was expected, and there were remarkably few objections.

This 1922 meet was a spectacular success for the DOC, with Carleton's three jumps of 150 feet, 142 feet, and 151 feet leading the field by over thirty feet compared to the next two from Dartmouth. Fred Harris himself cleared 107 feet. There was only one accident, and this was the seventeen-year-old Hanover high school student, Charles Proctor, who with his first leap of 114 feet showed excellent promise, but he cracked two ribs on his second try with a 137-footer. But accidents were not necessarily bad; as one newspaper headlined, "More Than 40 Falls Add Thrills to the Day's Program."

The voyeuristic pleasure of watching danger and play at the same time helped bring in the crowds.

In all, the famous amateur record of 111 feet by Bing Anderson of Berlin "was smashed time after time"—in fact, eleven times during the competition, watched by an estimated three thousand spectators. "So many of the contestants wanted to try the jump again," reported the *Boston Globe*, "that another contest will be held in about ten days." Brattleboro business interests realized immediately that money could be made from winter sporting. There was the occasional naysayer. Mr. Rollin Child complained of the "community spirit which disregards much hunger and discomfort in village localities [and yet] establishes a costly and veritable death trap which may send more than one young man to an early grave or life disability . . . it was a leap in the dark for supposed fame—or eternity." No one paid attention, and the meet proposed for ten days later again lived up to expectations.

The local paper thrilled its readers with such headlines as "Anderson Establishes New Eastern Amateur Mark in Ski Jumping" and "158½ Feet in Flawless Jump." The Nansen Ski Club had come south, the Dartmouth men were back, and jumpers came from the Laconia Winter Club and from New York City's Norseman Ski Club, and also from Montreal. About two thousand had turned out to watch. Second-best was Rolf Monson of the Norseman, whose last jump was a spectacular 134 feet. He was followed by Canadian champion Frank McKinnon, with a leap of 132 feet. Hanover high school's Charley Proctor was back and, in spite of his ribs, with very good lengths of 117, 119½, and 124½ feet. One other matter of note was that Nansen Club youths had performed extremely well. There was plenty of competition in New England then.

As if all this had not been exciting enough, some of the jumpers wanted to try and break the U.S. national record of 176 feet by Sig Steinwall out in Colorado. Brattleboro's unique lip was raised, and, indeed, the distances increased, but the top four all fell immediately on landing. Bing Anderson had flown 168 feet, the DOC's Maxwell had made 158 feet, and the Nansen's Michelson and Sverre Knudson had fallen at 151½ and 139½ feet—they had outjumped the sloping landing area. Immediately the Brattleboro Outing Club announced that over the summer they would grade the landing hill 5 percent steeper "and go after the national amateur record again."

With the obvious enthusiasm and success of the 1922 meets, the leadership of the Brattleboro Outing Club had thoughts of expansion. First there were discussions on hosting the Eastern United States Ski Jumping Championships to be held in mid-January 1923, with a further meet on February 24. The path to ensuring this led through the newly formed United States Eastern Amateur Ski Association (USEASA). And even greater hopes were bruited: lobbying for the U.S. National Jumping Championship in 1924. That path led through the National Ski Association (NSA).

Eastern, as the USEASA was always called, came into existence after a ski meet at Saranac Lake in the Adirondacks of New York. E. H. Ned Stonaker proposed forming an organization to make skiing into a modern sport, that is, to regulate competitions and record results. These sorts of bureaucracies had been discussed as early as 1919, but nothing had ever come of the talks. After Stonaker's suggestions, members from six clubs—the Brattleboro Outing Club; the Dartmouth Outing Club; the Norseman Ski Club of New York City; the Nansen Ski Club of Berlin, New Hampshire; the Saranac Lake Ski Club; and the Sno Birds of Lake Placid—met at Lake Placid and elected Fred Harris of the Brattleboro Outing Club as president, a position he held until 1926.

The formation of USEASA was not necessarily a happy union. Brattleboro and Berlin had very similar wishes to become major jumping centers. The Dartmouth Outing Club was more bound to intercollegiate skiing than to Eastern's organization. The Sno Birds, although calling themselves the Sno Birds of Lake Placid, were not town-related at all but had ties to Melvil Dewey's select, anti-Semitic private club owned by the New York State librarian and advocate for simplified spelling. His son, Godfrey, very early on had visions of making his club "the St. Moritz of America." Guests at the club spent their time on Christmas snow hikes to find the Yule log, tobogganing, and skating. Ski competitions were called "amusements": all rather different from promoting equal conditions at ski competitions, equal opportunities to compete, the specialization of roles, quantification, bureaucratization, and the quest for records—the major signifiers of modern sport. And as more and more skiers crowded the logging trails, farm slopes, and even mountainsides, organization and regulation became increasingly essential. Here is the change from skisport to skiing.

Fred Harris, as we have seen in the chapter about the DOC, had an impressive organizational vita, and he brought to Brattleboro the impetus for sustained work in organizing the jump. It is no accident that he was honored when in 1951 the jump was officially named Harris Hill. Harris held the presidency of USEASA for its first five years. He was truly the fulcrum around which Brattleboro skiing became so prominent: he was the leader of skiing parties, he supervised children's hikes, and he organized jumping officials, gave speeches, and wrote articles, all of which added to Brattleboro's increasing importance for the growing popularity of skiing, that is, cross-country for family fun, jumping for bringing in the money. And he was "too much for Brattleboro," according to the Nansen Club's Alf Halvorsen: "He always wanted the Eastern ski meet there." There was trouble, enough that Halvorsen walked with Harris to the meeting "so the boys wouldn't give him a licking." All, then, was not well within USEASA's hierarchy, and there was some relief when Harris gave up the presidency and Henry Wade Hicks from Lake Placid took over. USEASA survived, and with the increasing number of skiers, club membership grew by leaps and bounds until there were 167 clubs in 1941.

To obtain the national championship, it was essential that the newly formed USEASA be affiliated with the National Ski Association. However, that association delayed the application. The national organization did not like the idea of an eastern division joining the association. Up until this time, there had been little questioning of the Midwestern, Norwegian outlook that dominated the NSA. Many of the Norwegians still felt that only those with Nordic backgrounds could really understand what skiing was all about. What would they make of one of Eastern's clubs, whose motto was "Soc et tuum"? But it was becoming obvious that the problem of managing a larger number of clubs that were increasingly dispersed created the need for regional associations. Eastern was first in 1922, the Rockies followed in 1923, northern Minnesota in 1925, the Midwest in 1927, and California and the Northwest in 1930. Eastern was the most powerful division and secured control of the NSA with the election of Fred Harris as treasurer in 1929 and Dr. R. S. Elmer as president in 1930. Into this mix, in 1924, came the first truly international winter world festival at Chamonix in the Haute-Savoie region of France, retrospectively called the First Winter Olympic Games.

The NSA had great difficulty in choosing competitors for this international meet, partially because the best prospects had become professionals, and although they had returned to amateur status, they had not done so within the stipulated time. It was feared that the eligibility of most of the jumpers would be questioned, but those who knew themselves to be the best were simply determined to go to France no matter what. Onetime professional Hans Hansen left Minneapolis to catch the boat for Europe. Ragnar Omtvedt was delayed but just caught the boat as the gangplank was being raised, and Anders Haugen, the best jumper, persuaded himself and presumably the NSA that once the International Olympic

Committee saw his record, they would permit him to compete. With the lone exception of Dartmouth's John Carleton, all members of the United States team were Scandinavian immigrants. Carleton appears to have been chosen because he was at Oxford University as a Rhodes scholar and was already in training at Chamonix. He was appointed coach of the team.

Although forming a team in this manner runs counter to our modern sense of order and fairness, it hardly raised an eyebrow at the time. Besides, the U.S. team presented no challenge in the cross-country events. None of the members was entered in the marathon, and Norwegians won the first four places, as expected. The jumping, however, was a different affair, and "affair" is the right word.

Anders Haugen led the field with a fifty-meter jump, followed by two Norwegians, each with forty-nine meters. But Haugen had thrown "all style aside and bent all efforts only on distance," reported the newsmen. A disinterested Englishman observed that "the American . . . jumped with fierce determination that was admirable, but his style was atrocious." That atrocious style brought Haugen down to fourth place, with 17.91 points (Tullin Thams won with 18.96, Narve Bonna had 18.68, and Thorleif Haug 18.00). The manager of the U.S. team lodged no complaint. It was suspected that Haugen had not been merely misjudged but that the calculations were incorrect. Yet nothing was done. Until at the Winter Olympics' fiftieth anniversary celebration in Oslo in 1974 the scoring was recomputed to show that Haugen had, in fact, gained third place. In a nice gesture, the eighty-six-year-old Anders Haugen received the bronze medal that Thorleif Haug had been awarded in 1924—rightfully his by 0.095 of a point. At those first Olympic Winter Games, the Norwegian cultural norm had damned atrocious style. Fifty years later, mathematics proved one man better by less than one-one hundredth of a point!

Two different events then played into Eastern's hands. When the team returned home from Chamonix, a number of the Olympic jumpers competed at Brattleboro. Haugen failed to place, and two others came in seventh and twelfth. It seemed that something had gone very wrong with the men the NSA had sent to France. Then a story circulated that the manager of the team, the mayor of Minneapolis, George Leach (only over there to convince the International Olympic Committee that his city should be the venue for the 1932 games), had seen his men only four times while they were in Europe and had scarcely visited Ragnar Omtvedt after he had broken his leg. "It was enough to make your blood boil," Harris reported to the Eastern establishment. Eastern was determined to have more of a say in future American participation in international competitions.

Oscar Oyass, president of the NSA, had much to be proud of when he assessed the 1924 and 1925 seasons: his organization had joined the American Athletic Union and the Fédération internationale de ski (FIS), thus raising its status at home and abroad. The NSA had sent a team to the 1924 Olympic Games in France. Oyass appeared particularly pleased that the 1924 national championships had been held in Vermont, for it signified the nationwide interest in the skisport. He was careful to note that 1,500 people attended the ball that concluded the event. And the NSA had been represented at the National Congress of Outdoor Recreation. "It will thus be seen," Oyass concluded, that the NSA "has become the acknowledged organization . . . not only on this continent but in the entire world."

After the brouhaha over the Olympics, Brattleboro produced an excellent USEASA Championship meet the following year. It was made excellent when the 2,500 fans roundly cheered when the record was broken by the Nansen Club's Bing Anderson, with 190 feet. It was not lost on anybody that Anderson had passed Detroit's Henry Hall mark by ten feet. Brattleboro was on its way to more than national prominence; it had become, with the Nansen, a real challenge to the dominance of the Midwest.

One might compare this with the 1925 meet held in Montpelier. The jump was "a bump compared to Brattleboro's," a newspaper reported. There was plenty of excitement "due to the jumping of prices, not the jumping." No price of entry had been advertised. The crowd of eight hundred "was forever getting in the way." Events were late in starting; there was no numbering of men; no score cards were sold; and there was no judges stand, no telephone, no flags, no music, no bugler, "no emotion." Few people seemed to know or care much who was who, or what was what, wrote the disgusted reporter. And the final indignity: "Even the spills were not as good as in Brattleboro."

The organization and management of such an event really mattered. Vermont governor Redfield Proctor had been thrilled at the 1924 meet, and had said "it was a splendid advertisement for Vermont as a winter sports region" and also "a tremendous incentive to the development of ski sport throughout the East." The "Winged Trophy," made by world-renowned jeweler Cartier, was valued at $750 ($11,535 in today's purchasing power) and was ready for the meet. Later this trophy was extravagantly described as the winter equivalent of the Davis Cup. It has remained one of the most coveted trophies in the United States. When it has been retired, meaning one man has won it three times, the Harris family has supplied a new one, and following Fred's death, his wife, Helen, and now his daughter, Sally, continue this tradition.

If there was to be development, with the jump being the major focus of Brattleboro skiing, then the structures not only had to be kept in good condition but would also need improvements to remain competitive with the jumps at Hanover and Berlin, as well as to keep up with Godfrey Dewey's insatiable promotion of Lake Placid. As already noted, Brattleboro Outing Club's immediate determination was to make the landing hill steeper. The following summer $1,000 was spent and, generally, as finances permitted, hill preparation made increasing lengths of jumps possible. In 1938, a $4,000 Works Progress Administration grant enabled the removal of over a thousand tons of rock, thus widening and steepening the hill. And success immediately followed: Norwegian Birger Ruud, at that time the most recognized jumping name in the world, cleared 212 feet for a new record. Further improvements followed, such as setting the "flexible takeoff" on concrete foundations, further grading of the outrun . . . and in 1941 Torger Tokle, newly arrived from Norway, leaped 223 feet, his twenty-seventh victory in thirty starts. With hope—even expectation—of receiving the nod to host the 1942 national championships, the entire hill was modified, with some alteration to the profile, with a steeper landing area. More rocks were removed and various uneven sections were leveled. A coat of loam was applied and the hill was reseeded with grass. Twenty-three planks were laid across the hill, each ten feet apart, to hold the snow. Jumping could now take place with only six inches of snow cover (as opposed to twelve). Jumpers approved, and officials praised the hill. Roger Langley, longtime Eastern leader and now president of the NSA, said that of all the hills he had seen in the country, "I believe that Brattleboro has the most nearly perfect 65 meter hill that there is anywhere in the United States."

These jumping meets were widely advertised in Massachusetts. In 1938, short pieces in the four major Boston dailies, the newspapers of Greenfield, Springfield, and Worcester covered the events, as did the two college town papers of Holyoke and Northampton. The total cost for attracting Massachusetts visitors was $155.54 (the equivalent of $2,776 in 2020). Four papers in Connecticut, including the state's premier Hartford *Courant*, four in Vermont, and three in New Hampshire were used in the effort to pull in spectators from the region. The total amount of $95.20 ($1,700 today) was spent on the *New York Times* and *Herald Tribune* alone. And appeal to Brooklyn's immigrant community was made through the *Nordiske Tidende* at a tidy sum, then, of $357.84

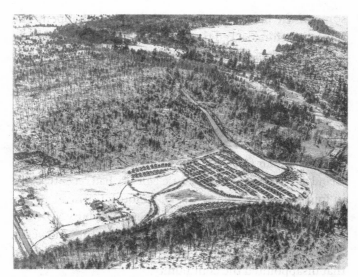

Figure 5. This aerial photo gives a good view of the vastness of the Brattleboro jump, showing all the component parts, from the parking area to top of the inrun, ready for competition in 1942. New England Ski Museum photo 1982P.014.002. Used by permission.

in all ($6,386 today). When the entrance fee in 1938 was $1.50, and about five thousand attended, the accounting shows that it was obviously worth it. Radio, too, was exploited; you could "listen to the Ski Stars in Person" on WKNE, the Keene, New Hampshire, station on Sunday mornings for quarter of an hour. Top performers coming from as far away as the state of Washington were featured. Best of all, "that foreign sensation, the nineteen-year-old Torger Tokle, out-jumping and out-gracing every competitor, highlighted the tournament with jumps of 188 and 189 feet."

For the 1941 meet, efforts to attract major jumpers from the Midwest ran into opposition from the central association. Its rules were simply that no jumper could participate out of the region if its own championship was taking place at that time. To bring nationally acclaimed jumpers from the Midwest, the Brattleboro organizers even considered flying some of the best men out, but that did not happen. The meet, therefore, lacked that special quality that Olympians and others from the Midwest would bring. What could take their place? The war, starting in 1939 in Europe and engulfing Finland and Norway, provided a patriotic possibility, for both the Finns and the Norwegians who were extremely highly regarded in their fight against Nazism and Communism. The town organizers sent word to Norwegian flyers at Lille Norge, their air force training camp located at the Toronto Island airport. A team from Little Norway had recently come in fourth out of seven at the Dartmouth Carnival. At the Norseman Ski Club of New York's meet at Salisbury Mills, one of the flyers had won the class B jump. This time, however, they were not given permission to come to Brattleboro, and that disappointed the community.

World War II took its toll: no meets at Brattleboro, and Torger Tokle, the meteor that had flown through the skies so consistently since arriving in the United States, was killed on the Italian front in March 1945. Brattleboro's first postwar meet made for an auspicious beginning: local lad Merrill Barber made the longest jump of 202 feet, and returning veteran Art Devlin from Lake Placid took first place with two two-hundred-foot jumps. In 1948, it was Torger Tokle's brother Art who was victorious, with jumps of 207 and 206 feet. Barber was third at that meet. A Norwegian, Reidar Andersen from Oslo, came in second. And from this year on, foreign jumpers—often exchange students—came to give Brattleboro a special cachet. Over the years, the band has had to learn many a national anthem; Brattleboro has hosted Norwegians, Finns, Austrians, Slovenians, as well as jumpers from the Czech Republic, Canada, Japan, and the Netherlands. A Ukrainian retired the Winged Trophy after his victories in 1996, 1999, and 2000. Slovenians placed first, second, and third in 2013, and a Turk won the 2015 meet.

The Brattleboro Outing Club jump put in a bid to hold the national championships in 2006. In spite of a new tower, new judges stand, and fence replacements, all made in 1957, and besides the addition of snowmaking in 1986, making the jump one of only three in the country that could ensure conditions, it did not come up to the standards in 2006. The last major jump had been a tryout meet to select the team for the Olympic games at Albertville, France, in 1992. Now the United States Ski and Snowboard Association (morphed from the NSA) refused to sanction the tournament because the jump was not up to international standards, nor was it safe. This national association, in addition sanctioning tournaments, also guaranteed the insurance for the meet, hence it was all-powerful.

The crisis in Brattleboro produced a nonprofit group that immediately estimated that one million dollars would be needed. This was later reduced to $400,000, of which about 25 percent could be in-kind donations. How to raise $300,000 to construct a new steel tower, remake the start and the inrun, widen the landing area, install safety boards, and replace the dangerous 302 wooden stairs with steel ones? Brattleboro was asked "To Step Up and Soar," and this produced $257,000 of local money. In February 2008 a totally unexpected foundation grant of $130,000 ensured success. Euphoria! In November, this same foundation gave another $188,000 to cover increased construction costs. And those 302 steps: eighty of them had been "sold" for $1,000 each, indicating real local support for the jump: Brattleboro had its ninety-meter hill to celebrate.

The eighty-fifth annual Harris Hill Jumping Tournament was a triumphant success; the two-day crowd of about eight thousand saw the foreigners superior yet again: two Austrians split by a Slovenian came first, second, and third. The winning jump was 100.5 meters (332 feet). Lake Placid's Andrew Bliss came in fourth with one flight of 98.5 meters (323 feet). The best Brattleboro man was Willy Graves, with 88.5 meters (290 feet). One other factor was of great interest: five women competed, with the fifteen-year-old Vermonter

Tara Geraghty-Moats making an eighty-nine-meter jump (292 feet). Numbers two and three came in at 87.5 meters (287 feet) and 83 meters (272 feet). The year was 2009, and it was hoped that women's ski jumping would finally become part of the Winter Olympic Games. This was not to be, and there was even a lawsuit. However, the event was recognized at last at the Sochi Games in 2014, and first off the massive jump was Sarah Hendrickson of New Hampshire and Park City, Utah. We met her promoting the renovation of the Big Nansen in Berlin. Geraghty-Moats went on to win the first officially sanctioned Nordic Combined World Cup contest in December 2020, winning gold at the end of the truncated COVID-plagued season, receiving the globe at Oberstdorf in March 2021.

Has Brattleboro become America's Eastern Holmenkollen? No . . . its successes of the 1920s were questioned late in the 1930s, when the Big Nansen offered major competition from northern New Hampshire. The cachet of the name Holmenkollen was used, for example, in 1939, when competitors from not only New England and the Midwestern jumping heartland but also Norway, Germany, and Canada were expected to make the third annual "Holmenkollen of the East" a superb meeting "worthy of the famous name it bears." And in 1940, the *Ski Bulletin* reported on "the American Holmenkollen event held in Berlin." But still, that magic name never took hold. Maybe it carried so much Norwegian baggage that it simply could not be carried over to the United States. And one should not forget that Harris Hill, the ninety-meter pride of Brattleboro, was ready not just for American jumpers but for those who came in increasing numbers from abroad as well.

The war of 1917–18, of course, put any major skiing on hold, and in the 1930s came the drive for alpine skiing—Brattleboro's first Eastern-certified ski instructor was available at the Billings Hotel for the 1938–39 season. The skiing population of the 1950s, 1960s, and early 1970s seemed ever increasing, but it was alpine skiing that they enjoyed, not jumping. That remained for daredevils rather than city people, whose social weekends included downhill skiing with friends. The impossibility of schools and civic organizations paying for insurance precluded any sustained interest in ski jumping. The oil embargo of the early 1970s only added difficulties for those who might be among the spectator crowd.

Ski jumping is on a mild rebound in the 2020s. Some private schools have picked it up, and New Hampshire remains the only state to hold public school championships. Where there are small jumps with interested parents to support kids' programs, ski jumping flourishes. On the regional scale, those venues with the infrastructure in place, and, like Brattleboro, the will to compete, may well see a lasting contribution to American and international ski jumping competition.

Brattleboro is particularly well-positioned, since the centenary of the Harris Hill was celebrated in 2022. A sixteen-member committee set the weekend date of February 19–20 for onhill and surrounding events. A larger-than-life wire structure jumper floated above Main Street—certainly an eye-catching and novel introduction to "Jump Town Brattleboro." The celebration took place at the same time as the Beijing Olympics, so no Olympians were expected, but two Norwegians, an Icelander, and a Rumanian added spice to the competition, the Norwegians coming first and second. Reflecting the growing interest in all-round ski abilities, Nordic combined events (cross-country and jumping) were on the program., but the weather forced changes in the Friday night celebrations, so no bonfires, fireworks, bands, or hoopla. Weather-related problems caused delays on Saturday morning. The major jumping on Sunday, though, was in superb conditions and brought out an enthusiastic crowd. A centenary volume was available full of photos from local collections and museums. An online Harris Hill story project is ongoing, and these oral memories will have supporting photographs as well. "Step Up, Brattleboro, and Soar!" was a good cry in the past. We heard it again as Harris Hill came into its own after one hundred years.

CHAPTER 9

VERMONT SKI TOWNS

WOODSTOCK AND MANCHESTER

Among the fifty ski areas today served by the Vermont Ski Areas Association, twenty are alpine, and thirty cross-country. However, four skiing towns have developed, each with different characteristics, each in different decades: Brattleboro made its mark in the 1920s, Woodstock in the 1930s, Stowe somewhat later, and Manchester in the 1940s and 1950s. The decades are not exact, of course, but each provided a special aspect to the growth of skiing: Brattleboro had the jump, Woodstock had the rope tow and open slopes, Stowe had a single chair—the first in the state—and Manchester's growth relied on the capitalistic dynamism of Fred Pabst Junior of the famous Milwaukee brewing company.

Prior to World War I, there were other regions in the state where skiing took place. It was reported in 1895, for example, that skiing "seems to be a favorite pastime with the boys nowadays" at Whitingham, about half an hour west of Brattleboro. By 1899 it was reported that "skiing is becoming a popular sport" in Burlington. The *Brattleboro Reformer* wrote that Woodstock "bids fair to be the most popular town in the state with the usual opportunities for snowshoeing and skiing." In Brattleboro itself in 1914, undoubtedly influenced by Fred Harris, thirteen boy scouts hiked on skis to a rendezvous point about five miles away. There was ski activity with the Saint Johnsbury's Winter Sports Club. The odd exceptional account of climbing Ascutney and Camelback were noted. At Killington, "near the summit, the ski man thrust his arm at the end of the ski pole far down in the snow reading a depth of seven feet." This sort of skiing was a one-off newspaper read, enough to titillate the stay-at-homes beside their fires. In 1916 Appalachian Mountain Club members came north from Boston to try out the snows of Wilmington, about fifteen miles west of Brattleboro—precursors of a beginner and moderate ski center extolled by the *Ski Bulletin* in 1934, and eventually Haystack was made into an alpine ski area opening in 1964. After a number of owners, today Haystack is a member-club ski area. All this skiing activity, whether in the north, central, or southern sections of the state, lets us sense a general enjoyment in the snows of Vermont, but you had to get out and about. Fred Harris himself had promoted the state as early as 1912 in the *Vermonter*, asking, "What state presents better advantages and how many can offer charms which can compare favorably with our good old Green Mountain State? We should be able to boast of thousands of active ski runners and snowshoers! Let us then produce a race of men who love the out-of-doors who know and appreciate Vermont's great charms and who are active followers of the snowshoe and ski." It was quite a call.

And it was heard. In 1918, a large snowstorm closed down Brattleboro's shops and businesses and, according to the *Reformer*, brought hundreds out on skis. "Out-Door Needs" were advertised, and Wagner's promoted its "double-sole and heel boot especially adapted for skiing." In the 1920s, right on the Canadian line, Newport boys received skis for Christmas, "as skiing is popular lately." The Memphremagog Outing Club flourished. When Blondine Roberts fractured her leg skiing on Butterfield Hill in Derby Line, she was taken to the Orleans County Memorial Hospital in Newport. Newport, home of the Slalom Ski Wear manufacturing company, was the skiing hub of this section of northern Vermont. This activity all took place before the mechanization of skiing, before the fast-paced alpine *Schuss* made its appearance in the Green Mountains. Yet, in 1935, that is, after the invention of the rope tow, after the Arlberg technique became de rigueur, Narada Coomara gave an assessment of the state's skiing: Brattleboro, Woodstock, and Mount Mansfield were the main centers. Of course, there were other places where locals skied; Coomara singled out the Finnish communities around Ludlow who have "their own specialization of cross-country." Two Finns from the Chester Outing Club had come tenth and eleventh in the ten-mile cross-country national championship at Brattleboro in 1924. Yet when discussing Finns in the area the *Vermont Tribune* and the *Vermont Journal* make no mention of their skiing. A photo exists of Finnish skis made and used in Dover, Vermont, soon after 1900. Coomara, whose base was in Craftsbury Common, recounted that it was visited rarely in winter, and only in spring were some outsiders seen on skis. The accommodation was "scant in Vermont," with about two hundred beds listed in Stowe, and a few more in Woodstock; Brattleboro alone was well supplied with hotels. Generally, though, the lack of support, judged A. W. Coleman, a man who had a finger on the pulse of ski development, "was due principally to the local lack of general winter sports enthusiasm." This was borne out by a state of Vermont assessment for the 1937–38 season that concluded that it was "still questionable whether skiing was going to be a permanent factor" in the state.

WOODSTOCK, VERMONT

All this was about to change. The shift in skiing occurred first in Woodstock, the only town in the state that could argue that it had a tradition of winter sporting going back to the opening of the impressive Woodstock Inn in 1891–92. The inn looked out onto the village's large oval green, flanked by patrician white clapboard New England houses. The churches' Paul Revere bells pealed for the increasing number of summer people as well as for the local agricultural community; there was no industry in town. The Woodstock Railway was completed in 1875 and ran the fourteen miles from White River Junction into town. Horse and buggies met the train in summer, and in the winter horses and sledges took guests to the inn that had been equipped against winter cold. The inn was under the direction of Arthur Wilder, a skiing enthusiast whose 1912 photograph of speeding down a hill in bowler hat with one pole is well known. The rail line was in operation until 1933, the year before skiing's rope tow revolution began, but by that time, automobiles had become prominent for those with a degree of wealth and a desire to ski. Taxi and bus services were also available.

What Woodstock also prized was its rural landscape. Here was the escape from the increasingly industrialized urban centers. For the winter tourist it was a return to the kind of America depicted by Currier and Ives. For skiers, there were open and rolling hills, splendid farm lanes, and a local population ready to bundle up visitors for moonlight sleigh rides to vantage points where a bonfire was lit and hot drinks made ready. And skis? Remarkably few. In 1914, we get an excellent account by a visiting Englishman, a Mr. Tennant, who took himself to the inn resembling a "first class Norwegian hotel in many ways." After breakfast, everybody prepared for the day's outing. Mr. Wilder had laid in a large stock of skis, but all but two boys and Mr. Tennant were outfitted with snowshoes. The majority had never seen skis before. They were so impressed that for the afternoon all but the elderly forsook their snowshoes and took to skis. A very good slope was found for practice on the golf course. It was all by self-experiment, for there was no instruction. Meanwhile, Tennant and the two youngsters had a glorious afternoon run over the neighboring hills. Tennant imagined the possibilities of crossing the countryside to small towns twenty to thirty miles away, where adequate accommodation could be found. He reveled in the area's rolling hills and found the woods not too thick. The region was rather like the hilly part of the south of Scotland, he told his British audience. Yet, as late as 1928, another Brit could write that the Green Mountains were "not developed yet for skiing." His experience of the superdeveloped Switzerland-for-the-British contrasted with a trip he was enthusiastically proposing on the Long Trail from Williamstown, Massachusetts, to Jay Peak in the very north of Vermont. It would be the antithesis of the hotel sport he knew from Europe.

In the 1920s, the early enthusiasm for winter sports centered around the inn seemed to wane. It was as if nearby Dartmouth College, with its athletic youth, its annual winter carnival, its gown-town ski relationship, and its close proximity to the railroad at White River Junction played to its advantage, not to Woodstock's. From White River, skiers were taken to Dartmouth's own Mount Moosilauke in New Hampshire. When there was something to report from Woodstock, it was Dartmouth graduate Fred Harris's hundred-foot and six-inch jump in 1921, a mark that held for four years. In the south of the state, Brattleboro carved out a special niche in the spectator-driven world of ski jumping in the 1920s, even holding a national competition in 1924. Due to the Depression, the Woodstock Inn closed for nine winter seasons.

At first, this appeared to create an economic disaster for the town. But in 1932 arrived J. Dwight Francis. Francis came from a background of wealth in Pittsfield, a divorce from Hollywood star Kay Francis, and skiing honed on the Berkshire hills of Massachusetts and the mountains of Europe. Francis announced that Woodstock simply had New England's finest open-slope skiing. He backed this up by founding the Woodstock Ski Runners in 1932, with an impressive membership that brought immediate recognition and authority: John Carleton was president, and Alec Bright vice president. Recognizing, too, that alpine skiing was the attraction, rather than cross-country outings, Francis sought an instructor from Europe. Swiss Fritz Steuri, endorsed by Arnold Lunn, round whom British skiing produced a sort of athletocracy, and Lunn's Swiss friend Walter Amstutz, one of his alpine-style students, arrived from Grindelwald, trailing an enviable record as three-time national Swiss champion in cross-country, and with many wins in alpine events. He was a much-respected mountaineer as well as mountain guide. The invitation for the first meet of the Woodstock Ski Runners went out to the Hochgebirgers, the Amateur Ski Club of New York, and other patrician ski clubs. Francis assured everyone that Steuri would be on course. Harald Paumgarten of the Austrian team was coming, and so was Hanover's Charley Proctor. You could hardly have a better drawing card. At the race for the Hochgebirge Cup run on Moosilauke, Steuri came in first in just over seven minutes, with Charley Proctor over a minute behind. Steuri had eclipsed the record, but he had taken "a short, unofficial cut off." The course had been changed slightly, and the announcement was made just before the race; Steuri, as well as others, had not heard it, so his record was debated. Officials tried to clear up the matter, not that it really mattered: Steuri had won the race, and by a large margin. But then two poor snow seasons damned Francis's efforts, and Steuri went home. Francis took to promoting the first ski cruise to the Alps in 1935, a week each in Saint Anton, Davos, and Wengen, a forerunner of the foreign ski vacation package.

Some Dartmouth men acquired a cabin north of town at Cloudland. This provided an opportunity for the "ride and run" method of skiing, publicized in Woodstock and listed on the town's "Winter Sports Map." Skiers coming from Woodstock drove up to the Cloudland school house, where they extracted themselves and their equipment from their car or taxi. A two-and-a-half-mile run down over four open slopes back to the village was the reward. The brochure advised that it would take about two hours. This ride and run combination was quite popular, but other ideas for making down-the-hill skiing easier were in the making during these Depression years.

Enter the White Cupboard innkeepers Elizabeth and Robert Royce, three of their wealthy, European-inspired guests, engineer-tinkerer David Dodge, and farmer Clinton Gilbert, and the first rope tow rose up Gilbert's pasture on

Sunday, January 28, 1934. Seventy members of the Ski Club Hochgebirge and the Amateur Ski Club of New York were on hand. What excitement! The rope tow appealed immediately to Dartmouth College students who had a cabin at Cloudland. They were joined by the newly formed Harvard ski club, the Schussverein, who had an option on an ex-hen house nearby, on condition that they fixed it up. There was, then, a top clientele as skiing at Woodstock—and elsewhere—began its mechanized and industrial phase.

Since this rope tow mechanized and revolutionized skiing, its tale will be told later. Suffice it to say here that rope tows immediately seemed to sprout in odd out-of-the-way villages. "Unspoiled Vermont," the slogan for the promotion of the state, boasted thirty-nine winter resorts, seven of which were new for the 1936–37 season. The state, said the *Boston Herald*, "refuses to be stampeded into skiing." One problem was the blue law prohibiting various activities, such as attending movies on Sunday. The state's attorney general said that paid admissions at skiing centers would not be permissible, so use of tows, sales of gas and ski wax, and use of special bus transportation on Sundays would not be allowed. Somehow that did not seem to apply to Woodstock!

Bunny Bertram, Dartmouth class of 1931, created a small area, Hill 6, and served it with three rope tows. The steepest slope ran down the far side toward South Pomfret. Bertram named that slope Suicide 6. In our safety-conscious age, just naming a ski trail "Suicide" would give any adman sleepless nights, but in the 1930s, with the advent of the tows, speed of descent and derring-do counted for just about everything in this new alpine delight. The best skiers competed for the record—no real course, just top to bottom. In 1937, Alec Bright held the record at 56.8 seconds, in 1939 it stood at 35.6 seconds, and ten years later it was down to 31.8 seconds. There were gold pins awarded for breaking the record, silver ones for those making the hill in a minute or less—a minute and a half for women. No one who was part of the growing fraternity of alpine speedsters "would be caught dead" wearing the bronze pin. Suicide 6 had become a rite of passage, and it came to mean Woodstock. An effort was made to see if over twenty-nine thousand feet of skiing—the height of Mount Everest—could be achieved. With a vertical drop of 650 feet, one man made thirty round trips in an hour, nineteen thousand feet, but 45 ascents would be required to equal Everest.

Bertram had one other promotion in mind having to do with speed. Recognizing its lure, he persuaded the Underwood Company of South Boston to manufacture the "Speed Tow," "The New Thrill! Operates on Level Ground." And the clincher: "Speeds up to 100 miles per hour." Wendy Morse of Trinity College, in Hartford, Connecticut, managed ninety-one miles per hour, and Nancy Nye of Chestnut Hill, near Boston, was clocked at sixty-five. Just after the speed skier

Figure 6. Austrian Siegfried Buchmayr playing his usual role as the captivating center of attention, this time at Woodstock, where he taught for many seasons. New England Ski Museum photo 2014.084.017. Used by permission.

let go of the rope, there was a small bump, and a local girl managed forty-three feet off it. The novelty did not last long; skiers needed their own thrill of speed, and the rope tow provided the means to get up to the top of a hill, increasing their own skiing time spectacularly. This automatically improved their expertise, and it also popularized skiing; it eliminated the uphill grind and left the skier ready for a grand alpine *Schuss*.

In 1961 Bertram sold Suicide 6 to Laurance Rockefeller, who also bought the Woodstock Inn. The town was moving up in the skiing world just at the time when New England was losing—in some ways, had already lost—its premier place in American skiing to the resort towns of the Colorado Rockies and California's Sierra Nevada range.

MANCHESTER, VERMONT

The town of Manchester is so bound up with Fred Pabst and his Bromley Mountain that it is difficult to realize that he was only able to make such a success of Bromley because he found in the town exactly what he had been looking for, namely, a civic-minded group prepared to support such an endeavor as winter tourism, promoted by skiing.

Over four generations the town had turned itself into a summer haven for wealthy city people. Some inns had been built, and the Equinox House was raised to patrician status. It had hosted four U.S. presidents. Abraham Lincoln's son had built the massive complex of Haldene—now a museum. The railroad arrived in the 1850s, the years that the town started to lay down marble sidewalks; there was nothing tawdry about Manchester. In winter there was an eccentric soul here and there on skis, such as the editor of the *Manchester Journal*, who wore "no special boots, no bindings, no poles" as he skied in the area of the Congregational Church around 1910. In 1916 a large Appalachian Mountain Club party came north from New York and Boston for several days of snowshoeing, skiing, skating, and coasting at Manchester.

In March 1920, the *Manchester Journal* found "a skiing trip worthy of mention," one taken by three local boys to Dorset Cave. They found it a "marvel of icy glory, heavily encrusted with stalactites and stalagmites of ice, some were nine inches in diameter and long in proportion." The descent, the article concluded, was a matter of minutes, "pure unadulterated sport of the first rank." Here, then, for the first time were the winter attractions of viewing a geological site combined with the sport of skiing.

Perhaps it was this little expedition that, some months later, bolstered enough interest in "a project to make Manchester a winter as well as a summer resort." This was not just talk. A meeting was called "to see what can be done in the way of "encouraging winter sports such as skiing, snowshoeing and skating." The innkeepers were wary, suspecting that "there would be quite a loss for a year or so at least." For the 1921–22 winter season, the Mount Aeolus Inn in East Dorset, a few miles north of Manchester, was planning on staying open. It was joined in 1927 by Wallingford's new hotel half an hour away.

While all this was going on, Fred Pabst, born in 1899 into the famous Milwaukee brewing family, had become an enthusiastic skier, enough to convince the University of Wisconsin to build a jump, and in 1920 he brought the ski club to compete in the Marshall Foch Trophy—part of the intercollegiate competition at the Lake Placid Club. After a year at Harvard Business School, Pabst joined the family brewery, built ski jumps in Milwaukee, started some junior ski programs, and in 1926 went off to Europe to learn "the theory of downhill techniques." It was said that he enrolled in twenty-five different ski schools. Patently, the beer business was not as exciting as skiing. On returning home, Pabst toured the western United States, looking for alpine areas that might do for skiing: Mount Baker, Snoqualmie, Yosemite, Soda Springs, Arrowhead, Mount Hood "too much snow, too much red tape or both." He also considered Ashcroft, the old mining settlement outside Aspen, Colorado. None seemed quite right. But up in the Laurentians of Quebec, Canada, he found what he was looking for: small towns willing to contribute, close to large population centers, in this case Ottawa and particularly Montreal, with a rail line going north into the hills. By 1936, he had options and leases on six possible hills, and his newly formed business, Ski Tows Limited, put up a rope tow on Saint-Sauveur's Hill 70. He would eventually run four tows in the area.

Pabst also scouted out New England and found the winter-minded folk in Manchester, Vermont, particularly receptive. He formed an American branch of Ski Tows. He was impressed when Manchester's Outing Club was renamed the Winter Sports Club and then constructed ski trails— with additional help from the Depression-spawned Works Progress Administration—on the Long Trail from Peru to East Dorset. With rope tows going up at Battenkill and at Mount Aeolus, the town and Pabst combined to make of Manchester a ski town. But Pabst wanted to capitalize on the growing number of alpine skiers elsewhere, and put up tows in New Hampshire as well. For the 1937–38 season, he was running ten altogether, three of them around Manchester, two in New Hampshire, three in New York, and two in the Midwest. By 1942, two more were added in Michigan, three in Saint-Sauveur, and one at Stowe. This was "chain-store management." It soon became clear that so many tows, stretched from Milwaukee to New Hampshire, could not be handled from the Ski Tows headquarters in Manchester. So much of the ski business was unpredictable, and condi-tions in the Midwest could be very different from those in New England. Logistics, too, had to be considered. It was five hours by train from Chicago to Wausau, only two hours by train from Boston to Chester, Vermont, the drop-off station for Manchester. Greyhound and Vermont Transit busses ran specials from Boston. That sort of arrangement was impos-sible in the Midwest. Pabst began dismantling his tows and bringing them to Bromley, and by the 1941–42 season, hardly an auspicious moment for ski development, he invested in alpine lifts. There were wartime restrictions on the use of building material, as well as gas and food rationing, and many of his skier clients were on war service, causing him to liquidate his chain store operation and concentrate on Bromley. The railroad ran to Chester, about half an hour from Manchester. Pabst arranged a transportation service—the Big Bromley Club. In the 1943–44 season it made $302, and in 1944–45, over $1,500. The Manchester Winter Sports Club ran a bus service too. Bromley was ready for the postwar boom. It did appear to bear out the ads that in 1942 Bromley was "the NEW winter sports paradise, and biggest ski area in the East."

In 1948 the *Baltimore Sun* compared Bromley favorably with Stowe and Pico Peak. It was "the finest area this side of Sun Valley, Idaho, with facilities for quick transportation to the top, even greater than that famed resort." The following year the *Boston Globe* added that the lift capacity was up to 2,460 per hour, the "highest in the country." In 1955, the figure was up to 5,400 skiers per hour. Ten years later, all those skiers were assured of skiable conditions: 71 percent of the area was served by snowmaking equipment.

Pabst also promoted his slopes as excellent competition venues: the interclub races of New York City organizations, the Amateur Ski Club, the Dartmouth Outing Club of New York, the German Ski Club, the Skidreiverein, the AMC, the Penguin SC, and the Norsemen all held their competitions at Bromley. The Amateur Ski Club ran a fathers-and-sons race on Shincracker Schuss. An idea developed in the late 1930s that Vermont skiing should be divided geographically; a Mid-Vermont Ski Championship, for example, was held at Randolph. The Southern-Vermont Downhill and Slalom was at Bromley in 1939, 1940, and 1941. Interestingly, the downhill was a no-fall race. What had happened by the end of the 1930s was that racing downhill had produced many accidents, and a no-fall downhill was one way to curb speed. Another was the giant slalom. And the Dartmouth men had started wearing helmets.

In 1942, the Southern Vermont Team Championship was held on Bromley's Shincracker. The slalom competition, however, was on Snow Valley's Grand Slam. And that introduces us to another aspect of Manchester skiing: competition between, and, one senses, among ski areas.

But Snow Valley was rather different. In one sense, it would be difficult to find a more impressive instructor list anywhere else in the United States: the Rath boys, Dolf and Walter (Dolf had been a contender for the 1936 German Olympic team); Sig Buchmayr, whom we met at Peckett's, Woodstock, and on Mount Washington; Otto Lang, Schneider's number one instructor in Saint Anton, who then served at Peckett's, Mount Rainier, and Sun Valley; and Fred Iselin, coworker with Lang at Sun Valley, and later running the ski school at Aspen with Friedl Pfeifer. How did the just-opened Snow Valley collect such luminaries? How was it possible that only five miles out of Manchester, and a little more than a mile from where Fred Pabst already had such a going and well-publicized area that Snow Valley could land such prize instructors when Fred Pabst appeared to dominate Manchester skiing?

It is an unlikely tale. In the late 1930s, Paul Kollsman, German immigrant totally unknown in the ski world but a star in aviation circles, acquired about eight hundred acres of land from the International Paper Company. His two nephews, Dolf and Walter Rath, both excellent skiers, had, with their uncle's backing, searched the United States for possible skiing land development. Kollsman had an engineering vita from universities in Stuttgart and Munich that he parlayed into an aircraft instrument making company. In 1928, he founded his own company, and the following year had a contract with the U.S. Navy for three hundred of his altimeters that had tested perfectly in a fog. By the mid-1930s, his altimeters dominated the growing aircraft industry. In 1940, he sold the company for $4,000,000 . . .

and bought the eight-hundred-acre parcel of skiable land outside Manchester. The Rath brothers were the men-on-the-spot developers. They knew their skiing world; living on the edge of the Schwarzwald (Black Forest), Dolf had had a possible shot at the 1936 German Olympic team, but injury forestalled that. In America, they were stalwarts of the German Ski Club of New York, Dolf coming fourth in the 1¼ mile Barton Trophy Downhill in the spring of 1940, and Walter was sixth in a field of thirty-one. At Pico the next year, Walter was seventh in the downhill, and Dolf eighth in the slalom. Clearly they valued the racing ambience, and the potential advertising it gave them, even though their glory days were past.

The years 1940 and 1941 were not the easiest for German immigrants, especially Jews. Almost immediately after war had been declared, the Raths found themselves in a Rutland, Vermont, prison awaiting official immigration questioning. Sig Buchmayr was also taken into custody. They were released, and Walter Rath went on to serve in the U.S. Army. Buchmayr went back to ski instructing. The Raths ran Snow Valley until 1950.

The war had another startling development. Kollsman must have known how to pull strings. A few days after Sun Valley had closed, Otto Lang, then in charge of the ski school, and a man who had been at Peckett's in 1935, had written one of the most popular how-to ski books, and had then gone on to run ski schools on Mounts Rainier, Baker, and Hood, received a phone call: "Would I come East with some of my instructors and open a ski school there?" The call came from Snow Valley. Lang queried his friends and coworkers Fred Iselin and Elli Stiller, who agreed to join him. So he accepted, but, he said, "right from the beginning I sensed that this would not work out." Lang was to run ski schools at Pabst's Bromley and at the Kollsman-Raths' Snow Valley, "three instructors at each of the resorts." That was how it was supposed to work out. "The competitive jealousy," Lang wrote in his autobiography, "between Fred Pabst, the

American brewing scion of German ancestry, and the Snow Valley group of Jewish ownership reminds me of a fight of attrition between two mafia factions." Never stated but often underlying resort situations was the anti-Semitism in the 1930s, 1940s, and 1950s.

Summer resorts were known to be frank about restricting their patronage to Gentiles, said the Reverend Ritchie Low, who was speaking in Burlington on the growing paganism in the state in November 1941. Low criticized the roundabout way of keeping Jews "in their places" that was now being used in Vermont. The words "Restricted Clientele" appeared in ads in Stowe in 1939–40, as they did at the Barrows House in Dorset. In the years 1939–42 these warnings appeared in the *American Ski Annual* for inns in Franconia, New Hampshire, Buck Falls, Pennsylvania, Tremblant in the Laurentians, and, of course, Lake Placid. Melvil Dewey (of the Dewey Decimal System for organizing books in libraries), owner of the Lake Placid Club around which all skiing swirled, had already been dismissed as New York state librarian in 1905 on grounds of anti-Semitism. In Vermont, in the north, Stowe seemed particularly concerned as its stature as a ski resort grew. After World War II, Robert Kahn, who had been in the African campaign, had flown forty-three missions over the Rhineland and southern France, and had been a prisoner of the Germans for eight months, tried for a room at the Lodge at Smuggler's Notch. He was refused. The *Burlington Free Press* found out from the Stowe-Mansfield Association that twenty of their forty-five members had a policy of restricting clientele. No one appeared to tackle what was considered a problem of owner's rights.

Still, Snow Valley seemed to be a success, and it was remarkable that the $100,000 of development work began with forty-eight laborers on October 1, 1941, and by December 5 workers were finishing up two rope tows of 700 and 1,200 feet, a parking lot for five hundred cars was ready, and the 3,500-foot "Boomerang slope" was the "prize attraction." A new design for the clubhouse, "The Snow Man's Rest

Lodge," incorporating a restaurant, lounge, ski shop, and offices, promised a far more comfortable and welcoming warm-up than the rough old camp with one large fireplace, and earthen floor, and an outhouse. It really did seem to be "All New . . . the place for YOU in '42."

Snow Valley was easily accessible from the major cities of Boston and New York, as well as the urban centers of Massachusetts and Connecticut, all on some rail line, and, like Pabst's Bromley, could expect skiers from Albany and Schenectady. On January 1, 1942, the area was "to open very soon." Three weeks later the first skiers came to enjoy three inches of powder on a twelve-inch base. By February, a bus service from Manchester touching at Little Bromley and at the Snow Valley Club House was available for twenty cents each way for residents, fifty cents return for out-of-towners. This was the Manchester Winter Sports Club at work—exactly what Fred Pabst had hoped—but now, after all, it served his competitor too. As we have seen, Pabst started his own transportation service.

These two Vermont towns, Woodstock and Manchester, developed skiing in a different way from Brattleboro and Stowe. All four had summer mountain attractions, but in winter there were major differences due to geography and promotion. Brattleboro's ski energy was concentrated on the spectacle of jumping. Stowe built its hotel/motel nine-mile semiurban corridor from the village to Mount Mansfield that, for the most part, succeeded in maintaining a Vermont/ Alpine look. Woodstock and Manchester, both with established five-star inns, had a town in place to provide winter lodging, dining (never "eating"), and shopping, and from which skiing could be enjoyed in all its facets for those of all levels of expertise. World War II intruded on all this development, but, as these chapters show, all four Vermont ski towns, having gone through many changes, survive as centers for enjoying a New England winter on skis.

CHAPTER 10

STOWE

SKI CAPITAL OF THE EAST

I owe much thanks to Stowe, for it was here that I first learned how to ski. From 4 p.m. to 1 a.m., I was a bar waiter at The Whip, the rather classy pub of the Green Mountain Inn, so I had all day to ski. While serving Tom and Jerries and Glühwein (this is in the mid-1950s), I overheard odd snatches of conversation: "I depend on Markers but, of course, Cubco's front throw. . . ."; "that second flush I dug my pole . . ."; "mark you, on my Riesenslaloms . . ." "Moguls," "aerials," "Stein turns," "Schusses"—incomprehensible language.

Up at the mountain the next day, outfitted with an ex-10th Mountain Division pair of edgeless white skis, poles that were too long, boots that were too tight, overdressed and full of enthusiasm, I confidently stalked off to the rope tow. What a mistake! I had not tried the boots in the bindings, and they did not fit. Those bindings were a hopeless mass of iron and rings, straps and buckles, and then the wire-clamp thing that was supposed to go round my heel: impossible! I went into the repair shop. How easy it was for Dieter to fix me up. So, off to the rope tow again.

Although I had watched carefully how he had put my boot securely into the toe clamp, when I came to do it, it was not the same thing at all. I had seen him clamp my heel down, then push the lever forward. He had then wrapped the strap around my ankle and buckled it with ease. On snow, now, I dropped the skis on the ground and pushed and thrust with one boot until it finally went into the clamp. Sweating profusely, feeling increasingly inferior to everybody, I stood unsteadily on one ski and, trying to put the other in place, fell. It is not easy to get up, and already I had an audience of two ten-year-old girls.

The second ski I placed parallel to the one to which I was so firmly attached, kicked my boot into the clamp and succeeded in sending the ski flying a good ten yards away. I followed it grimly, falling twice and giving unprecedented pleasure to my two small friends, who were now offering differing advice.

I had a stroke of luck: arriving at my wayward ski, I had placed the one ski on which I stood, quite inadvertently, on top of the erring one. It remained firmly in place. Now, could I remain upright while getting my right boot into the clamp? I did it and, bending double, put the monstrous heel clamp in place and pushed the lever forward, clamping one begloved finger with it. Solicitously, most solicitously, I eased the lever backward and reclaimed my finger.

On skis at last.

It is one thing to stand up on skis quite still, looking every inch a true-blue enthusiast. It is quite another matter to move across the snow. How to control the six feet or so of cambered hickory and steel (mine were actually ash and had no steel edges)? How to walk with that easy gait, let alone go up and—worse—come down the hill? And then that terrifying rope tow, that heavy, sodden, dripping, glove-ripping, twisting rope that pulled people (for fun) at high speed up two tiny iced tracks to the top of a near precipice—for such was the Toll House nursery slope in my eyes.

In the end, the tow operator refused to let me on. I had fallen twice in line, taking two ladies on the first tumble and an elderly gentleman on the second. I had stabbed someone's leg with a whirling pole and trodden on I don't know how many skis. I was not popular. The operator suggested a lesson, or at least that I practice walking before making an attempt at the tow. There was nothing else to do but comply, and after half an hour I progressed from slithering forward two feet and sliding back three to glissading forward three and slipping back two. Not much, but it was something.

I approached the tow, and the nearer I got to my turn, the faster it seemed to go. I hardly heard the man intone,

"Right hand in front, poles on left wrist, left hand behind."
He slowed the tow down and I got into position and grabbed
the moving rope with my right hand and found myself flat on
my face four or five yards up the icy track. I had learned the
first lesson of rope tows. The next effort was much better.
I let the rope run through my hand loosely and only grad-
ually did I tighten on to the quickening hawser. I slithered
up the icy hill about sixty yards before one ski strayed from
the rut and I fell in a hopeless heap. Two of the people who
followed me on the rope failed to get past, and we tangled
ourselves nicely. They extricated themselves and I was left.
I scrambled away from the tow and slowly considered the
problem of going down the hill. I was not about to remove
my skis and walk down.

To the left was the tow, a thing to be avoided at all costs.
At the bottom, the queue of people in line stretched ten
yards out onto the slope, and to my right was the wide-open
novice area, choc full (as it seemed) of skiers of incredible
ability turning this way and that at will—they were, in fact,
snow-ploughing neophytes.

"If they can, so can I, damn it!" And a wild slide ended
after twenty yards in a flurry of ski poles, snow, and me.
At least I was away from the tow, and with luck I wouldn't
crash into the line of people. There was nothing to do but
go straight—and in a triumph of speed and senselessness, I
stormed down the hill and sat down to avoid streaking into
the parking lot at the bottom.

What a run, what skiing, what a hill, what falls!

I had a happy time that evening serving drinks at The
Whip to crazy fools who went out of their way to break their
necks and talk about it, now as one skier to another.

Thank you, Stowe!

That Toll House rope tow had been erected in 1937, over
thirty years after a few loggers such as Craig Burt had gone
into the woods on homemade skis. Then immigrant Swedes
skied in the valley in 1912. They had inspired some youngsters,

mostly in and around Moscow (a couple of miles out of Stowe, toward Waterbury), and had made them skis. Stowe, already a summer tourist center, boasted a Toll Road that led to a Summit House on Mount Mansfield, 4,385 feet high, in use since 1858. Although Dartmouth's librarian, Nathaniel Goodrich, had climbed the Toll Road on skis in February 1914, and the kids from Moscow, Stowe, and Jeffersonville had held carnivals with minor competitions, skiing began to be noted only after the 1921 winter carnival, when it attracted between one and two thousand spectators—skijoring at forty miles per hour behind a car on Main Street was the prize attraction. Still, only a few took to the sport until the 1930s, when two outsiders—one from the moneyed aristocracy of New York, Roland Palmedo, and the other an Austrian immigrant, Sepp Ruschp—arrived to make Stowe "the Ski Capital of the East." This is their story.

Roland Palmedo, from a privileged banking family of German forebears, had first learned to ski prior to World War I. He had taken a trip to visit his cousins, who had put him on skis in the Garmisch region of Bavaria, and from then on he was hooked. At Williams College, he had been a member of the ski team, had joined a Dartmouth Outing Club trip to Mount Washington in 1916, and had won the skijoring race at the Williams carnival. In short, he was already part of the growing collegiate and postcollegiate ski scene. As a naval army aviator in World War I, he had served with the British. Flying remained a passion, and after demobilization, he even flew a short mail route. He soon acquired his own plane.

In the 1920s, Palmedo began to gather round him a group of like-minded sporting men to play polo and go skiing. They spent their winter weekends searching out possible places to ski: they visited Hillsdale, just inside the New York state border near Massachusetts, and Egremont, Great Barrington, and other venues. Palmedo formalized this group to found the Amateur Ski Club (ASC) of New York in 1931. The word "amateur" was important both in the sense of love of the sport

as well as in keeping professionalism out of the club. The pro-
spectus announced that the ASC was "to promote skiing by a
congenial group of amateurs living in and around New York
City." About a hundred invitations were sent out to prospective
members, and by the end of the year the membership stood at
seventy-eight, including some Rothschilds and Rockefellers,
and the radio voice of America in the 1930s, Lowell Thomas.

As more people joined the ASC, they ventured further
north. Palmedo wrote to the postmaster of Stowe inquiring
about available facilities and possibilities for winter excursions. He and ASC member Jose Machado spent three days
skiing around Stowe. They went up the Toll Road on skins
in three hours and, to the astonishment of local skiers, came
down in twenty-one minutes. They also skied over on the
Smuggler's Notch side and reported in the *Ski Bulletin* that
"a week or ten days at Stowe with a different trip or circuit
every time" was quite possible. Although a long way from
New York, the railroad line ran through Waterbury, and an
electric trolley operated from there into Stowe village.

These were Depression years, and in 1933 the Civilian
Conservation Corps was ready and able to work under Vermont state forester Perry Merrill, whose man in Stowe was
Charlie Lord. Logging landowner Craig Burt, a man who had
actually checked his logging operations as early as 1905 on
skis, was enthusiastic about the development of trails and
refurbished the Ranch Camp at the base of the mountain.
Two dollars a day would get you a bunk and three meals.
The Bruce was the first trail cut, and the ASC and the Mount
Mansfield Ski Club (MMSC) held the first of their interclub
races on it in late February 1934. However, bigger plans were
already in the works. The Barnes Trail was completed in 1935,
a down-mountain trail that avoided the major impediments
such as drop-offs and boulders with a variety of turns while
still retaining its steepness. Perry Merrill renamed it the Nose
Dive, and with its "Seven Turns," it instantly became the
East's premier downhill racing trail and acquired a mystique

of its own right from the start: "It satisfies," wrote Abner Coleman, "at least temporarily [the skier's] craving for a glimpse of the world to come." Stowe's rise to the top spot in New England skiing had begun.

The increasing ski activity, not just in Stowe but also in the neighboring New England states of New Hampshire and Massachusetts in particular, meant that there were many new-to-skiing sportsmen and women who needed some form of instruction for self-preservation as well as for enjoyment. At this time, too, fascism was becoming increasingly virulent, particularly in Germany and Austria, so that a number of skiers fled to the United States. Some took advantage by styling themselves experts, holding forth in an English full of German technical terms to instruct you in the mysteries of turning. They parlayed themselves into instructor status just by being European. America, after all, was built by amateur capitalists. Max Barsis, a refugee from Vienna, found that Americans considered practically any Austrian competent to teach them how to ski. He took advantage of this, and during the 1938–39 season he had collected enough episodes to portray the antics of his students in a booklet. *Bottoms Up: An Unreliable Handbook for Skiers*, published by Steven Daye Press in 1939 was the first of his humorous takes on the new-to-skiing public.

The leadership of the United States Eastern Amateur Ski Association (USEASA) came to the conclusion that "the number of these self-designated ski instructors reached serious proportions and the fraud on the novice is almost a scandal." They decided to do something about it. The committee comprised Alec Bright and Roland Palmedo, both with much European and American experience of skiing and club activity, who were joined by two well-known Norwegian cross-country and jumping men, Birger Torrissen and Bjarne Langslet. It may come as a surprise to find the two Norwegians on a committee to certify alpine instruction, but still in the mid-1930s it was felt that a bow must be made to the Norwegian traditions. A plan was developed and then taken out to the Midwest to the National Ski Association. It was presented as "similar in nature but less difficult" than European models. It required that candidates had sufficient English and were between the ages of eighteen and fifty-five. No would-be instructor was to have ties to any ski business. Besides the various stem turns and Christies of the Arlberg technique, it also included—again a bow to Norwegian skiing—Telemark turns. Since all candidates were alpine skiers, and by this time the heel of the boot was firmly fixed to the ski via a cable, doing a Telemark was virtually impossible.

Also required was "sufficient English"! But not too sufficient. When Fred Nachbaur was interviewed for the ski instructor's position at St. Paul's Private School in Concord, New Hampshire, although he was American-born and -schooled, and also spoke fluent German, he was refused the job because his accent was not exotic enough! Seventeen applicants took that first exam given on February 14, 1938. Seven passed: two Swiss, Arthur Schlatter and Hans Thorner; three Austrians, Sig Buchmayr, Sepp Ruschp, and Edi Euler; and two Americans, John Holden and Fred Nachbaur. When I spoke to Freddie Nachbaur in 1982, he used his acceptance letter to jog his memory of that first exam. There were three examiners: Benno Rybizka, guardian of the Hannes Schneider Ski School in North Conway; Walter Prager, the Swiss coach of the Dartmouth team; and Charley Proctor, on the American team for the 1928 Olympics and mentor to many New England skiers. Rybizka never showed up. Apparently, there had been some agreement among the candidates that "if Benno was going to be the examiner, then we wouldn't go to the test." Why? "Because he was obsessed with the Arlberg system that he could not possibly be an impartial judge." When I queried Charley Proctor (also in 1982), he replied, "Any technique that seemed practical and could be demonstrated and explained clearly by the candidate was accepted." Three examinations were given in the 1938–39 season. Thirty-nine passed, including three women. That number did not include four U.S. Olympic women's team members who had received Arlberg certification, nor one other who had taught at Jackson, New Hampshire. Twenty-two of the thirty-nine were Americans, but they were under the Arlberg spell, a disciplined way to reach perfection, and it brought out the critics. Lowell Thomas, who often broadcast from ski villages, believed that "for their own good, the ski schools should give up the idea of trying to make an expert out of every duffer." The criticism was really about the insistence by these Arlbergers on perfection of one particular turn before being allowed to advance to the next one. Rybizka was considered "a Prussian sergeant." Learning to ski was becoming a chore, warned Thomas in the *American Ski Annual* of 1937. Lurking on the ski slopes, too, were the promoters of the Swiss Ski School, the Schniebs School, and the Proctor Ski School. The battle of the ski schools, originally between the Arlberg crackpot crouchers ("crouch and you'll make it") and those who continued with the upright Norwegian style, was far more visual and vocal on the increasingly packed downhill slopes. "Let's forget names and nomenclatures," wrote Lowell Thomas, "let's build up a style that is essentially American." This was not, in fact, an original idea; "The American Ski School" could be found at North Creek, New York, where Otto Schniebs held forth after his stint at Dartmouth, and Paul Lamere's American School could be found at Whitefield, New Hampshire. In 1939, you could join Oscar Cyr at Bristol, New Hampshire's "American Ski School for American Skiers."

By the beginning of the war, seventy-six Eastern-certified instructors could be found in Massachusetts at Northampton, in New York at Lake Placid, in Illinois at Chicago, and in California at Yosemite. There were seven in Vermont and eight in New Hampshire where certified instruction was guaranteed. The next examination would be held when World War II was over, in January 1947.

It is hard for us to realize now that the ski heroes were not the racers but the instructors. In the 1930s it was Sepp Ruschp, Siegfried Buchmayr, Otto Lang, and, of course, Hannes Schneider who were the names all skiers recognized. Behind the scenes, individuals played key roles: Roland Palmedo, Alec Bright, and Katharine Peckett have their share in this book. Although in the 1930s, Dick Durrance was certainly a racing name to be recognized and admired, it was only in the postwar decades that speed stars such as Jean-Claude Killy, Toni Sailer, and—in 1964 finally—twenty-year-old Americans Billy Kidd from Stowe and Californian Jimmie Huega out of Squaw Valley won Olympic slalom silver and bronze medals at the Games in Innsbruck. We make much of Schniebs and Walter Prager coaching the Dartmouth College teams, and so we should, but we should realize that in the latter twentieth century Willy Schaeffler, a German immigrant, and Bob Beattie, originally a New Hampshire boy, had perhaps a more far-reaching influence on media, money, and the development of racing.

As the problem of ski instruction became increasingly worrisome to New England ski leadership, a letter arrived from Austria—one of eighty sent to American ski hill managers—from a Sepp Ruschp of Linz, inquiring about the possibility of a ski teaching position, listing his credentials both as winner of the regional cross-country championship that year as well as his state teaching experience. He was certified in an examination by Hannes Schneider. Schneider's name was increasingly recognized in America because making a ski trip to Saint Anton in the Arlberg region of Austria was a must-stop for the wealthy. They took a course in Schneider's Arlberg technique that absolutely dominated Alpine skiing by the mid-1930s. Skiers might well have seen one or two of the films Schneider had made under the direction of Arnold Fanck, and possibly the more committed had actually seen him perform at the Boston and Madison Square Garden ski shows.

The president of the Mount Mansfield Ski Club, Frank Griffin, eventually offered Ruschp a room and a desk in the Toll House Lodge, $100 a month, and 50 percent of any sum over $100 he received for lessons. He also arranged for Ruschp to coach the University of Vermont and the Norwich University ski teams. Ruschp arrived in Burlington on December 10, 1936, and was driven over to a Stowe with little snow and lots of woods. The Austrian instructor had arrived.

In Europe—Alpine Europe—going to ski school and passing tests was considered the right way to improve your skiing. Ski instructors were the gods of the village, especially at Saint Anton, where Hannes Schneider held forth as *Skimeister* to the world . . . and Sepp Ruschp had passed his exam under Schneider's eye. But Americans lived in a country made by do-it-yourselfers. They did not take readily to authorities telling and showing them how to enjoy themselves. Besides, those types were professionals, getting paid to show people how to enjoy themselves. Somehow it didn't seem right.

Sepp Ruschp had arrived in the United States as these arguments were heating up. At first, he did not have many students, so he took to traveling around locally and giving lessons here and there. He took the full amount for himself and did not pay the 50 percent to the MMSC. It was the first of many disruptive moves in Stowe's growing importance in the ski world.

Meanwhile, Roland Palmedo had taken it upon himself and the Amateur Ski Club to organize and sponsor teams for the 1935 Fédération internationale de ski (FIS) championships as a trial run, as it were, for the following year's Nazi-controlled Winter Olympic Games to be held at Garmisch-Partenkirchen. These games were for the first time open to alpine disciplines, downhill and slalom, and they were open to women for the first time too. Palmedo had more than a willing partner in ASC member and well-known habitué of Saint Anton, Austria, Alice Wolfe, whose skiing pedigree included a second in the old class in the 1931 Parsenn Derby, the great ten-kilometer downhill race out of Davos, Switzerland. Together they organized the 1935 team. Palmedo—"our Arnold Lunn"—borrowed American-born Helen Boughton-Leigh, who was racing for the British by way of her marriage to an Englishman, to captain the team. She and two others of the FIS team in 1935 went on to the Olympics the following year. Alice Wolfe was the chaperone on both occasions.

Two other matters concerned the skiing community at Stowe. The first was the increasing fascist quality of the sport of skiing in Europe; Mussolini was providing *Dopolavoro* (after-work) trips for young skiers and building up the Alpini, Italy's mountain troops; and Hitler's skiing clubs were now organized by *Gau* and led by *Gauleiters.* Pressure was put on Austria to become part of the "New Germany," something that actually happened in the Anschluss of March 1938.

The second concern was the competition among ski regions, even among ski centers (the term "ski area" was not in use until after World War II). In December 1936, Averell Harriman, friend of Palmedo, opened America's first destination ski resort, turning the wilds of the Sawtooth Range of Idaho into Sun Valley. Two or three hours from Stowe, New Hampshire's Cannon Mountain was served by a tram, ready in 1938, that could whisk twenty skiers to the top of the mountain in eight minutes, while every little village seemed to advertise a rope tow.

Palmedo was very aware of these developments; he had skied all over the place in the 1930s, not just in Europe (Mürren, Kitzbühel, Grindelwald, Davos) but also in Massachusetts, at Sun Valley, and around Assiniboine in the Canadian Rockies. Everywhere where Alpine skiing had taken off, he saw how important efficient lifts could be, whether they were funiculars, trams, rope tows, J-bars, T-bars, or Harriman's first-in-the-nation chairlift. Lift services brought about an astonishing rise in the amount of skiing a person might get in a day.

In 1937, Palmedo started talking about a lift at Stowe such as that found at Harriman's in Sun Valley. This undercurrent of talk was brought to the fore when he inspired some 1936 Olympic team members to come to Stowe for the 1938 National Downhill Championship on the Nose Dive. Of course, they had all been lift skiing in Europe, and here, at Stowe, they had to walk up to the start. "Where are the lifts?" they asked. Where indeed?

In May 1939 serious scouting of a proposed chairlift line was carried out by Palmedo and J. Negley Cooke (Cookie), accompanied by state foresters Perry Merrill and Charlie Lord, as well as Sepp Ruschp. Here was the nucleus of Palmedo's Mount Mansfield Lift Company. All that was needed was the raising of a large sum of money. But then Godfrey and Sterling Rockefeller were on board, and Lowell Thomas became a director. In all, fifty-seven stockholders put up about $100,000 to finance the chair. Work began in June 1940, and the first ride up was on November 17 that year. It was a disastrous opening: there was a wicked snowstorm, and the lift failed. Still, as Philip Palmedo writes in the biography of his father, "That day Stowe became No. 1 ski resort in the East," with a 6,330-foot line carrying eighty-six chairs some two thousand feet up in fifteen minutes, with a lift capacity of two hundred skiers per hour. A total of 57,266 rode the lift that first winter season.

With war raging in Europe, and with the United States veering ever closer to involvement, this was not the most opportune time for large-scale investments in pleasure. Then came December 7, 1941, and Roland Palmedo signed on in the U.S. Naval Air Force and saw service in the Pacific.

Meanwhile, at home in Stowe, the growth of skiing had led to construction on the mountain road: bunkhouses, inns, and shops. More trails were cut, and the whole operation of skiing was becoming—had become—a mishmash of conflicting goals. Palmedo and his stockholders were in charge of the chair that ran across both Craig Burt's private land as well as land owned by the state of Vermont. There were now two rope tows, four mountain lodges, two ski schools (Jacques Charmoz, a French Olympic team member, had arrived), and a hotel company with part ownership of Sepp Ruschp's Ski School. It was pretty unsatisfactory for all concerned. And Palmedo was very much worried about the growing glitz of après-ski life . . . where was his *gemütlich* Alpine village, why did busloads of hoi polloi come to the ASC's mountain? After his return to civilian life in 1946 he began to search somewhere else with increasing fervor.

At the time Palmedo, Cookie, and Charlie Lord were casting about for a would-be ski venue, arguments emerged over who should upgrade the trails served by the chairlift; it was obviously going to cost a lot of money and labor. And then Palmedo discovered that Sepp had gone behind his back and applied to the state for a permit to build a second chair. He sent a blistering letter questioning Ruschp's standard of business conduct and reminding him that the ASC was the first group of skiers who had come to Stowe. Who had suggested and arranged for the CCC to cut the first trails, and even paid for beer and refreshments for the men? Who was responsible for Stowe's first ski patrol? How did the National Downhill Championships take place at Stowe? Who had organized the first Women's Downhill Championship, and who had suggested, organized, and publicized the first Sugar Slalom? Who had the Shaw Trophy designed? And who paid for it? From where did the money for the Edson Trail emerge? Who brought the Bolivian and Chilean ski teams to Stowe? And who got the lift that in the words of the president of the Mount Mansfield Ski Club was "the greatest asset that Stowe had—without it today the region would not be in the running as a major ski center"? And—finally—he asked Ruschp if he had forgotten Palmedo's "efforts to welcome you and to help you and your school when you were first starting?" It was quite an indictment. We don't know what Sepp thought of this. He was already on safe ground with

Stowe's new man-with-the-money insurance magnate C. V. Starr. Stowe's postwar top spot in America's skiing in the 1950s resulted from this Starr-Ruschp cooperation. In 1949, Palmedo's Mount Mansfield Lift Company sold out to Starr. Meanwhile, he had found new ski land, some half an hour south of Stowe, at Mad River Glen. His mountain was not going to tolerate "belly dancers, discotheques and other side-show attractions." Mad River Glen remains a Palmedo monument, even to the extent of running the only single chairlift left in the lower forty-eight.

CHAPTER 11

SOUTHERN NEW ENGLAND

"I KNOW HOW TO MAKE SNOW!"

Driving along the Connecticut coast, between the densely populated centers of Bridgeport and New Haven you come across the town of Milford, an unlikely spot for the birthplace of today's multimillion-dollar snowmaking business.

An engineering aircraft division of Chance Vought happened to be located in nearby Stratford during World War II. Immediately after the conflict ended, using technology developed during the war, some engineers created a bonded aluminum ski, called it the ALU-60, and began to manufacture it. Chance Vought, though, was not supportive, so three engineers founded the TEY Manufacturing Company in 1947. The ALU-60 sold quite well until the weather turned bad in the winter of 1949–50, meaning very little snow. Wayne Pierce, one of those engineers, came to work on March 14, 1950, announcing to his partners, "I know how to make snow!" Thus, snowmaking got its start.

In fact, there had been other ways to make snow. In 1934, Louis Geib, the technical director of Warner Brothers Films, chopped up large blocks of ice, put a fan behind them to blow the chips, and lo! he had a snowstorm for the film "As the Earth Turns." More or less the same things had happened to provide indoor snow for the Boston and Madison Square Garden ski shows of the mid-1930s. The method had also been used at the outdoor jumping extravaganzas of the Hollywood Bowl in 1935 and at the Los Angeles Coliseum in 1938 and 1939. And during the war, Canadians Dr. Ray Ringer and his team, trying to control the rime ice on aircraft wings, had sprayed water into the air at the entrance of a wind tunnel, turned on the engine, and out had come not rime ice but snow. Not a thought was given to patenting the idea or method.

Pierce and his partners Art Hunt and Dave Richey at TEY Manufacturing ("TEY" coming from the last letters of their surnames) used an old paint sprayer to force water into cold air and so create snow. It sounds simple enough, and so it was, using a garden hose and close-at-hand water supply. The photograph of the prototype shows a box about twelve by fifteen by eight inches with a short hose and simple nozzle: patent number 2676471. The experiments were publicized on the front page of the *Boston Globe* and the *Wall Street Journal*, and Lowell Thomas gave it nationwide coverage in one of his radio broadcasts. The patent was applied for in 1951 and granted in April 1954.

By this time, Pierce and his cohorts were more interested in making skis for an obviously growing clientele, plus others were imitating and experimenting with snowmaking devices. TEY was sold to Emhart and resold to the Tropeano Brothers,

Figure 7. In the United States in 2020 it has been computed that a low-snow year costs the ski business over $1 billion. Much of that cost is from making snow. Hard to believe that it all comes from this tiny experimental box of the TEY company engineers in 1950. New England Ski Museum photo 2022.001.001. Used by permission.

who had already helped Pierce install their equipment. They, too, entered the snowmaking business, having excellent experience with fruit-tree-spraying machines using their own antifog nozzle. Test equipment was in operation at Mohawk Mountain in northwest Connecticut and in the Poconos in Pennsylvania in the 1950–51 season. It was successful enough for Grossinger's in New York to run the system for the next season. In the seventy years since, snowmaking machines, one type now called a "snow gun," can produce enormous quantities of snow overnight. The latest marvel comes from Israel, where IDE Technologies has a "VIM" (vacuum ice maker) all-weather snow maker that can produce 560 tons of snow a day. There is a larger model that can make 1,120 tons; Zermatt, Switzerland, has installed one of these. So far, there is none in the United States, but with global warming, an efficient VIM able to produce snow at ninety degrees Fahrenheit may be the answer.

In the United States, all was not well. In spite of the Tropeano brothers holding the TEY patent, when it was discovered that a Canadian team had, in fact, made snow before them, a court case against the Tropeano's TEY patent was heard. Ringer's experiments showed that snowmaking had, indeed, not originated with TEY, and the patent was declared null and void.

This was the situation in the late 1940s and 1950s, when into the winter world skied Walt Schoenknecht, who during the war had also worked at Chance Vought and who knew Wayne Pierce and his friends. Schoenknecht had his eye on Mohawk Mountain, some ten miles west of Torrington, in the northwest snow corner of Connecticut. The mountain was 1,683 feet high and comparatively easy for rope tow development. Schoenknecht leased one hundred acres and opened trails for the 1949–50 season, and with good snow came a good profit. The 1950–51 season was different; there was minimal snow, but Schoenknecht chipped off ice and blew it on trails served by the rope tows. It may not have been profitable, but it was great advertising. "Walt sprays 450 Tons of Ice over Bare Mohawk Slopes, Breaks Even," trumpeted *Eastern Skier* in February 1951. The next season Schoenknecht put a TEY system in place and opened for business in January with four inches of granular snow on a seven-inch base.

Schoenknecht was born in New Haven in 1919 and had taken to skiing on local golf courses and undoubtedly on some of the CCC cut trails, such as the 1¾-mile trail "wide enough to check speed" at Pound Ridge Reservation in South Salem, just across the state line in New York. A ski tow at Bethany, a few miles north of New Haven, boasted one of the first ropes in the state, and Schoenknecht had also been a promoter of the Quinnipiac Ski Club, also just north of the city.

It all sounds small beer from seventy years on, but Mohawk is one of six Connecticut areas still in the ski business and today run by Schoenknecht's daughter. He moved on to southern Vermont in 1954 to create Mount Snow from Mount Pisgah. Schoenknecht never forsook the smaller areas; he encouraged them, seeing them as not only good for the local economy but also as feeder hills for his larger project, Mount Snow. He advised on the construction of the YMCA's Camp Jewel Hill in North Colebrook and was volunteer chair of the camp's ski program. He was also a member of the Governor's Connecticut Tourism Council.

It was still typical in post–World War II American ski development that individuals played major roles in proving what was in fact an old winter enjoyment but now in modern form—one based on alpine skiing and providing the industrial infrastructure requiring vast amounts of dollars.

This was a long way from the Scandinavian immigrants who had made the northwestern corner of Connecticut a ski region. We know very little about the beginnings of skiing in the state. In Hartland, for example, there is documentation to show that an Ole Simonsen made skis for the owner of the village store, a Mr. Willis Hayes, in 1899. Here is evidence of the transfer of old country knowledge to new world enjoyment. The skis may be seen today at the local historical society. "On Skis in Connecticut" appeared in 1905, written by a reasonably knowledgeable practitioner, but there is not a hint of where the experiences described actually took place. In New Britain, in mildly hilly country close to Hartford, an emigrant woodworking instructor from Norway had his high school class making their own skis in 1910. The following year, the Norfolk Inn "intended to make this house as attractive as possible for winter house parties." Skiing became popular with Trinity College students in Hartford as they slid the hundred yards from Bishop Brownell's statue toward Broad Street. When Hartford had a run of six days of snow in February 1916, the favorite hill was just east of the golf course. At Storrs, University of Connecticut students practiced on Valentine Hill. When a good snow came, the newspapers commented how that brought out young men and women. There is a fine photograph of seventeen UConn students obviously enjoying themselves on skis in 1923.

These are the very few instances that remain of early skiing in the state before the arrival of the Sætre brothers (immediately Americanized to Satre) to wake up Salisbury to the joys of skiing. How to attract people to the sport as competitors and as an economic incentive? Build a jump . . . and they will come. In 1926 Johan Satre, as member of the Swedish Ski Club in New York City, had won the Metropolitan twelve-mile cross-country championship on the North Jersey Country Club course in Paterson, New Jersey. He arrived in Salisbury with job in hand as chauffeur to the local Wilmer family. The following year, brothers Magnus and Olaf came, then Ottar. They were a formidable skiing family. In 1919, Johan had been founding member and first president of the Vestre Trysil Idrettslag (the West Trysil Sports Club) in Tørberget, some 115 miles north and east from Oslo (in those days called Christiania; the name changed to Oslo in 1925).

The brothers had jumped at Holmenkollen. On arrival in Salisbury, they formed the Outing Club and built a jump and put on the first tournament in January 1927, to which two hundred spectators came to see such a winter novelty.

The Satre boys immediately made their presence known on the American jumping scene. In February 1928, at the U.S. National Championship in Red Wing, Minnesota, Magnus was first, Johan second, and Olaf fifth. "The Eastern team," commented the editor of the 1928 *Year Book*, "was treated in a highly courteous and friendly manner." That this remark warranted inclusion was indicative of the growing influence of New England skiing in the face of general and decades-long midwestern superiority. The Satre brothers were forcing the pace. At Lake Placid's cross-country events in December 1928, Magnus again came first, Olaf two fifths of a second behind him, and Johan third. Lake Tahoe, California, held the nationals in 1932, where Magnus came in fifth and Ottar eighth. At the pre-Olympic trials held in Lake Placid in 1934, Ottar jumped to first place and Magnus was the combined winner—that was the occasion attended by Mrs. Eleanor Roosevelt, one of the hoped-for five thousand spectators. Both these Satre brothers were chosen for the 1936 Olympic Games to be held in Garmisch-Partenkirchen, Germany. Salisbury was certainly on the U.S. ski map, and it was a remarkable fact that only six years after the Satres had founded the outing club they could put on the national championship.

And here is another extraordinary fact: less than twenty miles to the east, the village of Norfolk also had a contingent of Norwegian skiing stars: Harold Sorenson, Birger Torrissen, and Ole Hegge. These three competed against the Salisbury team, which now included one American-born, Richard Parsons. In 1934, for example, the Norfolk Winter Sports Association had piled up snow to ensure its cross-country and jumping meet would go off on schedule. In the ten-mile cross-country run, Magnus Satre beat Ole Hegge by thirty-six seconds. In the jump, Ottar Satre came out on top.

He won the "Ladies Cup"—a Scandinavian tradition given to the most graceful jumper. Birger Torrissen had come fourth, and Harold Sorenson fifth. No one could beat Alf Engen, jumping for the Sun Valley Club in February 1938. It is of note that Salisbury could attract the very best of American jumpers, and all the way from Idaho.

Yet another Norwegian, Anton Lekang, lived down the road at Winsted. That town's ski club was founded in 1933 and leased land on Spencer Mountain in Colebrook. They built what was advertised as the biggest jump in the world: 1,138 feet long with a maximum jump area of three hundred feet. Lekang was the outstanding jumper at the opening meet on January 14, 1934. He came from an island north of the Lofotens and had won events, broken hill records, received Ladies Cups at Narvik, Svolver, Tonsberg, and had been chosen to represent northern Norway at Holmenkollen in 1924. Like the other Norwegians of the area, Lekang too had a skiing pedigree that few could better, and quickly established himself as prime contender for jumping honors in New York, New England, and eastern Canada. At the Olympic Games in 1932, held in Lake Placid, he foreran the jumping competition, as his citizenship papers had not been completed in time for him to be a member of the American team. That same year, this "wingless flyer of the snows," as the *Reno Gazette-Journal* described him, won the U.S. amateur title at Lake Tahoe, and at Seattle he had the longest jump, in addition to winning the Ladies Cup, and he made the longest jump at the Portland, Oregon, meet, and so on.

Lekang turned professional in 1934 and helped to find, design, and build the huge jump at Winsted. He was able to attract Alf Engen, then the reigning professional, who made two massive jumps of 172 and 170 feet before a crowd of ten thousand. That same year, Lekang and Strand Mikkelsen found a suitable hill in Massachusetts at Ayer. They designed and directed the building of the seventy-meter trestle. Lekang was first off the hill . . . and broke his ankle. This led to a second skiing career as adviser and coach for Yale University teams, for young women at upscale Miss Porter's in Farmington, and at Saint Margaret-McTernen School in Waterbury, where Lekang was in charge of the ski program for over thirty years.

Lekang from Winsted and the Satre brothers from Salisbury, along with the Norwegian boys from Norfolk, made of northeast Connecticut a veritable ski destination, with both villages reporting snow depths to the *Ski Bulletin*, New England's go-to publication of eight rather flimsy pages for up-to-date news. By this time, the early 1930s, as we have seen, Alpine skiing was gaining interest, and especially so once the rope tow era began in 1934. This coincided with the regular snow train schedule that, as we know, was launched in January 1931 by the AMC and others with the Boston and Maine Railroad. But northwest Connecticut was not near any of B&M's tracks.

Mrs. R. Graham Bigelow, a Lake Placid Club regular, knew Norwegian Olle Zetterström of Canaan (a village between Salisbury and Norfolk). She invited all the local skiers—soon known as "Mrs. Bigelow's Norwegian team"—to form the Norfolk Winter Sports Association. They cut trails, kept adults and children under their skiing eye, and in 1932 broke ground for a natural sloping jump requiring no scaffolding, that is, in the Norwegian tradition. A junior jump was built alongside.

Fair enough, but ski jumping is not the same as skiing. With the increased interest in cross-country, especially the derring-do required for skiing those winding hilly trails with an occasional quite steep slope, the thrill of speed on an outing led to an increase in what became known as "downhill skiing." Mrs. Bigelow had her pulse on what was happening . . . and with her wealthy New York connections arranged to have the New York, New Haven and Hartford Railroad trains stop at a "snow station" just beyond an inn. In 1935 began the NYNH&H snow train from Grand Central Station in New York City to Norfolk. Representatives from the well-heeled Amateur Ski

Club of New York, the Skidreiverein (so named because they always occupied car #3 and sang German *Lieder*), the New York chapter of the AMC, and the Dartmouth Outing Club of New York arranged for 509 people to take the first snow train to the Norfolk hills. Even a traveling sports store was included, where equipment was available for rent or sale. The round trip cost two dollars. The price was no problem for the club members, of course, but for lesser lights of society, it was not prohibitive either. In those days a stenographer's weekly wage was twenty-five dollars, and a bookkeeper's thirty to thirty-five, but the *Ski Bulletin* was quite clear that there were many aboard who had "learned their skiing in the Alps or at New England colleges." Mrs. Bigelow arranged to have guides around to send the skiers off in the right direction. The day trip was an immense success if Monday's metropolitan papers can be believed. Later that season 261 enjoyed the February 12 trip, and another 110 three days later. With all these ski trains leaving, Grand Central administrators provided a roped-off area for the city's public to view this new breed of sportsmen and women bedecked in strange costume and carrying thin and narrow boards. The AMC's *Appalachia* commented in 1936, "Skiing as an intimate sport practiced by a close-knit and limited group of devotees is a thing of the past," and, indeed, the "snow train" began to give way to the "sun tan special." No wonder clubs like the Skidreiverein always sat and partied separately in the third car on their way north to snow country.

The "close-knit and limited group of devotees" such as the Skidreiverein operated quite happily near Mohawk Mountain. With Otto Schniebs, who at this stage was the pied piper of New England skiing, as adviser, the club cut trails at Cornwall Bridge. They arranged with the NYNH&H to discharge skiers before going on to the Berkshires. A Dr. Clark arranged transportation from the train to the slopes and trails of Harlow Mountain. It was there that the Skidreiverein challenged the ASC of New York to a slalom race. The best four from each team counted, and the ASC won by seven seconds—a grand match. Later they enjoyed moonlight skiing with Schniebs, and the following day he provided on-snow instruction. Here were the elite who were in the process of making modern skiing possible for the lesser lights of society while clinging to their own sequestration when possible just as they remained prime movers in the modernization of skiing. Reported in the *Ski Bulletin* of March 1, 1940, the first sanctioned downhill and slalom competitions held in the state took place in West Goshen on the Mohawk State Forest run, three-quarters of a mile long with a vertical drop of six hundred feet. Result in the downhill: Sverre Satre first, Magnus Satre second, and Olaf third. In the slalom Magnus prevailed, followed by Sverre and then Olaf. Those Satre boys moved with the times.

Increasingly, as more and more people skied, as more and more improved, bigger and varied terrain was the draw, and, as like Walt Schoenknecht himself moved north from Mohawk to Mount Snow, the northwestern ski areas of the state went into decline. After the war, a new group of entrepreneurs brought a return to the great jumping days of Salisbury. In 1950, the jump was restored, enough to hold the Eastern Championships there in 1952. Two training jump hills of twenty and thirty meters were built. Then the sixty-five-meter hill was replaced by a modern steel construction, snowmaking equipment was borrowed in 1980, and ten years later a permanent system was installed. Salisbury was back on the ski map with a contract to host the eastern division meet of the junior national championship starting in 2011 every five years. The 2020–21 season would have been a major one for the club, but the COVID virus postponed activities. Expectations were high for the 2021–22 winter, and the Salisbury Winter Sports Association's Jump Fest in February was a grand success, with males and females competing in a variety of competitions.

There were also a number of short tows built in the northeast part of Connecticut at Brooklyn (that's where Stein Eriksen gave a clinic using the three-hundred-foot rope tow), and at Pomfret Landing. These were close to the Rhode Island line, and perhaps it was this availability that slowed down the building of tows in Rhode Island. No matter what, skiing is a tough sell in Rhode Island, where the mean height of the land is two hundred feet. Rhode Island is, after all, the Ocean State, with its America's Cup heritage, International Tennis Hall of Fame, and patrician mansions in Newport; these are not exactly attractions for the ski-minded. The highest spot in the state is right on the border with Connecticut: Jermoth Hill, at 812 feet, nearer those two Connecticut ski tows mentioned above than to Providence. Since 2014, Jermoth Hill has been owned by the state, but Brown University retains the right to build an observatory. That is, there is no skiing there, and there will not be in future.

As early as the 1913–14 winter season, the NYNH&H Railroad advertised train connections from Newport for winter vacations, "ski-ing" being one of nine sports suggested. The unfortunate Mrs. Baggott of Providence had taken the train to Saint Johnsbury, Vermont, where, using a mop as a staff while learning to ski, she pierced herself in the lower abdomen; the mop came out of her body at the shoulders. A tough day on the slopes. Happily, she was reported to be making remarkable progress. Obviously Rhode Island was no ski mecca. Therefore it may come as a surprise to learn that when, in 1935, "Stinging Wind Sends Transportation Toppling," Newport "enjoys winter sports," as the *Mercury* detailed on January 18 that year. The sport was becoming popular and could be enjoyed "on the long slopes of Miantonomi Memorial Park"—a mildly sloping picnic area today—and on the hills around Green End and Lily Pond. This was, of course, exceptional. At least locals could have a try.

But between 1936 and 1939, Diamond Hill was open for hiking up and skiing down. A staggering 17,245 spectators turned out for the first Rhode Island Ski Runners Club

(RISKI) meet in January 1938. A cross-country race of two miles, a downhill, a slalom, and jumping competitions went on all day. All events were won by RISKI members from a field that included Brown University students, members of the Agawam Hunt, and the AMC. It was a grand success and has been continued on to this day. Well after World War II, two double chairs served the steepish hill, but they were removed in the 1970s and replaced with rope tows until 1981. At the height of Diamond Hill's popularity, there were even Austrian instructors from the Hannes Schneider Ski School. One skier remembered how her instructor had such a thick accent that she understood only a word here and there. Ski Valley shared the same hill as Diamond, just a different side of it! Here T-bars, a double chair, and instructors (one certified) teaching the American Technique in 1973 could not keep the area afloat beyond the mid-1980s, but the RISKIS took their skiers to Massachusetts areas and to North Conway in New Hampshire. Their sixty-eighth meet in February 2022, scheduled for Wachusett, Massachusetts, had to be cancelled because of COVID.

Another area also closed in the early 1980s was Pine Top, named for the pine glade skiing in the 1960s. At its height it too had over a dozen instructors. Snowmaking kept it in business, and was supplemented with night skiing. But by the 1980s skiers who had enjoyed themselves there as kids moved on to bigger hills, and driving their cars to areas in Massachusetts and beyond appealed more and more.

Sometime in the 1930s the city of Providence tried out an area between Killingly and Plainfield Streets, west of the city center, on the Johnston line. Very little is known about the two rope tows that constituted the area called Neutaconkanut Hill, now a city park. Indeed, it was the superintendent of parks in Providence who sponsored a "straightaway run and ski jump." It opened formally for the 1935–36 season and was well enough patronized that the run was extended to the top of the hill. I am told you can still find remnants of the pilings for the suspension of the tow. The website NELSAP has a good aerial photograph, and another one shows how it is now virtually all grown in with mature trees.

The one remaining ski resort, which doubles as a water park in summer, is Yawgoo Valley, in Exeter, about half an hour by car south of Providence. Remarkably, it boasted Rhode Island's first chairlift in 1965 and now has two of them as well as two rope tows. There is snowmaking and grooming along with night skiing on all of the approximately three kilometers of trails serving a 150-foot vertical drop. Yawgoo is financially family friendly, with an adult ticket at forty dollars and kid's day pass at thirty-five. I have seen lower rates advertised. However, when I cast my eye along the cars parked at Waterville, Loon, and Cannon on a weekend, there are not a few with Rhode Island plates.

CHAPTER 12

THE MODERNIZATION OF NEW ENGLAND SKIING

One legacy of the Great War that ended in November 1918 was that there had been troops on skis. American army personnel guarded Alaska from their base at Fort Davis, and in the Midwest, the garrison at Fort Grant in Illinois trained on skis. In New England, cadets at Norwich University in Vermont took to skis. The R & R (rest and recuperation) service provided skiing activities for the American Expeditionary Force in France at Mont Revard, near Chambéry in Savoie, near the border with Italy. Meanwhile, at home the growth of industrial cities produced not only the mechanized marvels of cars and trains but a workforce determined to relax. Much of their disposable wealth was spent by these urban populations on comparatively cheap out-of-doors leisure activities, whether watching baseball games or enjoying the beach. Automobiles and trains enabled people to go quickly from city to countryside. In winter, skiing began to appeal to increasing numbers of the wealthier sectors as, perhaps, an alternative to baking on the Florida coast. Because it was also not expensive, it appealed to the increasing numbers of office workers.

Everyone's skiing was dominated by the Norwegian *ski-idræt* ideal, but by the end of the 1920s notable changes were already taking place. They would guarantee a different—and mechanical—ski experience in the 1930s. The skisport would change to the sport of skiing. The Midwestern-centered National Ski Association (NSA) was pressured into a divisional structure. The United States Eastern Amateur Ski Association (USEASA), founded in 1922, took the lead. Whereas the NSA thought in terms of club tramps, urban skiers from

Boston and New York widened the summer hiking trails to accommodate ski excursions. Later it would be these city dwellers who would become addicted to speed.

The 1920s also saw a shift in the way that people skied. Imported from the European Alps was a style of skiing called alpine. Downhill and slalom, the foundations of this new sport, were first experimented with at Dartmouth. These new disciplines—pay attention to that word—appealed first to those wealthy enough to travel to Switzerland, Germany, and Austria. They returned to the United States delighted to pass on the heady lure of being able to ski at speed. This lure was attached to both a British attitude to skiing and an Austrian Arlberg technique enabling them to do it. All this was very different from the leftover muscular righteousness of Norwegian *ski-idræt*.

When Dartmouth's librarian, Nathaniel Goodrich, spent a ski vacation with the British in Mürren, Switzerland, in 1928, he couldn't resist a side trip to Saint Anton in Austria, where he "had a glimpse of Hannes Schneider." That was enough stimulation for one day! Appalachian Mountain Club (AMC) member Wilhelmine Wright was a wealthy vacationer who spent two months in Kitzbühel, where Schneider's Arlberg technique—a way to ski and a way to teach—was in full force. "Anyone caught doing a telemark is considered a criminal," she reported. The ski school regimen was as follows: first year, stem; second year, Christiania turn. After five years, Wright was told, she might ski reasonably well. There was to be no advance to the next stage until perfection was achieved.

From his winter belvedere of Mürren, across from the Eiger, Mönch, and Jungfrau, Arnold Lunn was simply the "Ski Pope." When he died in 1974, Boston's White Mountain Ski Runners were reminded "of the debt all Alpine skiers owe to his enthusiastic involvement in the development, popularization and organization of the sport." "He opened up a new epoch," wrote his Swiss friend Walter Amstutz, "and it bore his personal stamp." American skiers are particularly indebted to Lunn for three interrelated influences. First, he was skiing's most forthright publicist, and he waged a running battle, not always friendly, and occasionally impatient, with the Norwegians as he strove to reduce their influence in his Alpine world. His arguments peppered not only the Ski Club of Great Britain's *Year Book*, which he edited from 1920 until he died fifty-four years later, but also the French, German, and Austrian ski journals. Second, he invented modern downhill and slalom racing. He was tireless in obtaining recognition for these Alpine disciplines in world competition. And third, he held administrative positions on many international committees and represented Great Britain at Fédération internationale de ski (FIS) meetings.

Lunn's first love was mountaineering, and both downhill and slalom would help to develop the kind of technique suitable for ski mountaineering. The open slopes above Mürren could be run straight, meaning with no turns—hence early downhills were often called "straight races." But if you wanted to go from Mürren to the valley floor at Lauterbrunnen, you also had to be expert at tree running. Lunn invented the modern gate slalom as a substitute for racing through trees. In 1922, he was convinced that "the only satisfactory method of testing the power of moving among obstacles is a slalom race, i.e. a race down a course defined by *artificial* obstacles such as flags."

At Hanover in 1925, eight pine branches were stuck in the snow on a gentle hill dropping all of one hundred feet: the slalom had arrived in America. Reporters did not know what to make of it, describing it as a "British test in ski proficiency gauged by four flags at 75 to 90 degrees right and left down the steep hill." Slalom was included in the intercollegiate races in 1927. "My inspiration for this," wrote Dartmouth physics Professor Charles A. Proctor, "came from the British Ski Year Book." In 1927 he was elected an honorary member of the Kandahar Ski Club.

Downhill was also initiated at Dartmouth College on the suggestion of the Hungarian coach, Anton Diettrich (a better fencer than skier) in 1925. The 1927 downhill—parts of the course actually went uphill—was won by Charley Proctor, Professor Proctor's son, who went on to become mentor to many of New England's well-known skiers of the 1930s. The race was held on the college's own mountain, Moosilauke. In 1931, the course was described as "very steep and twisty for the most part through heavy woods," a race defined by nature, dropping 2,500 feet in 2¾ miles. "I was in that race," one contestant remembered fifty years later. He crashed on top of another runner in the trees. Having disentangled themselves, he reached into his pocket for a flask. "How about a nip?" Both finished in the middle of the pack.

As increasing numbers of people took to skiing, organized club instruction was begun by the Appalachian Mountain Club in 1928. Prior to this, teachers had been hired individually and attached to particular inns. Strand Mikkelsen made a name for the Weldon Inn at Greenfield, Massachusetts, and another "Norwegian expert," John Knudsen, was at the Shattuck Inn in Jaffrey, New Hampshire, known as the quiet place where Willa Cather finished *My Antonia*. During the Depression, his salary was reduced to thirty dollars but increased to one hundred in 1936 because of the number of guests. Knudson retired in 1938 after eleven winters. When the AMC started club instruction in Boston with the idea of getting ready for the 1928–29 season, what had once been a ten-minute indoor chat on how to ski was expanded to four weekly talks on the new Arlberg technique. In December, the club instructor, Otto Schniebs, gave three sessions on the "crouch technique," followed by an anticlimactic explanation of waxing. In 1930 regular exercises in the gym were added. Schniebs both wrote and was written about in the Boston papers, thus the Arlberg reached a widening audience. Once winter set in, AMC members felt that all the practice had really paid off as they enjoyed "Lunging, Crouching, Jumping and Hip Swinging." The Telemark "incognito" was barely permitted—once all the alpine Christiania swings had been mastered.

Here, for the first time in the United States, organized club schooling was offered to recreational skiers. A new clientele, drawn chiefly from clerical and professional groups who were neither athletically developed nor in proper physical condition, such as employees of the Revere Brass of Fall River and Hope Finishing Company of North Dighton and Taunton, constituted a group very different from the college down-mountain thrill seekers. Skiing was becoming popular. By 1931 the number of AMC members who skied had risen from twenty-five to over three hundred.

With new skiers on the trails, the search was on for more places to ski. Automobiles and trains were the industrial means to spread social skiing in New England. While his AMC friends traveled on a club trip to the Laurentians, north of Montreal, in 1928, John Holden was among the skiing crowd leaving Munich's Hauptbahnhof (Central Station) for the Bavarian mountains an hour away to the south. Holden's reports to Eastern and to the AMC stirred enough interest in the leadership to persuade the Boston & Main Railroad to try a ski train season. Of course, people had traveled by train with their skis before Holden's reports came in, but this was the start of a regular service. For the initial January 1931 experiment, the B&M announced a trip "to some winter sports center whose skiing, snowshoeing, and other winter forms of activity are at their best." The final choice of destination would depend on snow depth and weather reports. Three days before departure, Warner, New Hampshire, in the lee of Mount Kearsarge, was chosen. Of the 197 on the train, 115 were AMC members, and most of the rest were from Harvard and the DOC of Boston. Once in Warner, most practiced on pastureland. The train was used as a "club house [for] naps between exhilarating and strenuous exercise." All were jubilant over its success. All, that is, except the natives, who did not think much of the invading city folk tramping through orchard and field. A month later, Epsom, New Hampshire, was ready for 605, who were met with "smiles, conveyance, and directions." Twelve trains took 8,371 people from Boston that first winter of 1931. That spring, the AMC took stock of the ski train initiative and concluded that it had "opened up a new era in New England skiing."

Indeed it had; the snow trains captured the imagination of younger desk-bound office workers. That first season, for example, a February 15 trip for eighty employees of Harris Forbes, a Boston bank, enjoyed their ski outing at Greenfield in Massachusetts. Skiing, however, was not the only attraction of the ski train. "A great many people came up to raise hell. To put it plainly some of them did a marvelous job at it," recalled a north-country shop keeper. A former Dartmouth ski team captain disliked this city hoi polloi, "a whole Coney Island of people skiing where you wanted to ski . . . it was sort of a disaster, a mess; they'd just engulf you." The years of hair shirt- and *ski-idræt*-imbued youth were giving way to proletarian fun. It could be uncomfortable to the old guard.

In 1931 the snow train's destinations were the flatlands of Warner and Epsom, and by 1933 they were depositing "ski larks" for down-mountain skiing. In 1939, Harvey Gibson bankrolled a short film called the *Ski Larks*, emphasizing his Eastern Slope Inn, and in 1948 the New Haven Railroad promoted the Ski Lark, a train that would take you to a score of the popular northern New England winter resorts! Around that time, part of Grand Central Station was roped off in response to the fact that New Yorkers' "newest spectator sport is to watch the ski trains depart." The B&M hired well-known skiers to give advice on their snow trains as well as instruct at the destinations. Rentals were available, and by 1940 you could board the train straight from your office and get out at Plymouth, New Hampshire, in your rented ski togs. With rented skis and poles on shoulder, off you would go to a session of prearranged instruction and the promise of a sunny *Schuss*; the ski train provided easy sociability. "You'll have a glorious Sun-day," advertised the B&M, promising both a suntan and a stem turn.

These ski larks were headed for the hills that now sported uphill devices. A rope tow had been discussed at DOC meetings in 1915 as a means to get jumpers to the top of the trestle. Nothing came of that idea. In Europe, the rope tow as we now think of it was patented in Switzerland in 1931. In North America, Alex Foster, a former Canadian college jumper, rigged up two thousand feet of rope on to the axle of a Dodge at Shawbridge, Quebec. Any skier with the price, meaning the strength, could grab on anywhere he liked; tickets were for gents only.

Foster's Folly was copied at Woodstock, Vermont. Three New Yorkers, having had a wonderful experience at Kitzbühel due to the "funicularity" there, and a very poor last day of the season at Woodstock, suggested that the Royces, their innkeepers, do something about it. David Dodd put together "an endless rope which runs over pulley wheels attached to a timber horse guyed to a tree at the top of the hill." A Model T powered four or five skiers up about nine hundred feet at five to ten miles per hour, depending on how hard the driver put his foot to the pedal. Seventy members of the Ski Club Hochgebirge were on hand. "Nowhere in New England did skiers enjoy so much delightful downhill skiing with so little uphill effort." The Amateur Ski Club of New York found that the tow required some skill and considerable strength. "One gets almost as much of a thrill going up as in coming down." Or was it, as the *Ski Bulletin* put it only partly joking, "another sport gone softy?"

The White Mountain Ski Runners, another Boston club, took Ted Cooke to a meadow near Gilford, New Hampshire. To his surprise, they did not want a rope tow to serve the slanting field but one to rise up the mountain way above the meadow. Here the WMSR would have downhill pleasures. Cooke came up with a "Tow-Way," the longest rope tow in the world, an arm-wrenching three-thousand-foot haul up for skiers to get one thousand feet of vertical downhill. In spite of many inconveniences that first season—the slow trip up, the twisting rope—Cooke was sure those could be handled with lifting the rope on rollers: "Our equipment is perfected for all practical purposes, and we can look for only minor improvements in the future." Homemade tows appeared in New Hampshire, first at Lisbon in January 1935, and after that in Brookline, Rochester, and Franconia. They also cropped up in Vermont at Putney, Shrewsbury, and Corinth. At Bousquet's in Pittsfield, Massachusetts, on a Sunday in January 1936, the tow had "well over fifty at one time" until a chain broke. Jockey Cap at Fryeburg was Maine's first rope tow. Brookline's 320-foot claim to fame was that two youngsters got twenty-five thousand feet of downhill running in one day, "comparable with any Swiss ski center!" In the later 1930s, out of Seattle, the portable Sweden Speed Ski Tow proved attractive to small-time operators in New England.

The rope was important too. An immediate problem was that not only did the rope drag in the snow and thereby become wet and heavy but also that early ropes were notorious for twisting. To counter both those problems, Amco of Brooklyn came out with an all-weather manila rope, and one of the New Bedford Cordage Company's advertising lines was that it did not twist. Realizing almost immediately the strenuous pull on muscles unused to such exertion, Ted Cooke designed a steel pronged handheld claw that you twisted onto the rope, thus making the trip up much easier than managing the sodden twisting hawser by hand. It was even believed that a ride now would be "in close approximation of overhead tramway comfort." Clarence Bousquet had success with his contraption that took pressure off the arm by being attached to the skier's belt. Dartmouth produced a "new ski tramway," an early edition of the J-bar. Some DOC students closed their eyes at the "immorality of the machine" as the number of skiers increased 100 percent that first season. The T-bar, known in the early days as the "He-and-She-Stick," made its first appearance at Pico, near Rutland, Vermont.

In New England, two firms were involved in major ways in making winter sports structures such as toboggan chutes, jumps, and then rope tows. Hussey's of North Berwick, Maine, was the best-known, but as rope tows became ubiquitous, Underwood's of South Boston and Peter Carter of Lebanon, New Hampshire, provided models, Underwood even making "the new speed thrill," a tow advertised as running one hundred miles per hour on level ground. In fact, one man at Woodstock, Vermont—the only place where that tow appears to have found favor—reached ninety-three miles per hour . . . but the tow was withdrawn after one season! We may be wide-eyed about the safety angle, but in the 1930s, skiing was promoted by such derring-do, as skiers tried the "Devil's Dip," the "Undertaker's Delight," and the "Coffin Cheater." New England's most famous race was "The Inferno."

In December 1936, one of the most important civilizing (meaning the most industrial ease making) machines of the sport came out of the tamed wilds of Ketchum, Idaho: Sun Valley's chairlift. Some thirteen months later, at the Belknap Recreation Area, New Hampshire, the "modern tramway of the sit-down variety" was to New England what Sun Valley's chair was to the West. It started operations in January 1938, the year Roland Palmedo began the serious business of soliciting funds for his six-thousand-foot chair up Mount Mansfield at Stowe.

And then—as we have seen in an earlier chapter—Alec Bright advocated a tram car, European-style, for Cannon Mountain. "No avenue of contact with the mountains for the older or the physically untrained offers so much, so intimately and with so little encroachment of civilization on the sanctity of the mountains," he argued and, it must be added, nothing better could serve the newly cut Richard Taft Racing Trail in 1938. New Hampshire now proudly owned the first tram in the United States that was operational for summer tourists and winter skiers.

These aids, some would now say requirements, for alpine skiing were made by mechanizing the sport. However, there were side effects, not all seen or understood by those involved. You might arrive by automobile and rail at the venue, but all sorts of things had gone into making that possible: the mechanization of skiing made the modernization of skiing. It changed the culture of winter sporting on snowy slopes. Just to enter a downhill race, you needed to be in a club, for that would authenticate your application. You needed also a certain amount of expertise, which you obtained from European immigrant instructors. And then there was the up-ski to get you to the top of the course. Should you crash badly during the race, you would also need medical help—a ski patrol is yet another necessity brought on by the alpine form of skiing.

The problem was articulated by David Brower of the Sierra Club in 1938:

> The golden age passed when bindings were mechanized with rigid toe-irons and severe tensions. For with mechanization came a mania for speed. Steeper and steeper slopes were sought. Caution was cast aside. Mountains became mere proving grounds for exhibitions of tricks and techniques. Men worshipped perfection in *tempo, vorlage*; were consecrated to mastery of controls and schusses, corridors and flushes; talked of waxes and edges, ski-meets and records. They admired their apparel while the peaks went unnoticed. They slashed trails in the forest, built elaborate lodges, gashed mountains with highways, wired peaks with funiculars. They conquered the wilderness. Men now ski superbly. But what have they lost?

With the growing number of skiers on the slopes and race courses, the production of skis moved from individual ski makers in the old centers, such as the Norwegians in Berlin and the Finns in Newport, to small manufacturing companies like Craftsbury, just four miles from Stowe village. The Midwestern factories of Martin Strand and Christian

Lund had been operating since before World War I. Seeing the enormous growth in New England skiing, Lund opened a branch in Laconia in 1936 and went on to supply skis to the 10th Mountain Division during World War II. Lund's Northland models manufactured specially for racing, jumping, and touring in December 1932 were advertised as "known and used by 90 percent of American skiers" and in 1934 were chosen by the Byrd Antarctic Expedition. Wright and Ditson, a major Boston emporium, also stocked Northland. Groswold of Denver, Colorado, entered the eastern market in 1934. The era of small-time manufacturers was over. By this time, the ski was not just a plain board, grooved on the underside, with a tip at the front. Now it had steel edges. The "Lettner" edge, invented by Austrian Mathias Lettner and patented in 1927, made turning on skis easier and sharper. Hambro's soon promised "steel edges precisely attached" to the old edgeless skis. Whereas in the cross-country world, a corner might be made by swooshing the ski round, and for the experts a stylish Telemark turn would be applauded, in alpine skiing, you put your ski on edge and followed its curve with the up/down motion of the body, showing off your Arlberg technique.

That you were able to do this was also a matter of a binding that no longer left the heel free for the stride across the snow but now iron clamps held the toe in place, while the heel was kept in place by a cable that could be tightened enough to keep the boot firmly on the ski. Later, in order to fix the heel even more firmly to the ski, an Amstutz spring was attached. The Swiss Dr. Amstutz was one of the first adherents to Alpine skiing. His idea was soon picked up by Skisport in the United States, and "tempo springs" were on the market in December 1934. Advertising by use of key words, in this case "tempo" referred to the technique that Austrian *Slalommeister* Toni Seelos achieved. Skiers in the United States were quick to pick up the lingo, especially when it came from the Arlberg region of Austria; it gave authority to their skiing.

Early skiers used their winter boots; they were strong enough for crossing fields or slipping along logging roads, but downhillers required all the control they could get. Boots specially designed to give support were on the market in Maine, for example, in the late 1920s by such a well-known firm as L. L. Bean. Bass was selling "Men's water-proofed Ski Shoe with a Plain Toe, Hard Box, Ski Heel and Norse Last" in 1927. Still, the best boot for those with enough money was the German immigrant Peter Limmer's boot, with its heavy, tough leather and very firm sole. It was the most desirable boot on the market and—sign of the times—the Hannes Schneider model was a prize possession.

All these needs produced a winter economic boom even as the Depression seemed never-ending. The new equipment was put on view at two ski shows, in Boston and at Madison Square Garden in New York. At the first shows in the pre-season of 1934, the stalls of the exhibitors were mostly from equipment manufacturers and those supplying accessories, such as rucksacks, to skiers. But three years later, there was not much equipment on view. The tourism industry was in full swing with destination advertising of hotels, pistes, and ski centers—the German State Railway system enticed people to come to what was touted as "The New Germany." In 1935, the Hamburg American Steamship Line took out a full-page ad in the *American Ski Annual* advertising that the Bremen and the Europa would be making the crossing in four and a half days, docking alongside boat trains at Cherbourg and at Bremen, and then only thirteen hours on by rail to the winter games at Garmisch-Partenkirchen. Political conditions became more unstable in Europe. The Nazis marched into the Rhineland three weeks after their Winter Olympics had ended. The takeover, the Anschluss of Austria, in mid-March 1938 and the imprisonment of Hannes Schneider shocked the ski world. In America, those unsullied western mountains, the Rockies, the Sierra Nevada, and the mountains of the Northwest took on a greater appeal. It is no mistake that a vast ski area "the size of Zermatt" was planned for Mount Hayden, just out of Aspen, Colorado. So even before the world war, the Northeast, in spite of its obvious growth, was already finding those larger mountains with consistent and massive snow depths now being praised in terms with which the Northeast could not compete, no matter how much they mechanized skiing.

CHAPTER 13

SELLING VENUES, TRANSPORTATION, AND EQUIPMENT

Skiing came to the United States in the mid- to late nineteenth century just at the time when the country moved into its powerful capitalistic mode. Advertising was partly a cause and partly a result of this. Newspapers and magazines were readily available, and in the 1920s, and especially in the 1930s, radios became household items. Scandinavian folk attitudes defined the skisport. When skiing became part of the industrialized leisure economy, towns competed for the honor of putting on skiing events. They advertised their advantages. States began to lure skiers and would-be skiers to their hills with posters. Manufacturers offered equipment and accessories galore to the increasing number of people taking to the new alpine sport. These neophytes followed the dictates of those alpine downhill experts who virtually removed the *idraet*-inspired northern Europeans from the hills. Ski advertising did not take place in a major way until skiing itself became a sport,

We have noted how skiing was brought over by Norwegians, Swedes, and some Finns, all immigrants who did not bear the physical or political odor of Italian and Balkan immigrants. They tended to settle among their countrymen in the Midwest. In New England, communities from these northern European states provided the initial thrust for the use of skis in the region, places such as New Sweden, Maine, and Berlin, New Hampshire. The immigrants made their own skis; in Maine, as mentioned earlier, they were on view at the state fair in Lewiston in 1885. Homemade late nineteenth- and early twentieth-century skis may be seen at the New England Ski Museum in Franconia, New Hampshire. Very soon, following the lead of Norwegian immigrants in the Midwest—such as Martin Strand advertising his "biggest Ski Factory in the world," and Christian Lund, "The World's Largest Ski Manufacturer"—ski manufacturing on a semi-industrial scale began in the East. Tajco Skis, the brand name for Theo Johnsen of Portland, Maine, were the most prominent in New England, although, in fact, his products turned out to be too expensive, and he went out of the business after two or three years, but not before he produced America's first how-to-ski book that doubled as a catalog.

New England stores of all sorts stocked skis: Peirson Hardware, "Right in the Center of the City," of Pittsfield advertised in the *Berkshire Evening Eagle* in January 1915: "Genuine Ash Skis Any Length at $2.50 to $4.50 a pair, Pine Skis at $1.25 to $2.00." In 1922, they were selling pine, ash, and maple skis. Belden's Sporting Goods Company of the same town were the Northland agents, having received a big shipment of skis and poles, of all kinds and all prices, in December 1916. Only two weeks later, they announced the arrival of a shipment of a hundred pairs of skis, and in 1920 they had "an almost unlimited stock of Snow Shoes and Skis in all sizes." The Barris-Kenyon Company, dealer in hardware, paints, and mill supplies, also carried "skiis, skates, sleds or toboggans." In Woodstock, Vermont, if you wanted skis at L. P. Ward's, all you had to do was "Ask for SAM, He's one fine fellow." In Bangor, Maine, the General Paint and Electric Store had four-foot ash skis for sale at seventy-five cents, and 4½ feet for a dollar. Six-foot skis cost $1.75. A 1920 dollar had the buying power of between thirteen and fourteen dollars today. However, as late as 1936, you could still "Make Your Own Skis" quite easily; Hoopes Bro. and Darlington of West

Chester, Pennsylvania, would sell you 1½-by-4¼-by-8-inch ski billets for $3.50.

Both Strand and Lund continued to pitch their products nationally in Eastern's *Year Book*, taking out full-page ads in 1929 and 1930, Lund's Northland adding the imprimatur of American champions Lars Haugen and Nels Nelson (both Norwegian immigrants) in 1930. In 1933, Northland claimed that 90 percent of American expert skiers were on Northlands, and in the following year was delighted to report that Admiral Byrd's expedition was equipped with Northlands. In 1939 Byrd and Schneider "agree on one thing: Northland Skis." In New England, Tubbs of Maine was a major player in the late 1920s, taking out a full-page ad in 1929. Other indications of the growth of skiing were two quarter-page ads in the National Ski Association's (NSA) *Year Book* of 1930: Norge Ski from Oslo, and Wearhouse Incorporated of Hanover, New Hampshire, announced "Imported Ski Equipment" along with Ostbye and Brattlie waxes from Norway.

However, in the early 1930s, with the arrival of the mid-European alpine immigrants, the manufacturing of skis became big business and Eastern's *Year Book* virtually a national year book for the skiing community. It carried a full page for Northland, and quarter pages each for Strand and newcomer Groswold of Colorado. Patently these western firms realized there was a market in New England to be exploited. Groswold was selling his "Schniebs Ski," and Otto Schniebs himself, still playing the pied piper of alpine skiing, not just at Dartmouth, where he coached until 1936 but also regionally, was used as the authority to buy from Groswold. That same season, 1935, there was competition from local Craftsbury Ski Company in Vermont, Gregg skis from Minnesota, and from Seattle, Washington, came Anderson and Thompson with their A & T laminated skis. Imported Gresvig Norwegian skis were advertised by a shop in Boston. In 1936, from Ontario, the Peterborough Ski and

Tobogganing Company entered the U.S. competitive market. Nearer to home, in New Jersey, Hydrocyl made its entry: "faster, stronger," ear-catching words echoing part of the Olympic motto, and rightly so, since 1936 was the first year of alpine competition for both men and women at the Olympic Games to be held in Garmisch-Partenkirchen, Germany.

There seemed no ending to the production. Anderson & Thompson announced "12 laminations" for its Sun Valley model, another was the Otto Lang, "fit to carry this great instructor's name" (who by this time had relocated to the Northwest), and the Silver Ski was as "outstanding as the race it is named for" on Mount Rainier and run between 1934 and 1942, and again after the war in 1947 and 1948. Laminated skis were the rage, and Allen's, the famous old sled company in Philadelphia whose "Flexible Flyer" had become part of winter Americana, turned out the Splitkein laminated ski in 1939. Northland engaged Hannes Schneider, the "World's Foremost Skier," who had recently been sprung from a form of house arrest in Germany, to join some of his Arlberg instructors already over in the States. The strength of skis was a concern, and Groswold advertised first aid for broken skis in 1937, using the insignia proposed for the National Ski Patrol, which would be officially founded the following year. One of the newer sports shops in New York, the Alpine Sporting Goods Company, advertised "Repair Work our Specialty." Repair often had to do with broken or missing metal edges.

The Austrian Lettner edge had been patented in 1927, but in the 1930s a variety of edges had come onto the market: Schniebs promoted Lignostone edges in 1936, Spearhead edges competed with the Serr-Edge, claiming that it may not have been the cheapest but it was the best. No matter what, Hambro promised steel edges would be "precisely attached" in 1934, that is, you brought your wooden skis to Hambro, who would rout out the edges and screw the steel slivers in. For ski bums like me in the 1950s, this is what we still had to do.

Boots became specialized in the 1930s. Well known out-of-doors manufacturers such as Bass of Wilton, Maine, had started to make special boots for skiing in 1912. The Berkshire Shoe Company's "High Storm Shoes" were "ideal for skiing, skating, any outdoor activity where snow, ice and cold are encountered" in 1916. "Heavy Shoes" were available in Pittsfield in 1924. With the rising interest, Bass saw advertising in 1928 as a way to capitalize on skiers' enthusiasm. Bass launched its downhill boot by putting a square toe on a logger's boot. Yet using the word "Norwegian" in advertising was still an attraction, even as alpine skiing took hold. Norwegian immigrant Oscar Hambro relied on it for advertising, and in 1932, the Boston shop of Wright & Ditson was still selling "Norwegian type ski boots." In the 1930s, Ski Sport of Boston, Edwin Clapp of East Weymouth, Massachusetts, L. L. Bean—the Northeast's doyen of outdoor clothing—and Bass itself now advertised its ski boots as "European style, American price." German immigrant Peter Limmer, with cobbling experience in Garmisch-Partenkirchen, began his hand-sewn styles in 1935. In 1937, Sandler of Boston had a boot "approved by Birger Ruud and styled by Hannes Schneider," in addition forty other styles ranging in price from $3.50 to $15 in 1938. Just before the war, a popular shop in New York, André, stocked Les Trappeurs, the boots worn by rising French star Emile Allais. It is of note that no company advertised special boots for cross-country skiing, although the Chippewa Shoe Manufacturing of Chippewa Falls, Wisconsin—real cross-country terrain—would advertise in the *American Ski Annual* of 1940–41, "Fine Quality Ski Boots for forty years."

Bindings were not advertised at all in the 1920s. For cross-country work there were the well-known Norwegian leather-and metal-contraptions leaving the heel free. The Haug binding was carried in 1932 by Boston's Wright & Ditson, and specialty ski shop Hambro's was the place to buy Gresshoppar, Marius Eriksen (father of Stein), and Bredesens

Polar Ski Bindings. The Dartmouth Coop carried the popular Unitas from Germany.

Alpine skiing, though, required a firmly-kept-in-place heel, and that produced Ski Sports' Schuss downhill model, Northland's Micromatic, Dovre's Kabel, and T. Elliott's New Spearhead Toe Iron, all advertised in 1934. Then came the Cam-Lock, Spearhead's High Hitch Toe Irons, and Asco ski bindings. Dovre's were "purchased by the Byrd Antarctic Expedition." Northland's Reverse Throw Cable came with an explanation that defies understanding: "The front lock throws towards the boot, eliminating the possibility of catching and jerking open." The Superdiagonal was available in the season before the war. In the early 1930s, Swiss Walter Amstutz devised a spring connecting the boot to the ski at the back, providing a modicum of security.

Poles—single, in pairs, and two that could be clamped together as one—were all on the market by Theo Johnsen in 1905, but generally, at that time, men simply cut stout, straight branches of ironwood, hickory, and oak, as Fred Harris did in 1904. Early advertisements for poles start in 1931 in the *Ski Bulletin*, where, for example, Hambro simply includes them in a list. Tonkin, bamboo, and, in 1938, all-metal poles were available for $7.50 a pair.

Far more important for the skier was the ability to ensure that the skis ran well in all sorts of snow conditions, which in 1905 could be described as "downy, fluffy, powdery, sandy, dusty, flowery, crystalline, brittle, gelatinous, salt-like, slithery, and watery." No wonder, then, that wax and waxing played a major role in any ski outing, and, of course, in all race meetings. Concoctions to allow the ski to glide well had centuries of trial and error behind them in Scandinavia. The first patented formula was granted to Peter Ostbye of Norway in 1913. Advertisements for his wax can be found in the NSA's 1930 *Year Book*. The most popular imported wax was Victor Sohm's Red (speed), Blue (dry, cold snow), Green (wet snow), imported by the Dartmouth Coop in 1932. By

1936, a new Sohm's wax was on the market, "adapted to U.S. snow conditions"—whatever the difference was remains unsaid! Schniebs recommended Sohm's, and it was stocked by Hambro, who also carried North Star, Seeberg's, Finse, and Mika waxes at forty cents a tin, or three for a dollar. Skigliss by J. C. Reimann of Newtonville, Massachusetts, made its entry in 1934. Schneider endorsed Angra, the Farr-West Company in Seattle producing Red Head Lac Wax: "At last a liquid that actually stays on the skis!" Schniebs was selling Duro Speed, and from Ashtabula, Ohio, F. Maenpa was the agent for Finnish Kiva Skiwaxes, used in the "1937 50 kilometer race by numbers 1, 2, 3, 4, 6, 8, 9, and 10th finishers." In 1936 at the Olympic Games, thirteen of the first twenty-three runners in the fifty-kilometer race waxed with Kiva. And it cost only thirty-five and forty-five cents. Gsellin made its appearance in 1938, and the Mack Miller Candle Company supplied Base Wax and All-Purpose Wax for twenty-five cents each. The American Grease & Stick Company of Muskegon, Michigan, also had an All-Weather Ski Wax—probably better to stay with what Osborne and Hambro offered.

Before sealskins were readily available, men tied thin rope under their skis for climbing up. A climbing sock, a canvas sleeve slipped over the back of the ski and fastened to the front binding, proved a low-cost and easy-to-carry and -install alternative. There were other forms, most of them not very successful, such as the Jerns Ski Climber (from Seattle), a mini blade affixed to the base of the ski at the foot placing that stuck down when the skier was climbing up and flattened as he leveled off or went down the hill. The Alta Ski Climber was a permanently fixed small strip of retrograde hairs under the ski that acted in similar fashion as the Jerns climber. This New York firm's use of the name of Alta shows, once again, how important keeping up to date was; Alta, Utah, was an up-and-coming ski area just outside of Salt Lake City in the late 1930s and would become competition to the neighboring developing Colorado centers.

Only when the speed of the skier increased was it necessary to have goggles. Until then, dark glasses sufficed, but from 1935 on Polaroid supplied Eye Togs; Blodjer, non-fog visors; and the Ski Specialty Shop of New York City had a No Glare Ski Cap for sale.

Mitts, too, were vital. Parker Brothers of Littleton, New Hampshire, sold the SarAnaC, a brand name recognizable from the ski country around Saranac Lake, where the United States Eastern Amateur Ski Association got its start. Morris-Shutts Manufacturing out of Grinnell, Iowa, advertised its Trailmaster gloves for men and women—the Instructor and Towmaster for men only in 1939. Many skiers simply wore their old woolen winter gloves.

Care of equipment and of person needed to be taken, and most important was the care of skis over the summer months. The problem concerned the camber and the tips. What emerged was usually some sort of spreader, a system of keeping tips and tails together and blocking the center part of the skis apart, whose probable origin was the Swiss-made Davos Press. Ski Sport produced a metal press with an adjustable spreader for the tips. The Dartmouth Coop carried the Swiss Hespi Ski-Spreader, and Speed's Ski Spanner, "Swedish designed, American made," was on the market in 1938.

Boots and leather straps needed long-term care too, and various oils and greases were marketed by outfits such as Snow-Proof of Middletown, New York, "Leather's Best Friend." Sole oil for boots was available from Ome Daibar in Seattle.

As more women skied, Nepto Lotion assured them in 1931 that "Winter Sports [were] safe for the complexion." Ultra Tan was developed by a group of doctor-sportsmen, and Elizabeth Arden's Sports Gelée was popular with the upscale skieuse. Most popular of all was the original Swedish (but now made in the United States) Skol, used by instructors Otto Lang and Benno Rybizka, both very well-known from the Hannes Schneider Ski School in Saint Anton—Lang now in the far northwestern United States and Rybizka holding forth in New Hampshire. For men whose skiing exceeded the capability of their desk-bound muscles, there was always Absorbine Junior.

And then there were accessories. The earliest ads were for trophies, pins, badges, and the like. In 1928 and 1929, three New York City firms advertised: Heather-Mathews, Robert Stoll, and Gorham's (the latter even had a booklet of suggestions). L. G. Balfour of Attleboro, Massachusetts, advertised regularly from 1934 on. He was joined in 1935 by Boston jeweler H. P. Zeininger and in the late 1930s by another Boston firm, Dorretty. Charles Arcularius of New Canaan, Connecticut, offered ski motif jewelry such as cuff links for men and bracelets for women in the season 1940–41.

Equipment was sold by three sorts of shops: old established emporia, such as Filene's in Boston; shops that were not new but had been involved in outdoor activities, such as Alex Taylor's in New York, "the house that sports built." Wright & Ditson, L. L. Bean, and A. G. Spalding were active along with a growing number of quite new specialist shops, such as Hambro and Osborne in Boston. A number of established merchants simply included a Winter Sports Department, and some provided a special corner of the store for the snow train clientele. Usually these specialty departments were staffed in one form or another by a well-known skier who added authority to what they were selling, men such as Charley Proctor at the Dartmouth Coop. However experienced the big-name stores were for outdoor clothing and equipment, far more helpful for skiing information were the specialist shops, and it is no coincidence that they opened for ski business in Boston before they sprouted in New York. As we have shown earlier, Boston was in many ways the fulcrum around which modern skiing emerged in the Northeast. The two most prominent shops were Hambro on Carver Street and Osborne on High Street, both considered "more as a club than a store." In 1931 Hambro carried "Norwegian Skis, Poles, Wax, and Clothing" as well as the "finest hand-made Norwegian boots. Toques and caps were available from Norway, Lapland, and Switzerland." Bjarne Johansen defined himself by pro-claiming "A Norwegian Ski Shop," and Anton Lekang, ace jumper from the Lofoten Islands, manned the winter sports section of the Yale Coop. This Norwegian aura still lent its authority to skiing. Yet ski enthusiasts were turning to alpine enjoyment, and King & Dexter in Portland, Maine, provided "Everything for the skier" in 1936. A Tempo Ski Shop was advertising that year, too—using the buzzword of the times, "tempo," the turn *Slalommeister* Toni Seelos was perfecting.

Equipment was one thing, clothing another. Although the first ski outfit for women was on sale in Norway in 1889, special clothing for skiing appeared in Europe only just before World War I. In the United States, although you can find advertisements for "Tweed and Corduroy Knickers" for skat-ing and skiing ($5 and $5.50 in 1922), it was not until the 1930s that the ski clothing industry became a reality. That is, it was part of the change from the Scandinavian cross-country scene to the alpine down-mountain *Schuss*, that change from skisport to skiing. Long winter dresses worn, for example, at the prewar Dartmouth Winter Carnivals gave way to more manageable clothing for speedier skiing. In Europe there had been much argument over the wearing of trousers. In the United States, that played little or no role, but almost immediately fashion became a staple argument in the sell-ing of women's ski clothing. Chic B. Altman & Company had Katharine Peckett scout out Europe for the latest styles. Dartmouth Coop's John Piane personally endorsed clothing available for men. Right from the start there was an appeal to society's more wealthy sectors. "Winter sports trousers to be more voluminous but will keep a very neat waistline at the same time," skiers were assured by Vermont's *Poultney Journal* in 1932. A zip fastener could keep waists "terribly trim and trig." In 1937, Sporting Tailors of Boston claimed that "men, women and children were outfitted from tip to toe in the most approved fashion." What had once been a hair-shirt manly physical experience had turned into social play, something that accounted for vast economic changes.

So that you could ride the Snow Train with a minimal amount of preparation, Armstrong had its own shop car of equipment and clothing for rental or sale on the Boston & Maine trains. The B&M hardly needed to advertise, since announcements became a regular Friday column in the Boston papers, but even so, they ran copy in the *Ski Bulletin* of January 23, 1931, and again in December 1932. In the *American Ski Annual* ski trains in the Northwestern United States are featured in 1935, including the New Haven Railroad and the Central Vermont too. The B&M took out full-page ads in 1938 and 1939. The statistics were impressive:

1931	8,371 passengers
1932	10,314
1933	7,703
1934	14,974
1935	17,943
1936	24,240

These mostly new-to-skiing folks belonged to clubs. In the Northeast, the ski clubs of the 1920s were all cross-country and jumping clubs; the Nansen had been established in the nineteenth century. In Maine, the Chisholm Ski Club of Rumford was well established. the Lancaster Outing Club in Massachusetts and the Brattleboro Outing Club in Vermont were important vehicles for the promotion of cross-country and jumping. As alpine skiing became prominent, towns and villages organized local skiing around club activity, which often included rope tows. In 1930, Eastern's club roster stood at thirty-eight; by 1935, it had risen to 112, and in the winter of 1940, it was up to 181. Even in out-of-the-way villages, it was presumed that the local organization "will be a racing club." Roger Langley, a longtime official at Eastern and the NSA, judged that "you more or less had to belong to a club if you wanted to be a competitor." In Eastern's first modern annual yearbook of 1934, thirty-one of its 174 pages were devoted to "Results of Competitions," ranging from the U.S. National Championships to the Junior Intra-Club Meet of the Lebanon Outing Club.

Members of clubs came from different social strata, but the many ex-collegians gave their club the old ambience. These men, too, often had their start in New England's private schools. Half a dozen schools took out ads in the *American Ski Annuals* of the 1930s: Putney School in Vermont, Vermont Academy of Saxtons River, Clark School, Cushing Academy, Saint Mary's-in-the-Mountains, Eaglebrook, Williston, and the one that had promoted skiing since the 1920s, and was associated with the Lake Placid Club, Northwood.

All skiers had to have a place to stay, and it is not remarkable that among the many advertisements for places to ski, available accommodations were listed. Two Brattleboro hotels advertised in 1929. In 1932, the *Ski Bulletin* had one ad for Gray Rocks Inn up in the Laurentians, and two ads for New Hampshire, the Hanover Inn and Jaffrey's Shattuck Inn. The White Hart Inn at Salisbury, Connecticut, advertised, and, sixty-three miles from Boston, so did the Toy Town Tavern in Winchendon, Massachusetts. In the *Ski Annual of 1934*, ten hotels from New Hampshire took out ads, two from Massachusetts, one from Vermont, and two from the Laurentians. In the 1936 annual, the Eastern Slopes of the White Mountains in New Hampshire had four pages listing fifteen inns alone, such was the swift attraction of alpine skiing. Many came in their own cars. By the end of the 1930s, the Forbes Roof Rack could hold seven pairs of skis and was available for $3.95, while its running board model cost $6.50. Forbes had an Auto-Top Ski Carrier also carrying seven pairs of skis for $6. Crandall-Hicks's model, holding six pairs of skis and poles, cost $8.50.

Skiers often arrived in their ski togs. Some clothing manufacturers seemed to almost own the cloth and style of the
specialized jackets and trousers. In the Northeast, the best-
known was the B. F. Moore Company of Newport, Vermont,
with its well-publicized line of Slalom Ski Wear, relying on
the use of the alpine slalom to guarantee authenticity. In 1933,
prominent instructor and author Charles Dudley was available to assist buyers. That same year B. F. Moore's clothing
had been chosen by the Byrd Antarctic Expedition—another
superb recommendation. Gabardine and Irish poplin were
popular, as was cotton covert, what we might know today as
twilled cloth. Later in the 1930s, the "Tuckerman," a smart
windbreaker; the "Tempo" ski jacket, a "Mount Hood" lady's
parka; and a "Mount Mansfield" for men were on the market.
One major competitor came from Seattle: the White Stag
line from Hirsch-Weis.

The number of shops where clothing and accessories
could be bought increased. The already mentioned house
that sports built, Alex Taylor, was the only shop advertising in the 1929 annual. In 1931, three Boston shops took
out ads in the Boston-based *Ski Bulletin*. In 1936, six shops
advertised, as did others from New York, B. Altman touting
Katharine Peckett as their buyer for ski clothes. Saks Fifth
Avenue already had a shop out in Sun Valley, Idaho, and
Abercrombie and Fitch were lampooned in the *Ski Bulletin*
in 1941:

> Many a girl who looks well on the ski train
> Proves herself to be quite without ski brain.
> Bonwits and staid Abercrombie and Fitches
> Daily outfit lots of ignorant ladies.

Where to go skiing? Destinations for snow trains did
not even have to be considered by the majority of skiers;
they were simply deposited north of Boston by the B&M,
or from New York in the hills of northwest Connecticut

and, especially, in the Berkshires of Massachusetts. With the growth of alpine skiing, certain villages became part of the ski lore of New England. Hanover, because of the activity of the Dartmouth Outing Club, was the first renowned ski village. Then Woodstock, in Vermont, because of its 1934 rope tow. The rope tow revolutionized skiing down hills, and homegrown tinkerers put up tows all over New England. Plymouth Cordage and New Bedford marine rope found new outlets. The early problem had to do with twisting ropes, and very soon rope tow grippers were on the market; Bousquet's had one that pulled from the belt, Ted Cooke planned "to eliminate fatigue," by manufacturing a claw, designed to "grip the rope without even touching it." J-bars and T-bars appeared, and Gore Mountain in New York state became prominent because Otto Schniebs moved there, trailing his Dartmouth appeal wherever he went. By 1935, Franconia was calling itself the "Ski Center of the East," branding that really did seem true once the first-in-the-nation tram was in operation in 1938.

And there was the call of faraway places to tempt the skier—a major factor in the development of alpine skiing. In the early 1930s, in *American Ski Annuals*, the nearby hills of Quebec's Laurentians promised untamed and almost foreign skiing. Vaster terrain was advertised for Sun Valley (opened in December 1936), Yosemite, and the Banff area of the Canadian Rockies. Mount Hood, with its spectacular Timberline Lodge, advertised in 1938, followed by a two-page spread for Oregon skiing the following year. And alpine skiing was, after all, alpine, hence foreign travel to the Alps of Europe was a tempting possibility for those with disposable wealth. In 1928—before the downhill craze—the Norwegian American shipping line promoted its "Direct to Norway" excursions. In 1935, Mussolini's ultramodern resort at Sestrières competed with the Austrian Tourist Office advertising "one hour to the Winter Olympics," as did the Hamburg-American line—offering North German

Lloyd's "Famous Ships" as transport to the 1936 Olympics at Garmisch-Partenkirchen. Full-page ads extolled skiing in Japan and Switzerland, and the German railways and an "Austrian Ski Boat" listed sailings. What a wealth of possibilities! And more: New Zealand entered the quest for clientele in 1937—"Try your skill, challenge your daring"—along with a sixty-one day trip (of which twenty-five days were actual skiing) to Chile. In 1938, Pan-American Airways promoted summer ski trips to South America too. Heady stuff!

As the war drums beat in Europe, Americans in the New England region dwelt in a winter wonderland that retained much of its pristine beauty and unspoiled character even as it built an infrastructure that was the base for the massive move to modern skiing emerging in the 1950s and especially in the 1960s. That was when New England lost its premier slot to the Rockies and western mountains in the U.S. economy of winter sporting. Even so, New England's great advantage lay in the region's urban centers. Advertising to city populations that, as the Depression eased, seemingly had ever-increasing disposable wealth kept the ski centers going. The oil embargo of the early 1970s broke the pattern of development. Let Attitash's monorail never getting beyond the planning stage stand for the immediate disruption . . . and then came snowboarding, but that is a story in itself.

CHAPTER 14

CLOSING SKI TOW SLOPES

When you are driving through New England, you may be amazed to learn that you could pass (though not always actually see) 605 known ski areas that are now defunct. The New England Lost Ski Areas Project (NELSAP) lists them in the very north of Maine at Fort Kent and Madawaska, in the south at Wilton and Norwalk in Connecticut, and from the Vermont-Canadian border towns of Richford and Newport to Cumberland, Rhode Island, just north of Providence. Maine has 79, New Hampshire 172, Vermont 119, Massachusetts 172, Connecticut 59, and Rhode Island 4. There is a wealth of adventuring in these usually overgrown areas, which can be unrecognizable because of construction, and sometimes you might decide that the "Private Property No Trespassing Keep Out Ski Area," whose base area was part of a private aircraft landing strip, is simply not worth a detour to Southborough, Massachusetts. Besides, it is now high-end condo country.

The term "ski area" was not used in the 1930s. Since the actual place where a rope or ropes (and later J-bars and T-bars) were erected was usually bound by the size of a farm field or on one or two paths cut through woods, the original terminology was "tow." If there were many tows in one particular region or in the valleys up north, the geographic locale might become termed the "Eastern Slopes Region," such as those north and south of North Conway, New Hampshire. It was only when an individual mountain, such as Mount Mansfield in Vermont, drew entrepreneurs to build an industrial infrastructure that the ski area, with Roland Palmedo's chairlift, emerged. Instead of sliding off at the top of a rope tow for your run down the meadow, you now had many different ways down from the top . . . and these mountains provided the alpine ski enthusiast not just with trails but also with hotels and inns as an integral part of the ski area. This would become common only after World War II.

Back in the 1930s, to reach the top of the farmer's field, the moving rope could be anywhere from about three hundred feet to the longest in the Northeast, the Gunstock Ski Hoist in New Hampshire, an arm-stretching 3,100 feet. Many and perhaps most, certainly of the early tows, were put up by the homegrown mechanically minded who often were not interested in financial gain but merely wanted to give sporting possibilities to their children and friends and, generally, to the youth of the 1930s through to the 1960s. It is impossible to give accurate figures for numbers of rope tows, but what emerges from the statistics is that in the 1930s and 1940s over two hundred ropes were put up in New England. There was a flurry of activity after the first one went up Gilbert's Meadow at Woodstock, Vermont, on January 18, 1934, and there was a rope tow boom immediately after the end of World War II. The numbers dropped off steeply in the1950s, and picked up again a little in the 1960s, with very few built in the 1970s. Undoubtedly the lack of enthusiasm for ropes had to do with the economic disruption caused by the oil embargo. However, by that time, J-bars, T-bars, Pomalifts, platterpulls, chairs, and even double chairs had become desired, demanded, and provided. The old rope slopes began to close up shop.

The number of closures bears out these figures too. Of course, some slopes closed while their owners served in the armed forces during the war. After that, through the 1970s, a total of about 150 closed down. The occasional owner held on into the 1980s, but by then so many skiers were deserting the small hills with their ropes and T-bars for the mountains of the Rockies, California, the Northwest, and, for those with disposable wealth, the Alps of Europe. Even New Zealand was advertised as a ski paradise in the *American Ski Annual* of 1938–39. The changing pattern of ski area use was much affected by the airlines hooking into winter tourism in far-away places. Before World War II, a week was needed for an Atlantic crossing (and another week for the return trip) to the European ports and then connections by train to the Alpine resorts. After the war, transatlantic aircraft could land you at Geneva or Munich and you would be skiing the next day.

However, the magic names of Zugspitze, Matterhorn, and Mont Blanc did not really have to compete with Guptil's Pasture in Jackson, New Hampshire, since the standard of skiing for most in New England allowed a perfect day on the sloping meadow. The ferocious downhills of Garmisch, Kitzbühel, Saint Anton, and Mürren were impossible for those whose technique, equipment, and money would simply not be worth such extravagant outings. When the Rockies came into play can, I think truthfully, be dated to the opening of Averell Harriman's Sun Valley in the Sawtooths of Idaho. It really was new, since it was located off the beaten path but on the Pacific Union's railroad tracks. It was new, too, as the country's first destination resort (it was immediately dubbed America's Saint Moritz), and also new in that it was an instant Hollywood scene from its opening in December 1936.

It was all right, perhaps, to read of those goings-on—and there were plenty of them—but far better to join one of the increasing number of ski clubs emerging in all the states of New England, some of which would actually build their own tows. In Topsfield, a few miles northeast of Boston, the ski club leased a hill from Wheatland Farm, cleared brush, and acquired an ex-ambulance Chevy that they located at the top of the hill. They jacked it up to run a rope off one back wheel "at a pretty good clip." At the bottom, the club mounted an ingenious mini–A frame on skids so the tension on the rope could be eased or tightened. A safety gate at the top was wired to the ignition switch. "It was a neat old rig," remembered one ski club regular, appreciating in particular that the heat was left on so that "when you got cold you could climb in and warm up." Later, one handyman rescued a used electric motor from General Electric, the club built a housing for it, and the rope, supported on telephone poles, most with spotlights attached, ran for day and night skiing. There was obviously committed leadership that took care of problems as they emerged. In some places where that did not occur, vandalism was a problem. Ropes were cut, forcing closure at New Britain's Stanley Quarter Park, which operated from 1964 to 1975, and Abell Ski Slope in Braintree about the same time. Thieves stole snow-making pipes at Birchwood in Londonderry, New Hampshire.

Often rope tows were discussed and—usually—built by local towns, with Parks and Recreation Departments playing a crucial role. Jaycees, Kiwanis, Lions, and Rotary Clubs were moving forces, often providing funds and a workforce. Members of the Chelsea, Vermont, Rod and Gun Club were active in promoting and running the Fitts Valley Ski Tow at the junction of State Routes 113 and 110, twenty miles south of Barre–Montpelier. The YMCA in West Springfield was active, and so were the Boy Scouts in Spofford. An occasional religious organization had its own area: the Monadnock Bible Conference in Jaffrey ran the Ark Ski Tow in the 1940s, two tows, of five hundred and a thousand feet, serving a hill of about 150 vertical feet. One of the ropes actually operated until 1993. Evidently it closed because the Ark's clientele was becoming too good for the 150-foot vertical and began patronizing larger areas to the north. This was not unusual. Certainly, the higher price of insurance was also a factor— more about that later.

It is one thing for a town the size of Augusta, Maine, with a population in 1940 of 19,360, to organize the Hi Point Tow and get its municipal recreation department to man it both during and immediately after the war. It was not a huge operation, that's for sure, just one four-hundred-foot rope. We might compare how the Norway and Paris townships, each with populations of about two thousand, took over running a very similar operation as that in the city of Augusta. These two towns had a history of rope tow operation, and after the war, they cooperated as a Nor-Par venture. With the background of the Paris Manufacturing Company, a mainstay of Maine's ski production since before 1920, there was little persuasion needed to keep the well-supported tow running.

If the Jaycees (Northfield, Vermont), the PTA (Newbury, Vermont), the Men's Club (Monroe, New Hampshire), the Outing Club (New London, New Hampshire), and the Ski Club (Penobscot Valley, Maine) could fund and work a tow or two, it is not surprising that entrepreneurs of many stripes became enamored of the possibility of winter business. These endeavors were by country clubs, golf clubs, private clubs, and inns of greater or lesser degree. As might be expected, the country clubs and golf clubs offering skiing proliferated near the urban centers, and perhaps the best-known were the Brae Burn Country Club of West Newton in the late 1930s, only five minutes away by car to the Commonwealth Golf Club at Newton, which received a boost when Ted Cooke's Ski Hoist, as his rope tow was known, was removed from Mount Rowe, near Gunstock, and resurrected at the club in 1940.

From 1936 on, the wealthier establishments could buy a ski tow from Philip Carter in Lebanon, who was already advertising the six that he had put up ready for the 1937–38 season. In South Berwick, Maine, the Hussey Manufacturing Company, known for its construction of ski jumps and tobog-gan chutes, already in 1935 included in the small print of a full-page ad that it would build "a Slalom course with ski tow." Certainly, here was a means to get in more practice for those new-fangled races that required turning between poles. But it had to be done with speed. There was a move to capitalize on the appeal of speed when Underwood's "speed tow," claiming one hundred miles per hour on the level, was put into service at Woodstock. Its appeal soon faded, simply because speed while holding on did not have the thrill of individual expertise in making a fast downhill run, or, for that matter, competing in a slalom race. Underwood also advertised an unexplained "new type of rope tow." Perhaps new because of using New Bedford Cordage Company's Maritime Manila that resisted twisting and turning—the curse of early tows—and was flexible when wet or dry, as well as being rot-proof.

More comfortable, and certainly less exhausting, rides were already being sold. Fred Pabst's Ski Tows of Manchester Center, Vermont, for example, had four overhead cable-type lifts, with a narrow strip of webbing that you leaned against, up and running for the 1937–38 ski season, not only in Manchester but also two in New Hampshire and one at Lake George, New York. It was, however, Constam's T-bar at Pico Peak, "the first patented Constam ski lift in the United States," as the area trumpeted for the 1940–41 season, that caused a real change. The word "patented" was in there purposely! The Dartmouth Outing Club's director, Dan Hatch, had seen a picture of a Constam lift in Davos, Switzerland, and had more or less copied it. He had written to Constam to ask for possible design support and received the reply that it already had a Swiss patent and an American one was pending. The Split Ballbearing Corporation built the tramway that found some Dartmouth students closing "their eyes to the obvious immorality of the machine," and points to the fact that skiing was experiencing major growth. With the success of Hatch's J-bar at Oak Hill, in January 1941 Dartmouth agreed to pay Constam $450. By this time, Constam himself was in the United States interesting ski area operators—hence the ad of Pico's "patented" Constam ski lift.

These J-bars and T-bars, known in the early days as "he-and-she-sticks," were far cheaper to install and run than the "chair lift of the sit-down variety" at Belknap, New Hampshire, in 1938, or Roland Palmedo's single chair at Stowe in 1940, not to speak of the massive undertaking of the Cannon Mountain Tram opening in the summer of 1938 and ready for the next winter.

Many of the small-time slopes rigged up lights for night skiing. In the rope-and-T-bar era, après-ski revolved around hot chocolate in the miniscule warming hut. Night skiing, then, was local and popular. As one might expect, there were more lighted slopes in Massachusetts—I counted thirty-six in the NELSAP statistics—than elsewhere in New England: New Hampshire had twenty-seven, Maine thirteen, Connecticut seventeen, and three out of the four Rhode Island tows had lights. These stats should not be taken as definitive; more areas may well appear. In 2002, Jeremy Davis, who founded NELSAP in 1998, listed 430 lost areas, and he surmised that another fifty would turn up. The number in 2022 stands at 605! That is one caveat. Another is that many of the listed areas closed fifty or sixty years ago, and memory is not necessarily to be trusted. It is difficult, too, to rely on physical research; some areas have been bulldozed to make way for an interstate or two (such as at Warner, New Hampshire), while others have reverted back to dense wood and undergrowth. The statistical figures should be taken as a rough estimate. Still, it is impressive that about one third of the areas in eastern and central Massachusetts—thirty-six out of 106—had lights. In the western part of the state, in the larger centers of the Berkshires, only eight of sixty-two areas offered night skiing. Bousquet's in 1935, for example, hung up incandescent light bulbs on Russell Slope and advised car owners to keep their lights on if they came for night skiing.

We find also in the rope tow years that a number of family men built private tows for their children and friends. These were home engineered, seldom more than four hundred feet, and giving access to a cleared field with a one-hundred- to two-hundred-foot vertical. Inevitably, the children's expertise on skis outgrew their ropes, and they moved on to J-bar and T-bar areas, then to the growing number of down-mountain resorts that dotted the New England landscape after World War II. Still, you can find, east of Groton, Massachusetts, on Route 119, in a semiovergrown part of the hill, the remains

of a couple of poles of a private tow that was never enthusiastically supported by a family. More memorable was that
the father who built it occasionally used to land his small
plane at the top of the slope.

Another facet of skiing in New England—not so promi-
nent as in the Midwest but still a great attraction—were the
number of jumps, many of them comparatively small, say
thirty- and forty-meter hills, with fifty of the fifty-six in New
Hampshire, Vermont, and Massachusetts, not a few of them
built and run by private schools such as Dublin, Tilton, and
Holderness. Colleges, too, had jumps. The best-known was
Dartmouth's, but in Vermont, they rose on the campuses of
Saint Michael's, Norwich University, and Vermont College.
Jumping came to the United States from the Norwegian tradition, so it is no accident that where Scandinavians settled—
and there did not have to be many of them—you would
find a jump constructed. The three Satre brothers made of
Salisbury, Connecticut, a jumping center, the Big Nansen
at Berlin, New Hampshire, spawned a Little Nansen as a
training jump for high schoolers; and there were other jumps
in Berlin's section of Cates Hill. The Nansen, of course, was
special, as we have seen in the chapter on Berlin; most of
the jumps were in the range of thirty to forty meters, with
one advertising at ten meters.

It is not surprising that an area called Norseman's Hill supplied a jump to complement its rope tows. In Bolton, directly
east of Boston (on today's Interstate 495), a Swedish immigrant family had one son, Donald, who competed in the 1920s.
After World War II, he bought a hundred-acre parcel of land,
cleared three downhill slopes, and built his prize: a forty-meter
jump, on which he sprayed water on the run-out, providing a
pretty slick and fast finish to a leap. He drew in local ski clubs,
including the Scandinavian Ski Club of Worcester, and one
of the leading Norwegian jumpers in the Northeast, Strand
Mikkelsen, who had a ski shop in Worcester and, as we have
seen earlier, made of Greenfield something of a ski center.

Two other jumps show another side of Norwegian cultural ski tradition. At the Underhill Ski Bowl in Vermont, and at the Oak Grove School in Vassalboro (between Augusta and Waterville), Maine, jumps were built into a hill. Norwegian jumping originally came from the ideal that a skier should have all-round expertise. Contestants would start with a little cross-country, make their way down a slope avoiding trees, take a little leap over a mound, swing around a rock, and continue on down to finish their run across a meadow at the bottom. Soon, in the late nineteenth century, the jump became specialized, and primitive constructions emerged with the inrun built between trees to minimize winds. The leap would be off some sort of platform, and the landing on the outrun . . . that is, each section of the jump was planned to be incorporated into its natural surroundings. This was the goal that builders of jumps tried to achieve. However, in the United States, it was easier to construct the jump on top and use the natural hill as an outrun. At Underhill, the jump was built into the hill, more or less parallel with the slope served by a tow—the best of both worlds. It was used for high school meets. Underhill modernized and did not quit until 1982, having faced forty years of nearby Stowe's dominance.

At Vassalboro, the Quaker-related Oak Grove School (curiously, since it was a girls' school, and joined with the Coburn Classical Institute only in 1970) built a jump described by an alumnus as "unique in that it was dug into the ski slope." It seems likely that the jump was an addition made in 1970, when male students were admitted. Whether the builders knew of the Scandinavian tradition, I don't know, but it was quite possible, since in the 1970s and 1980s the Oak Grove–Coburn school had an advanced liberal outlook favoring environmental concerns.

A jumping competition brought spectators to town, and as such the event was heavily supported by local businesses. The more impressive the event, the better. Impressiveness was contingent on two factors: one, jumpers coming from different towns (the further away from the meet, the better) was considered a real plus, and two, the length of their records and the lengths of the jump that might be expected at the meet, which were often exaggerated. In Bristol, New Hampshire, hardly a major destination for skiers, the jump record stood at 118 feet, a distance that was broadcast far and wide in 1937. As alpine skiing was becoming increasingly popular, the continuing attraction of the high-flying jumpers provided the frisson for a crowd of spectators. Cross-country running and racing, by comparison, seemed merely sweaty boredom.

Jumping, as one aspect of skiing, was more or less on hold during World War II. Immediately after the war, there was resurgence, but alpine excitement proved far more attractive. Jumping declined and almost disappeared in the 1970s. It has made an extremely slow recovery in the recent decades, with New Hampshire as the only New England state that holds high school meets. There is renewed hope; Gunstock has invested in its jump, and the experience of Berlin's enthusiasm may well lead to greater activity in this important discipline of Nordic skiing. Salisbury is proud of its jumping heritage. And Brattleboro's efforts to become America's Holmenkollen have been chronicled in an earlier chapter.

Just as schools are playing a role in the revival of jumping, they played a role in lift-served skiing. Statistically, fifty-five universities and schools ran their own ropes and uphill contraptions—Dartmouth, for example, building a portable tow. Private schools were to the fore in providing early rope tow experience for downhill skiing, and many of the schools continue to this day with strong alpine ski teams. Gould and Fryeburg Academy (Maine), Holderness and Proctor (New Hampshire), Saxtons River (Vermont), Eaglebrook and Deerfield Academy (Massachusetts), and Hotchkiss and Taft, located in the hills of northwest Connecticut, used nearby Mohawk Mountain. Kent School (Connecticut) has made an on-and-off effort. At the February 1935 interscholastic meet held at Eaglebrook in Deerfield, Massachusetts, teams came from Mount Hermon, Berkshire, Deerfield, Cushing, Saint Marks, Hotchkiss, Middlesex, Vermont Academy, Leland-Grey, Choate, and Saint Pauls. That is an impressive outlay of enthusiasm; here were the future college team skiers. All of the above schools remain part of the U.S. ski world today.

With Dartmouth leading the way, other colleges and universities soon followed the Dartmouth Outing Club model, and before the rope tow era beginning in the mid-1930s, New England state universities (with the exception of Rhode Island) all fielded ski teams. Private universities such as Williams and Middlebury had local hills at their doors. In Boston, Harvard, Boston University, and MIT tended to follow the lead of well-to-do clubs such as the Hochgebirgers and Schussverein. Harvard's club leased a building near Woodstock, Vermont, in 1935, and then bought a house in Bartlett, New Hampshire, with easy access to the Eastern Slopes of the White Mountains, with their increasingly sophisticated uphill lifts, such as the unique Skimobile at Cranmore Mountain.

These high-tech lifts were one reason for the decline of rope tows. Another was that the ropes of the 1930s and even into the 1960s were built on slopes, not mountainsides, and after twenty-plus years of alpine skiing, skiers—especially the younger set—were requiring greater challenges, hence the change from a "ski tow" to a "ski area." This, then, was not only a matter of lifts but a matter of the entire infrastructure: the ski lodge became part of the ski business. Although a number of hotels had their own ropes and advertised them, in the years following World War II they provided insufficient enjoyment, hence they disappeared from the ski scene at the Eastover Resort in Lenox, Massachusetts, and at the Twin Town Inn at Tilton and the Esquimo Lodge in Dublin, both in New Hampshire, to give three examples from the two dozen that were once part of the inns' offering.

Although snow trains ran from Boston until the early 1950s, the era when they really brought masses of new-to-skiing people north was in the 1930s. After World War II,

America's love affair with the automobile, already established by Henry Ford in the 1920s, took off as increasing
economic well-being of the middling classes was invested
in a car that traveled on President Eisenhower's Interstate
91 to the resorts of Vermont, and Interstate 93 to those of
New Hampshire. The new ski resorts catered to weekend
crowds on the mountain slopes. What had seemed to be an
inundation to small villages with snow-train arrivals turned
into massive lines at the tows, and Cranmore put in an extra
tow for "rush hour." Crowded trails made for accidents.

The National Ski Patrol had come into existence in 1938
because not only had accidents risen to alarming numbers
but two highly connected skiers had suffered. Minnie Dole
had broken an ankle on the Toll Road on Mount Mansfield,
and it had taken two and a half hours before he reached
a doctor. And Greenwich socialite and big game hunter
Franklin Edson had died when he hit a tree at speed. Neither
had accident insurance, although that had been available
since at least 1933. "Some people believe in luck," ran Boston's
Arvid W. Johnson's advertisement, "Others carry insurance."
By 1936, one doctor in North Conway was celebrated enough
to find himself immortalized in the AMC's *Appalachia*:

> [Skis] upon whose surface wax is spread
> Whose devotees need Dr. Shedd.

Indeed, Dr. Harold Shedd was the first of the nation's doctors
who made their niche as ski physicians. The small areas had
instant patrollers, made up of the better high school skiers
and the regular dads. Later, an occasional rope tow owner
might advertise that he had a paid ski patrol on duty. Of
course, this was just another expense, and with declining
revenues as skiers left for the larger resorts, it meant the
demise of the smaller ones.

A very early legal case concerned a Ruth Morse, who was
injured at Bear Mountain, New York, in January 1939, when

she was hit by a sled even though there was a designated toboggan run. The *Ski Bulletin*, New England skiers' information source par excellence, editorialized that "it appears owners of area [are] liable for negligent operations." After the war, it was generally assumed—and proclaimed in a 1951 court case—that a skier accepted certain inherent risks for which operators could not be held liable. This opinion stood for twenty-five years. But in 1974 a twenty-four-year-old novice fell forward while snow ploughing, hit his head on a rock, and was paralyzed . . . and in 1977 was awarded $1.5 million. The Stratton Mountain case rocked the ski business. Most of the larger resorts survived the increase in premiums, but not the smaller tows. Anecdotally, it has been reported that Franklin Pierce's insurance cost went up from two hundred to four thousand dollars, and Mount Spofford's hundred dollar was upped to five thousand, astronomical payments quite out of reach. Whether or not correct, it is undeniable that many people who responded with memories of closed areas referred to rising insurance costs as one reason, and sometimes the most important reason, for closing.

To counter the Stratton Mountain case, ski area operators began to put in place a serious—and expensive—safety program. Very large and pricey grooming machines secured a perfect snow surface. Skiers quickly began not so much to rely on these for safety but to expect them for pleasure's sake. This was bolstered by snowmaking . . . and what area can do without it in these days of increasing evidence of global warming? In the northern hemisphere, the length of the snow season has fallen at the rate of five days every decade since 1970. That is twenty-five fewer days of snow in 2020 than in 1970.

Crushed ice, a Hollywood spin-off, was used in the 1930s. Snowmaking, as detailed in the Connecticut chapter, first appeared in 1952, the work of Wayne Pierce and his partners of the TEY Manufacturing Company, who sold their patent to the Tropeanos of Boston. Very quickly, efficient machines received patents, and all of this technical improvement was soon out of the financial reach of small-time operators—yet another reason for their decline.

Rental equipment, which in the post–World War II years meant lines of secondhand skis to be picked out of a row by beginners, was now chosen for the never-evers (today's term for those trying skiing for the first time) from last year's or even this year's models by a technician whose expertise in fitting bindings to the correct tension was vital for safety . . . and so on. These sorts of expenses were way out of reach of pockets of the individual small slope owner. No wonder, then, that the lost ski areas number 605 . . . and counting.

CHAPTER 15

ASSESSING THE SKI HERITAGE OF NEW ENGLAND

It is a remarkable fact that only since the 1970s and early 1980s has there been a concerted move to conserve the ski heritage of New England. The reason that it has happened only so recently—Norway had its first museum in 1923, and the United States National Ski Museum opened in Ishpeming, Michigan in 1954—is largely cultural.

In broad terms, from the time that immigrant Swedes settled in Maine in 1870 until approximately 1930, New England took to the sort of skiing that Scandinavians had brought with them, skiing we now call Nordic. But in those days, there was no Alpine skiing. Skiing comprised getting out and about on skis over hill and dale, through woods and over pasture land, along unploughed roads, and with an occasional race. Skiing also included ski jumping, and it seemed that every snow-covered village supported a small jump, mostly for fun for the local youngsters. In the 1920s, the Northeast was able to offer jumps of considerable size on which to hold national competitions. Men came from as far away as the Midwest, even from the state of Washington; no one came from California. Thus, until the early 1920s, skiing took place in its own unregulated way in New England, with no pressing need, as there was in the Midwest, for major organizing bureaucracies to keep records of events, come up with rules, and make them stick.

This is not to say that rules did not exist, but they tended to be entirely local. In Berlin, New Hampshire, for example, all records of the Nansen Club were kept in Norwegian until 1912. Around that time, Dartmouth College, with a very different makeup of wealthy Americans, organized their own regulations, initially relying on track models and turning to the Scandinavians for technical matters. But everything else, such as a different ambiance, was largely guided by a very few individuals; Fred Harris, for example, is mentioned in many pages of this book.

But around 1930, winter sport became something quite different. Often fleeing from fascism in Europe, a number of Austrians and Germans, but also a few Swiss and French, emigrated to the United States, bringing their particular brand of skiing with them. Alpine skiing comprised climbing up mountains and speeding down them as fast as you dared. Europe's Alps mounted up from cleared-for-farming valley floors, through forests, to the tree line, then offered a vast open arena to the top, perhaps a further thousand feet or more up. These Europeans enjoyed the downhill freedom of the pure snow on the mountain and then, perforce, had to wind themselves down through the trees. In racing parlance, these became "down-mountain races," the "straight races," and finally "downhill races." Through the trees became tricky tree running, turning races, gate races, and finally "slaloms."

Norwegians, as they like to say, were born on skis, whereas alpine skiers needed instruction, and such were the two cultures of skiing: the first thinking of itself as defined by the old country's *ski-idræt*, the second requiring an economic infrastructure to satisfy a pleasure economy. This was working itself out in the 1920s, with increased fervor in the 1930s, and then in the postwar 1950s and 1960s. But then came a divide that, for some years, appeared unbridgeable. And it was in those years that groups of people who enjoyed the ease of lift-skiing, the new comfortable but tight boots, the efficiency of metal skis, and the warm fire of the ski lodge began wondering how to preserve their own past. And all they had to bring it back was memories, and these they shared to advantage.

The first steps to keeping the ski heritage alive by creating a museum made their way into committee meetings, with discussions of venues, funds to be raised, and artifacts to be collected. Virtually no thought was given, for example, to the necessity of wood preservation or how bindings should be organized. There was just a lot of old stuff—trophies appeared seemingly everywhere! Their names were on them, and they wanted this and that cup displayed!

From simply amassing a bunch of the old stuff, ski museums have made significant progress in recent years with computerized collection management and archival treatment of wood, cloth, films, photographs, documents, and art. This sophisticated approach has required major financial support. In Maine and Vermont, the ski museums have become Halls of Fame, and Vermont's 2003 induction included the entire state's contingent of 10th Mountain veterans that could be located—all 260 of them! What follows is the state of New England's ski museums in 2022.

The senior museum opened in 1982. The New England Ski Museum (NESM) is located in Franconia, New Hampshire, in an entirely refurbished two-bay state garage. It is some thirty yards north of the base of the Cannon Mountain tram, and many visitors stop off to see local hero Bode Miller's five Olympic medals (Cannon Mountain can claim to be his home mountain). Inside, the building is overflowing with artifacts arranged permanently on the walls, while changing exhibits occupy large movable walls inside the center of the main building. Upstairs a room serves as library, a three-person workspace, a conference room, and a lunch area. You get the picture: too many things going on in too small a space. Downstairs, what used to be the Lowell Thomas Theater is now divided into two spaces. One space is used for showing films, hosting talks, and the like for a maximum of twenty-five people. The other is a packing space for the shop. The shop per se does not exist, but articles for sale, all ski-themed—and there are a lot—are ranged on shelves at the entry/exit of the inner display panels. Two televisions play a variety of films.

Figure 8. The building may be quite small, but the breadth and depth of the New England Ski Museum's collections are impressive. The museum hosts around twenty-five thousand visitors per annum. An original tramcar can be seen at left, and the Skimobile, in operation at Cranmore Mountain from 1938 to 1982, provides a good photo op. New England Ski Museum. Used by permission.

The history of the museum is bound up inextricably with its ability to raise funds. Starting in 1976, an interested but museum-inexperienced group of locals determined to save old skis set a course to collect artifacts relating to the sport: skis, boots, poles, bindings, and clothing were preeminent. A surprising number of old cups emerged. Films then came in at a rush, followed by many hundreds, and now thousands, of often-unidentified photographs. Besides those personal gifts, New England was home to a number of early journalist-photographers: Winston Pote, Charles Trask, and Christine Reid, to name three. Just recently the late Dorothy Crossley's archive has been donated to the museum, which included approximately five hundred photographs, most of which are fortunately identified.

In order to understand, document, and analyze the material coming into the museum (at certain times at an alarming rate), the directors established a library. The library has become a major asset of the museum, allowing fairly easy access to papers, magazines, articles, art, and books that supply the raw material for fifty-six issues of the *New England Ski Museum Newsletter* and, since the spring of 2002 with issue 57, has the *Journal of the New England Ski Museum* to rely on for their articles. The number of books soon outgrew the shelf space, and when Robert J. A. Irwin donated his entire collection, and Marie Chapman started a fund solely for acquisition and library improvement, it was abundantly clear that a major expansion of the museum was needed. An ex-doctor's office now houses the library, the growing collection of posters, films (now numbering seven hundred), boots, and clothing ... and it includes a room large enough to hold a thirty-person directors' meeting. The Paumgarten Family Archive Center—to give it its official title—came into operation in 2003, thanks to funding from the heirs of Harald Paumgarten, an Austrian racer of the 1920s and 1930s and local instructor at nearby Peckett's on Sugar Hill. Just as the building was moved and put on solid foundations— the downstairs holds six hundred pairs of skis and more— the museum was presented with the skis on which Harald Paumgarten won the Canadian *Langlauf* championship on a ten-kilometer course in 1928.

The Paumgarten Center also houses the collection of nearly five hundred posters and over seven hundred films, including the reels from which John Jay produced his annual influential films. A vast collection of journals rounds out the library and gives it its all-round excellence. It is one of the best ski libraries in the United States. It holds Olaus Magnus's work of 1555—famed for its woodcuts—and keeps up to date with the latest work of historians such as William Frank, Andrew Denning, Annie Gilbert Coleman, Roland Huntford, Thor Gotaas, Halvor Kleppen, and Christof Thöny.

At a regional level, journalists and local club and town historians have produced a wealth of books on fiftieth anniversaries, and in the case of the Dartmouth Outing Club, its centenary celebration. The printed word is far more reliable than some of the more ridiculous things you can find on the Internet: "Chiharu Igaya, when she was at Dartmouth . . ." and so on. There are anniversary volumes on Stowe, Mad River, Jay Peak in Vermont, Cannon in New Hampshire, Sugarloaf, Rumford, Shawnee Peak, and the Camden Snow Bowl in Maine. The museum also has club accounts, mostly from the wealthier sectors. The Amateur Ski Club of New York (considering Stowe its home mountain) put out a volume on its first ten years in 1941, and after the first fifty years did another in 1981. The Ski Club Hochgebirge has also produced a very short fiftieth anniversary account from 1931 to 1981 in which their deep involvement with the tram at Cannon receives a couple of lines only. On the whole, these constitute a very uneven historical record.

More important, then, are the collections of newspapers, especially those from Boston whose columnists, such as "Old Man Winter," filled the papers, especially on Fridays, explaining what New Hampshire and Vermont might offer for the weekend. There are a number of scrapbooks, especially those of Fred Harris of Dartmouth College and Roger Barbin of Berlin. Papers from leading ski journalists John Fry and Morten Lund, both passed on, are an important addition. Forester Henry Baldwin contributed a short *My Skiing Life* published in 1989 and revised in 1992. The museum also has important collections of papers, such as those of Snow Engineering, one of whose principals was Sel Hannah, Dartmouth team member and would-be Olympian of 1940 and one of the most influential ski area designers. Doc Sosman's papers are vital for any understanding of U.S. skiing and its relationship to the international community. Sosman was a U.S. representative to the Fédération internationale de ski (FIS) for thirty years. He worked as an official at six Winter Olympic Games between 1964 and 2002.

The poster collection numbers about five hundred, many promoting New England, but there are fine selections from elsewhere in the United States and Canada, and also from Europe. The museum exhibits are often enhanced by showing a few of these posters. Once created purely for advertising, they are now often classified as fine art, and some sell for thousands of dollars at auctions.

The exhibitions are changed annually. However, because of COVID restrictions, the present exhibit, "Before and Beyond the Lifts: Sketches of Backcountry Skiing," has been on view since 2019. Before that exhibition "Skiing in Southern New England" in 2018, "Skiing in the Granite State" in 2017, and "The Mountain Troops and Mountain Culture in Postwar America" in 2016 were the annual exhibits. These exhibits are supported by lengthy and well-illustrated articles in three of the four museum journals that are published every year. The fourth journal contains a major essay on some other New England skiing subject. Recently, for example, the article was on Arnold Lunn, the Brit who started the Arlberg-Kandahar race (always the A-K) with Hannes Schneider. There is frequently (though not always) a connection with Schneider, since he spent the last sixteen years of his life in North Conway.

This connection with Schneider has grown increasingly strong, supported by an annual fundraiser, now in its thirtieth year: the Hannes Schneider Meistercup, always held at Mount Cranmore in the spring. Two hundred and fifty racers compete, and the museum is proud that it disperses three thousand dollars annually from the proceeds to three or four worthy ski causes. Recently, the museum hosted an Austrian film crew of six working on a documentary of Hannes Schneider. Three prominent members of the museum were interviewed for the film, which will be shown on ORF (Austrian National Television) and elsewhere in Europe.

The interviews for the Austrian documentary were conducted in the museum's newly opened North Conway branch. The museum's board of directors had the confidence and fundraising ability to turn a building on Main Street in North Conway into a museum that pays special respect to

Hannes Schneider, and to the Mt. Washington Valley, as well as to Tuckerman—altogether an impressive addition to the museum's contribution of "preserving the future of skiing's past," as its mantra goes. *Yankee Magazine* was enthusiastic: "A small museum shouldn't be this good," the author commented after a visit in 2020.

The NESM is extremely fortunate to have board members who bring a wide range of ski interests to the museum: a FIS official, a leading ski documentary filmmaker, a ski historian, past executives of ski business and ski area managers, lawyers, insurers, and authors—enthusiasm abounds, with the support of around 1,500 members. The museum's speakers bureau provides experts on topics ranging from local ski history to the films of Schneider and Riefenstahl. Occasionally there are special performances; one time a tenor sang a seventeenth-century Sami ski-love song, something that was last noted in Longfellow's day! So there is a variety of activities that keep the museum humming rather than, as some, a display of static same-old, same-old.

The questions for all the ski museums are these: Just what are they collecting and why? And for whom? There is plenty of enthusiasm for collecting, and the arranging is left to executive directors, with possibly some help from board members. There is sporadic enthusiasm for producing something from the exhibitions. Take the case of the museum's seven hundred films, of which three hundred are in cold storage and twelve are digitalized. Not many have been used in their forty years. Richard W. Moulton's major documentaries *Legends of American Skiing* (1982) and *Ski Sentinels* (2000) employed much footage. Only very few from the museum's collection, such as John Litchfield's Dartmouth home movies, were used in *Sentinels*. The outtakes for *Legends* are housed in the museum and comprise a wonderful filmed oral history of some twenty-five ski personages, men such as Averell Harriman, and women such as Janet Mead. Have these been taken advantage of? Hardly at all. Others Moulton has used in short biographical sketches of the various inductees of the Vermont Museum's Hall of Fame and the New England Ski Museum's Spirit of Skiing award. Television station WGBY in Springfield, Massachusetts, interviewed a couple of board members, photographed appropriate exhibits, and scanned some photos from the archives for their forty-minute pre-sentation of skiing in the Berkshires, which, we understand, received good reviews. New Hampshire's WMUR has also featured the museum, and Austrians periodically request Schneider material.

This is the moment to turn our eyes to the east and com-pare what the Ski Museum of Maine is doing after celebrating twenty-five years of existence. Starting as an idea around Sugarloaf in 1995, the museum became a reality by hiring a director and rental exhibit space in Farmington (an hour south of Sugarloaf) in 2006. By 2009, it was back in Kingfield above the Sugarloaf Outlet store, where it seemed to have set-tled. I am not being critical; every homespun museum—that is, every ski museum in the United States and Canada—has its starts and stops, and at some point (it is never entirely clear at the time; witness the present case of the Canadian Ski Museum), something happens. The Maine museum's efforts of "celebrating, preserving and showing Maine's skiing heritage and history" is presently undergoing rigorous dis-cussion on the ways to assure continued success. A forceful historian with an enthusiastic board with multiple talents has produced enough support to pay for a "Mountains of Maine" exhibit. Another exhibit, "Maine Olympians," proved very popular, and both have been turned into successful traveling exhibits. There is a satellite exhibition with its own space in the Bethel History Association building. Discussion is underway to make this permanent.

Sometimes the biggest problem for ski museums is the actual buildings where the artifacts are housed and dis-played to the public. This has been a major problem for the Maine museum. It was at Kingfield (over two hours north of

Portland) and, as of 2022, has negotiated a move into part of a building about half a mile from the base of Sugarloaf. It is expected that the museum will occupy the entire building beginning in the summer 2022. The Maine museum remains extremely dependent on its core local support. Skiing visitors, five to fifteen per day on poor-condition skiing days; a total of three hundred and eighty visitors came in 2019. These are not numbers that will sustain a museum, hence the major effort at finding a much more suitable building.

This is the reason why, using the term broadly, outreach is so important. There was an extensive program of "Fireside Chats," illustrated talks given from North Kent to Portland, but these have been replaced by the "Cocoa Chronicles" and "Chairlift Chats," which are shorter and more personalized than structured lectures. Virtual exhibits and the exploration of different topics via Zoom are also in the planning stage. An oral history program was in full swing until the COVID-19 epidemic intervened. Of course, everything has been made more difficult by the epidemic. Important in connecting with the museum's 375 members is an annual glossy news magazine that is presently running a string of ski club histories, six in the summer 2019 issue of *Snow Trail*: Sugarloaf, Ragged Mountain (near Camden), Auburn, Penobscot Valley, Downeast, and Caribou Skee Club. These are chatty, illustrated, and each about a page long. A regular contribution is written on some recently acquired artifact or relevant topic, such as the history of ski brakes, often connecting with a display.

Support for these articles comes from the approximately 750-book library, collections of photos (with an ongoing accessioning program), and films—the highlight is *From Tree to Ski* and details the Paris Manufacturing Company. This effort—a curator was hired in the spring of 2018—has meant that professional care is taking hold. In the museum itself there is a reproduction of a 1930s ski shop, with classic equipment and fashions, as well as a children's corner, all overseen by an executive director. In addition the usual top four of the board—president, vice president, secretary, and treasurer—and about a dozen others meet quarterly. With the venue change, matters will be looked at from a new viewpoint.

Since 2003, a Hall of Fame has been part of the effort to keep the history of skiing alive. Inductees range from Maine's grand old man of cross-country skiing, Wendall "Chummy" Broomhall to local Sugarloaf worthies Amos Winter and Warren Cook. Filmmaker Greg Stump (*Blizzard of Aahs*) and Olympic standouts Seth Westcott and Julie Parisien have been inducted. Theo. Johnsen was elected posthumously in 2005. About six to eight are selected for inclusion every year, so already there are over one hundred who have been honored. Now that the museum is moving into new quarters, a strategic plan for the future is vital. The board of directors has been given that charge, and the setting of a new course for Maine's ski heritage looks very positive.

The next ski museum visit is to Vermont. After an enthusiastic lay start in 1988 by Roy Newton with a large room full of his private collection in Brandon, the town fathers of Stowe, ever mindful that it was the Ski Capital of the East, with an undisclosed sum of money, succeeded in 2002 in getting Newton's collection transferred to their care to become the Vermont Ski and Snowboard Museum. Meanwhile, a board of directors had been constituted, and they had acquired a magnificent building—storybook Stowe—next to that village landmark, the Green Mountain Inn. However, as a listed historic building, it cannot be changed, so the museum is confined to exhibition space on the main floor. The basement triples as office, workroom, and archive storage. The main storage area is the attic. One is overwhelmed when one walks in because there is so much on the floor, on the walls, and hanging from the roof! One hardly knows where to look. Exhibition space and storage are long-term problems and have been partially addressed by grants. The goal presently is to assess possible donations and manage the collection.

To do this, a fifteen-member board of directors comprising a few who have been associated with the state's ski industry—including public affairs specialists, writers, and a well-known filmmaker—has the depth to set a course for the future of the museum for the recently hired executive director and curator. They can count on the support of about three hundred members, and the Hall of Fame induction, dinner, and auction provides an astounding 25 percent of the annual budget. The year 2021 was a very difficult one for the museum, since the class of 2020 was cancelled because of COVID. Entry charges for the 4,500 annual visits provide 7 percent of the budget, which, along with membership subscriptions, donations, and grants promises a steady, if precarious, financial future.

Stowe's ski museum library is, of course, a necessity for the planning and research of exhibitions. There are very few visiting researchers. About a thousand books and a fair holding of magazines comprise the collection, along with some 180 films, a few of which have been digitalized. These are usually done in connection with a Hall of Fame induction. The most important are some of Hans Thorner's films. Thorner came from Switzerland in 1932, and operated ski schools in New Hampshire (Glen House), New York (Lake Placid), and Washington (Mount Rainier) before opening the Thorner House in Franconia, New Hampshire, ready for the 1940–41 season. In 1960, he bought Glebe Mountain near Londonderry, Vermont. He planned and created a Swiss-village atmosphere and mountain that he called (after Thomas Mann) Magic Mountain. He ran it with his two sons and sold it in 1985. Much of this history Thorner recorded on film—hence the importance of the collection.

As the New Hampshire and Maine ski museums put on talks and programs, the Vermont museum's regular Red Bench Speakers Series pulls in audiences of between twenty-five and one hundred. Given the drawing power of these talks, the Red Bench Speakers will be a regular program after the pandemic has passed.

What has emerged from these museums is that the New England Ski Museum is very much member-oriented yet retains an academic background, witness the footnoted articles in the journal, the collections of important papers, the depth of the library acquisitions, and their general availability to researchers. The museum has also supplied artifacts for an exhibit in England, is presently working with a number of Austrian historians, including contributing to an international conference zoomed from Austria, and has been visited by leading German and Austrian sports and ski historians, a Norwegian folk-historian, and a number of Canadian ski historians. It averages about twenty-five thousand visitors a year. It is the go-to center for skiing history in New England and, indeed, in some ways, in the United States; it has members in thirteen countries.

The leadership of the Ski Museum of Maine sees the NESM as a guide but wishes to remain local—one of its most successful exhibits was "Made in Maine." Remaining local, however, does not mean homespun storytelling; there is a seriousness of endeavor, a wish to have visitors understand just how Maine skiing fits into the mosaic of the American winter experience; it is the heritage of the sport that is most important. The new building will provide space enough for exhibits to explain and delight the state's contribution to the sport.

All this is rather different in Vermont. The museum at Stowe is part of the town's effort to attract visitors. It is another activity—so apt in winter—for skiers to get a view of skiing in days gone by, but is also a draw for those who visit in the summer. There is little concerted effort at explaining what went on over time in the state. There are artifacts aplenty but very little serious discussion of the museum's meaning or effect on the community. The showing of old equipment, boxes of wax, and one of Stowe's original chairs are quite enough for the visitor . . . and it is difficult to find financial support for keeping up the display. Not much looks like changing; there are more people inducted into the Hall of Fame than there are members of the museum.

The conclusion is that each of the states' ski museums has to decide what its goals are: the NESM, as its name implies, uses the region of New England as its base but realizes that skiing is not, and has never been, parochial. It has extended its interests; you simply cannot talk about Hannes Schneider without some historical knowledge of the Austro-Hungarian Empire, World War I, Saint Anton am Arlberg, and the Nazis, not to speak of Arnold Lunn and the A-K.

Maine is maintaining its emphasis on local state matters. Since there is a wealth of subjects that have some foundation for modern skiing, especially with the increasing popularity of cross-country skiing, past developments in Rumford and recent ones in North Kent, the Ski Museum of Maine's efforts to keep its history local could be well rewarded. There is an intrinsic interest, too, in the Swedish emigrants and Tajco equipment, and, as already mentioned, the popularity of the ski manufacturing film keeps alive the Tubbs and Paris names, once the major suppliers of skis to New England. The oral history program is in place, although now in abeyance because of COVID restrictions. When those are lifted, the museum intends to interview a further twenty-six people. It is hoped that excerpts from the interviews will add a personal note to the exhibitions.

There are other ski displays. If you travel to North Adams in the northwest corner of Massachusetts, occupying part of the onetime railroad station (and presently right by the parking lot of the bike trail) is a small exhibition entirely devoted to the Thunderbolt Trail—Massachusetts' answer to the Taft Racing Trail on Cannon Mountain. This is a permanent exhibition and even though limited is well worth a visit. Other exhibits in New England are of two kinds. As an example of the first kind of exhibit, at Thetford, Vermont, the historical society displays the handmade ski Mr. Gairey crafted for some Dartmouth student in 1879. In the historical museum in New Sweden, Maine, there are a number of pairs of skis of unequal length, some dated in the 1910s and others in the 1920s—the only such skis in America. In Hartland, Connecticut, the historical society boasts a pair of Norwegian immigrant-made skis from 1899. The second kind of exhibit is not really an exhibition at all but bears mentioning. Occasionally people with a deep interest in ski history have private collections of artifacts, some have libraries, and others have films and DVDs. If any reader becomes intrigued enough with ski history to start a collection of, say, ski stamps or old magazines, bindings, brochures, or trail maps, she or he will soon find out persons of similar interests.

Should you become such an enthusiast, you will need to add at least two other enjoyments: watching ski films and reading ski books. There are two sorts of films, and two sorts of books. The first kind are entirely devoted to instruction, the second provides entertainment. Published and produced for the increasing number of skiers who needed to be shown how to ski, some became extremely popular. The history of skiing was, at that stage, not a necessary ingredient for understanding skiing's importance. That would come at the end of the twentieth century.

German mountain film entrepreneur Dr. Arnold Fanck and Austrian *Skimeister* to the world Hannes Schneider made skiing a visual as well as a down-mountain sport. Down-mountain was Alpine; cross-country became Nordic. In a sense, the titles of the films made alpine skiing glamorous: *The Wonder of Skis, White Ecstasy*—words that simply could not be used for cross-country jaunts. These films presented the extraordinary prowess of Schneider and his ski school—all, of course, skiing the Arlberg technique, a low crouch and a lift and a swing into the turn. And with the tracks they left in the snow, the viewer had both a lesson in how to ski as well as a view of the perfection of the style among glorious virgin-snow mountains.

Fanck's films were shown in the United States, and when Americans traveled to Europe, they joined a Schneider

Arlberg class. In the 1930s ski schools in New England (actually all across the United States where alpine skiing provided the winter enjoyment), all promoted Arlberg specialists: Olaf, Matti, and Tor were replaced by Kurt, Otto, and Fritz.

At the same time, a few Americans tried their amateur hand at filming skiing. Winston Pote, a druggist, filmed 1927 antics on Tuckerman that started a trend. Much more important were the films of instruction. John McCrillis of Newport, New Hampshire, and Otto Schniebs were followed by Dartmouth alumnus and foremost downhiller Dick Durrance, who—following Fanck's success with the ski-chase theme—produced the *Sun Valley Ski Chase* in 1938 as a promotional film for Averell Harriman's destination resort in Idaho's Sawtooth mountains.

While those earlier serious attempts played an increasing role in attracting people to skiing, Kodak had sixteen-millimeter color film on the market in 1936, and this was first successfully exploited in *Ski America*. Sydney Shurcliff produced the first of the America ski jaunt films. He started a fall tradition of annual pre–ski season film showings across America that was followed by John Jay and Warren Miller. It was quite a surprise to learn that Shurcliff was a well-known landscape architect; he renovated Colonial Williamsburg's gardens. The filming of skiing was, therefore, very much an amateur effort in those early days. It was a local medical doctor in Hanover who filmed Toni Matt's Headwall plunge in the 1939 Inferno. Wealthy amateur Christopher Young starred and produced *Schlitz on Mount Washington*, twenty-two minutes of craziness on skis, narrated by Lowell Thomas. Shurcliff also had great success with his *Dr. Quackenbush Skis the Headwall*.

The travelogues of John Jay and Warren Miller had competition from a number of filmmakers who exploited the growing attractions of extreme skiing, packaging the instant gratification of novelties: skiers roaring down near-vertical chutes, leaping off cliffs, and doing impossible dips, twirls, and flips and other death-defying stunts. Some call it "ski porn." It appears as one aspect of today's ski culture. The only serious film with skiing as the driving force is the 1969 *Downhill Racer* starring Robert Redford.

For much the same reasons that ski museums became a reality, film histories of skiing appeared soon after. They did so because those museums held many old films, home movies, network broadcasts, and training films. Quite enough for Rick Moulton, an interested filmmaker brought up in Hanover, New Hampshire, to produce *Legends of American Skiing* in 1982. This documentary is still shown annually on a number of television stations and ran continuously in the Western Skisport Museum at Boreal Ridge, California, until that closed down. Moulton has also produced a film on the National Ski Patrol. *Ski Sentinels* drew positive reviews and is also shown annually. There have been a number of films on the 10th Mountain Division, the latest being a Slovenian production of a race on Mount Mangart, only a few weeks after World War II ended, between Slovenian resistance men and 10th Mountain men. Sergeant Walter Prager won the event.

When looking at the written record, many "how-to-skee" articles were published in a number of middle-class magazines in the early twentieth century. In popular magazines there were sixty articles published between 1918 and 1928, and 215 were published in the 1929–39 decade. My working bibliography shows that from the end of World War I to 1929, eight books on skiing were published. From 1930 to the beginning of World War II, twenty-eight were published, and 60 percent of those were in the three seasons of 1936, 1937, and 1938. There was, then, plenty of reading material for a would-be tyro, not to speak of what was available in the daily press; the ski columnist became a regular staff contributor for a number of papers during the preseason as well as covering all winter activities. For New England, Old Man Winter was a Boston favorite. For entertainment, a look at any one of Max Barsis's cartoon books will do: try *Bottoms Up! An Unreliable Handbook for Skiers.* It was an instant success in 1939.

When we come to the history of skiing, it is a different story. Historical essays appear in a variety of magazines before 1930, written by the likes of Fred Harris and extolling Dartmouth and Brattleboro. Later in the ski magazines some journalists—Morten Lund in particular—analyzed some aspect of skiing history, but there were no American written histories of skiing until 1935, when Charles Dudley published *60 Centuries of Skiing*. That remained the only history, and obviously covered more than just the United States, until my *From Skisport to Skiing: One Hundred Years of an American Sport, 1840–1940* came out in 1993, the first history of American skiing. Around the same time and also since then, there have been more detailed histories of regional skiing, such as Bill Berry's *Lost Sierra* (1991), Annie Coleman Gilbert's *Ski Style: Sport and Culture in the Rockies* (2004), and Allen Adler's short self-published *New England and Thereabouts—A Ski Tracing* (1985). Margaret Supplee Smith's *American Ski Resorts: Architecture, Style, Experience* (2013) gives an idea of the broadening of interests in the writing of ski history. Tenth Mountain veterans have related many an experience of their World War II escapades both at Camp Hale in Colorado and in the Italian mountains. John Fry published *The Story of Modern Skiing* (2006), which purports to be a history of international skiing post–World War II but is heavily weighted with American material. All this is positive, but we are far behind the Europeans.

It is always difficult to make any conclusion about a work in progress. But that is the present state of the heritage of skiing in the Northeast of the United States. Since skiing, using the word in all its meanings—social, technical, economic, visual, and cultural—is undergoing continual change, *Traveling the Old Ski Tracks of New England* gives a base to an understanding from where we have come. It may help us understand what has made this winter sport such a part of the regional culture of New England.

PG#   **Introduction**

3 *"alone as a wide territorie"*: Fred Harris, *Diary,* February 7, 1905. The diaries remain in the possession of the Harris family. In the 1980s, Mrs. Helen Harris gave me permission to use them, for which I am most grateful.

4 ski-idræt *(Norwegian) and* ski-idrott *(Swedish)*: Åke Svahn, "Idrott und Sport. Eine semantische Studie zu zwei schwedischen Fachtermini," *Stadion* 5, no. 1 (1979): 20–41.

5 *"than is generally supposed"*: Fridtjof Nansen, *The First Crossing of Greenland,* trans. Hubert Majendie Gepp, 2 vols. (London: Longmans, Green, 1890), 1:82–84. For the original, see Fridtjof Nansen, *Paa Ski over Grønland* (Kristiania, Norway: H. Aschehoug, 1890), 78.

6 *"sport into the club"*: Carl Tellefsen, presidential address at annual meeting of the Ishpeming Ski Club, April 18, 1904, ms. between pages 50 and 51 of *Records of the Ishpeming Ski Club of Ishpeming, Michigan* (Ishpeming: National Ski Hall of Fame).

   From Ritual to Record: Allen Guttman, *From Ritual to Record: The Nature of Modern Sports* (New York: Columbia University Press, 1978).

7 *"unbearable whiteness of skiing"*: Annie Gilbert Coleman, "The Unbearable Whiteness of Skiing," *Pacific Historical Review* 65, no. 4 (November 1996): 583–614.

   fun and health: Introduction to "An Oral History of the National Brotherhood of Skiers," *Outside Magazine,* December 2020, accessed February 1, 2022, Outsideonline.com/outdoor-adventure/snow-sports/national-brotherhood-of-skiers-oral-history/.

9 *"to beat the record"*: Stephen Hardy at April 1990 conference in Holyoke, Massachusetts.

11 Schlitz on Mount Washington: *Schlitz on Mount Washington,* directed, written, and featuring Christopher Young, with narration by Lowell Thomas (1935).

   "And pilgrims of the Northland meet": Craig O. Burt, *We Lived in Stowe* (Middlebury: Ranch Camp Publisher, 2003), 119. Used with permission.

Chapter 1: "Millions of Flakes of Fun in Massachusetts"

12 *states of the United States: Boston Globe,* January 14, 1887.

   have lived in town: Ninth Census, vol. 1, *The Statistics of the Population of the United States* (Washington, DC, 1872), 698. Department of Interior Census Office, *Statistics of the Population of the United States at the Tenth Census (June 1, 1880)* (Washington, DC, 1883), 495. *Report of the Population of the United States at the Eleventh Census 1890,* part 1 (Washington, DC, 1895), 632; U.S. Census, 1910, Vol. II, 276, xerox copy of pages concerning Massachusetts, Boston Public Library.

13 *"loudly applauded"*: For Dr. Christian and Trygve Frølich, see *Boston Globe,* January 2, 1910, and *Sunday Boston Herald,* Magazine section, February 20, 1910.

   "winter awakes again": C. Turner, "A Northern Winter's Welcome," *Outing,* February 1896, 416.

14   *national importance:* Fridtjof Nansen, *The First Crossing of Greenland,*
      trans. Hubert Majendie Gepp, 2 vols. (London: Longmans, Green, 1890),
      1:82.
      Punkatasset Hill in 1927: Information from Jeff Diehl, "Punkatasset Hill,
      Concord, MA, 1930's," New England Lost Ski Areas Project, accessed
      January 6, 2022, nelsap.org/ma/punkatasset.html.

15   *A "skee-man":* photos in *Appalachia,* new series, 17, no. 5 (May 1951): facing
      313; and new series, 18, no. 7 (June 15, 1952): facing 56.
      Boston Globe in 1912: Boston Globe, February 4, 1912.
      snowshoeing, tobogganing, and skiing: Brattleboro (VT) Reformer, Feb-
      ruary 18, 1914; February 9, 1915; February 15, 1916; and February 14,
      1920.
      Williams College: J. S. Apperson to F. B. Sayre, Schenectady, New York,
      March 20 and April 9, 1914, and Sayre's reply, March 27, 1914. MSS in
      Apperson Papers, Adirondack Research Center, Schenectady Museum,
      Schenectady, New York.
      "those alluring Berkshire Hills": Outing, January 1922, 183. *Boston Globe,*
      February 4, 1912.

16   *"before the season ends":* "Fashionable Sport," *Chicago American,*
      reprinted in the *Skisport,* 1912–13, 68.
      Berkshire Evening Eagle: Berkshire Evening Eagle, March 9, 1920.
      "thank-ee-ma'ams": explained as embankments that will throw you if you
      are not ready for them. R. Fisher, "Snow-shoeing and Skeeing," *Country
      Life in America,* December 1908, 175.
      "turns somersaults backwards or forwards": Boston Globe, December 25,
      1910.
      "longest ski jump": Boston Globe, January 13, 1918.

17   *"back next winter": New England Winter Sports,* brochure in Taylor Papers,
      box T7, folder: Green Mountain Club 1920, Vermont Historical Society,
      Montpelier, Vermont.
      could be generated: "New England's Winter Tourist Trade Proves Veritable
      Goldmine," *Atlantic Coast Merchant,* January 20, 1923.
      "ski races": Berkshire County Eagle, January 3, 1923.
      added to the festivities: Berkshire Evening Eagle, December 30, 1926.
      "Offers a Royal Welcome": "New England Offers a Royal Welcome," *Motor-
      dom* 23 (December 1929): 1213.

18   *AMC found Otto Schniebs: Bulletin Appalachian Mountain Club* 17, no. 1
      (June 1929): 285; *Bulletin Appalachian Mountain Club* 26, no. 10 (June 1933):
      470; *Bulletin Appalachian Mountain Club* 20, no. 4 (June 1934): 105; *Bulletin
      Appalachian Mountain Club,* new series, 1, no. 7 (November 1935): 431.
      Boston Evening Transcript: *Boston Evening Transcript,* December 7, 1929.

19   *were in use as well:* Charles M. Dudley, *When We Ski* (New York: Grosset
      and Dunlap, 1937), 18–19.

20   *"Coney Island"* and subsequent quotations: Selden Hannah in *Legends
      of American Skiing,* director Richard Moulton (Huntington, VT: Key-
      stone Productions, 1982). "The Old Carriage Road Runners," 2 MSS,
      New England Ski Museum (hereafter NESM), 1983 L.002.008 and
      2004.027.007.
      remembered one stalwart: Roger Clapp, interview by Susan Noble, Novem-
      ber 1, 1980, in E. John B. Allen, "Values and Sport: The Development of
      New England Skiing, 1870–1940," *Oral History Review* 13 (1985): 62.

21 *along on outings:* Natalie Hoyt correspondence, 1931–32, privately held.
    "advanced members": For Mount Holyoke skiing, see *New York Herald Tribune*, January 10, 17, 1937.
    "they just plain love to ski": Harriet Aull, "Smith College 'Shees,'" *American Ski Annual*, 1939–40, 72.

22 *"musical instruments appeared":* Newspaper clipping, dateline Greenfield, February 15, 1931, NESM.
    "daring leap from dizzy heights": *B&M Employees Magazine*, January 1925, 16–17; January 1926, 5; February 1927, 10; *Appalachia*, new series, 2, no. 7 (June 1936): 95.
    "Sun Tan Specials": *Boston Herald*, March 9, 1939.
    1939 and 1940: *B&M Annual Reports*, 1931–40, 3, 4, 6, 7.
    "in heated cabin": *Berkshire Eagle*, January 28, 1937.

23 *34,069:* Laurence H. Bramhall, "The History of Skiing in New England and the Lake Placid, New York Region" (master's thesis, Boston University, 1946), 137.
    "Temperature 20": *Ski Bulletin*, December 16, 1932.
    "ski runners only" and the like: Ibid.
    "The View from Toronto": Ibid.

24 *1939 to 4,000:* Statistics in *Ski Bulletin*, March 29, 1935; March 20, 1936; and November 1939.
    Boston Evening Transcript: Old Man Winter also was on regular Friday evening radio. *Boston Evening Transcript*, January 10, 1936.
    "a sort of gathering point": Rockwell Stephens, interview by Dale Rodgers, December 11, 1980, NESM Oral History Archive.
    "more as a club than a store": *Boston Herald*, March 13, 1936.

25 *"the bank did":* Stephens interview.

26 *snow train departments:* Photos in Cal Conniff and E. John B. Allen, *Skiing in Massachusetts* (Charleston, SC: Arcadia, 2006), 39–41.
    December 1935: *Boston Herald*, December 5, 6, and 9, 1935.
    drew nightly applause: *Boston Herald*, November 30, 1936, and December 2, 3, 6, 1938; *Ski Bulletin*, December 9, 1938.
    "more and more of a spectacle": *American Ski Annual*, 1937–38, 178–79.
    "crew of Austrians": Ruth B. Chase, "IV Boston," *Boston Herald*, November 30, 1936.

27 *"expected bated breath":* *Ski Bulletin*, December 9, 1938.
    "introduce thousands of skiers": Ibid.
    "next time they visit Pittsfield": *Ski Bulletin*, January 17, and February 7, 1936.
    level ground: *American Ski Annual*, 1942, 13.

28 *rope-tow gripper:* *American Ski Annual*, 1939–40, 7.
    "Snow Bus": *Ski Bulletin*, January 25, 1935.

29 *"a good deal more difficult":* *Boston Evening Transcript*, February 1, 1935.
    first race in 1904: *Aftenposten* (Christiania), February 16, 1904.
    1935–36 season: *Boston Herald*, December 16, 1935.

30 *Christmas 1938:* *Boston Herald*, March 9, 1938.
    "bug had bitten hard": *Appalachia* 20, no. 9 (December 1934): 258.
    "which can be solved": *Appalachia* 17, no. 3 (June 1929): 285.
    giant slalom: Otto Schniebs, "Sanity in Competition," *American Ski Annual*, 1938–39, 148–50. For the Greylock no-fall and giant slalom, see *Ski Bulletin*, March 3, 1939, and January 19, 1940.

throughout the 1930s: Statistics derived from lists of member clubs in the *American Ski Annuals*, 1934–41.

31 *skiing trails:* For what follows, see USEASA, *Ski Annual*, 1934, 120; *Appalachia*, new series, 1, no. 7 (November 1935): 443; *Boston Evening Transcript*, January 4, March 8, 1935; *Boston Herald*, December 21, 1937.

tobogganing, and snowshoeing: American Ski Annual, 1938–39, 33; 1939–40, 33.

835 yards: The Massachusetts Development and Industrial Commission, *Massachusetts: Paradise for Winter Sports*, 1938 and 1940.

33 *"the new sport of skiing":* Sherwood Anderson, *Home Town* (Mamaroneck, NY: Paul P. Appel, 1975), 64–65.

Chapter 2: Immigrants and Their Skis for a Maine Winter

35 *1,945 Swedes: Statistics of the Population of the United States at the Tenth Census (June 1, 1880)* (Washington, DC: Government Printing Office, 1897), 495, 512; *Twelfth Census of the United States, taken in the Year 1900*, part 1, *Population* (Washington, DC: U.S. Census Office, 1901), 759.

"ten feet in length": "Maine's Swedish Colony," *Frank Leslie's Illustrated Newspaper*, October 3, 1885, 101–2.

Beloit, Wisconsin: Billed-Magasin, May 1, 1869, 172.

In the Midwest and in the Californian: William B. Berry, *Lost Sierra. Gold, Ghosts, and Skis* (Soda Springs, CA: Western America Skisport Museum, 1991). Helen M. White, *The Tale of the Comet and Other Stories* (Saint Paul: Minnesota Historical Press, 1984), 128–51.

36 *commissioners of settlement: Report of the Commissioners on the Settlement on the Public Lands of Maine* (Augusta, ME: Sprague, Owen and Nash, 1870), 4.

Arthur and Harrison: William Widgery Thomas, Jr., *Sweden and the Swedes* (Chicago, IL: Rand and McNally, 1892), 1.

Aroostook County: Report of the Commissioners, 1879, 3, 5. See also letters W. W. Thomas, Jr., to Assistant Secretary of State, F. W. Seward, February 12 and September 16, 1864, U.S. Consular Letters, Gothenburg, National Archives and Records Administration, Washington, DC.

"Swedish snow-shoes": Reports of the Board and Commissioner of Immigration, 1872 (Augusta, ME: Sprague, Owen and Nash), 11–14.

"Yankee school house": Thomas, *Sweden and the Swedes*, 182. William Widgery Thomas, Jr., "Historical Oration by Hon. W. W. Thomas, Jr., Founder of New Sweden," in *Celebration of the Decennial Anniversary of the Founding of New Sweden, Maine, July 23, 1880* (Portland, OR: B. Thurston, 1881); and in *The Story of New Sweden as Told at the Quarter Centennial Celebration of the Founding of New Sweden, Maine, July 23, 1880* (Portland, OR: Loring, Short and Harmon, 1896).

37 *against the wall:* Clarence Pullen, *In Fair Aroostock: Where Arcadia and Scandinavia's Subtle Touch Turned a Wilderness into a Land of Plenty* (Bangor, ME: Bangor and Aroostock Railroad, 1902), 30.

villages along the Canadian line: "Smugglers Use Ski Sticks," *Barber County Index*, July 30, 1902, accessed October 12, 2020, newspapers.com.

38 *"The Warden Is Coming":* Frederick E. Jorgensen, *25 Years a Game Warden* (Brattleboro, VT: Stephen Daye Press, 1937), 65, 67, 96, 98, 122–23.

"snowshoed and red handed": Oral histories from Harold Day and Adin McKeown, nos. 678.037 and 1284.009, Northeast Archives of Folklore and Oral History, University of Maine, now the Maine Folklife Center.
"A going on a skee": Machias Republican (Maine), February 5, 1910.
lodge in Bethel: The Damariscotta ski is exhibited in the NESM in Franconia, New Hampshire, E89.6.1. The longest ski is at the cross-country lodge in Bethel.

39   *unequal length:* These are exhibited in the New Sweden Historical Museum.
"one long," in 1926: "When Skis were a Dollar a Foot," an interview with Henry Anderson in *Silver Birches,* published by students from Stockholm and New Sweden, Maine, n.d., 14–15.
small difference in length: These are exhibited in the New Sweden Historical Museum.
"skee-man": Photos in *Appalachia* 17, no. 5 (May 1951): facing 313; and *Appalachia,* new series, 18, no. 7 (June 1952): facing 56.
"swish-and-walk": New York Times, January 21, 1900.

40   Among the Clouds: Information from the late Susan Chandler.
"five feet long": Wilkes-Barre Times Leader, February 23, 1886.
"Maine this winter": Daily Mail (Wellington, KS), July 25, 1894.
"absolutely unobjectionable": Frank Leslie's Illustrated Weekly, February 2, 1893, 70.

41   *"starlight Saturday night": Bangor Daily News,* March 5, 1900.
spread the word: Theo. A. Johnsen Company, *The Winter Sport of Skeeing* (Portland, ME: Theo. A. Johnsen, 1905), 45–57 (on bindings), 48 (on push sticks), 53–54 (on footwear).
manual in his newspaper: Ishpeming Iron Ore, December 10, 1905.
"skees": Johnsen, *Winter Sport of Skeeing,* 42–54.
Bindings: Ibid., 45–57.

42   *"occasion may require":* Ibid., 48.
cheaper footwear: Ibid., 53–54.
"slithery, and watery": Ibid., 6–7.

43   *advertising in their language:* Advertisements in Finnish may be seen at the Maine Historical Society, Portland. They appear to have been prepared for publication but never actually used.
Journal of Maine: *Chamber of Commerce Journal of Maine* 29 (April 1917): 341.
for the 1905–6 season: Glenn Parkinson, "The Story behind the Winter Sport of Skeeing" in *The Winter Sport of Skeeing,* by Theo. A. Johnsen (repr., International Skiing History Association, 1994), n.p.
"up to the present time": Letter from Martin Strand to F. C. Barton, New Richmond, Wisconsin, March 10, 1914, 14 023 in Apperson Papers, Adirondack Research Center, Schenectady, New York.

44   *"cases of extreme need":* Johnsen, *Winter Sport of Skeeing,* 22.
"air for a distance": Ibid., 8.
"snowy shroud": Ibid., 6–8.

45   *"sports on a large scale":* C. J. W. Tennant, "Ski-ing in the United States," *Year-Book of the Ski Club of Great Britain* 2, no. 10 (1914): 374.
the most "real": Daily Eastern Argus (Portland, ME), February 19, 1916.
exhibition for the first time: Daily Eastern Argus (Portland, ME), February 22, 1917.

46   *Oscar Oakerlund:* E. John B. Allen, "Skiing—a Hundred Miles of Hell,"
Magnetic North (Winter 1986): 37, 40.
"real long race": Harold Bondeson, interview by E. John B. Allen, New
Sweden, August 29, 1990.
179-mile race: Rita Stadig, *The Ski Marathoners* (Soldier Pond, ME: Rita
Stadig, 1987), 65, 77–79.

47   *Houlton's 1934 concert lovers: Bangor Daily News*, January 25, 1934.
Miss Burpee: "My Lover He Comes on the Skee," by Henry Clough-
Leighton, published in 1901.
Schefferus in the seventeenth century: John Schefferus, *The History of
Lapland Wherein Are Shewed the Origin, Manners, Habits, Marriages, Con-
jurations, and c. of the People* ([Oxford]: At the Theater in Oxon, 1674),
99–100. E. John B. Allen, "The Lapland Lover," *Journal of the New England
Ski Museum* 87 (Fall 2021): 19–23.

48   *"winter sports picture": Boston Herald*, January 24, 1936.

49   *Waterford: Boston Herald*, November 30, 1936.
for the Olympic team: Bangor Daily News, January 28, 1938.
"various communities": Bangor Daily News, March 4, 1940.
"newly built lodge": Bangor Daily News, January 5, 1938.
"Eastern Slope Ski School": Bangor Daily News, January 5, 1940, and
March 15, 1941.
"climb up the ski slope": Bangor Daily News, February 12, 1944.
January 1941: Bangor Daily News, January 30, 1941.

Chapter 3: Berlin and Big Nansen

51   *coast to coast:* "World's Largest Ski Tower: Olympic Tryouts 5 and 6
March 1938," *Souvenir Program 1938*, Berlin, New Hampshire.
Brown Company sawmill: Nansen Ski Club, Oral History, Alf Halvorson,
interview by Eugene Anderson, 1972. This tape cannot be found. E-mail
from Walter Nadeau to author, February 4, 2022.
"1-8-9-0": Brown Co. no. A3937, in Brown Company collections, Spinelli
Archives, Plymouth State University, Plymouth, New Hampshire.

52   *"surrounding towns":* USEASA minutes of November 6, 1932, in minute
book, n.p., NESM 1983R.023.001.
"'The Ski Club'": Harold A. Grinden, "Away Back Yonder," *American Ski
Annual*, 1936, 137.
hut and so on: This information and what follows is drawn from the
Jones typescript, 1–4, kept by the Nansen Club in Berlin.
"you wouldn't be chosen": Selden Hannah in *Legends of American Skiing*,
directed by Richard Moulton (Huntington, VT: Keystone Productions,
1982).
modern skiing: E. John B. Allen, *The Culture and Sport of Skiing from
Antiquity to World War II* (Amherst: University of Massachusetts Press,
2007), 284–87.

53   *"is generally supposed":* Fridtjof Nansen, *Paa Ski over Grønland* (Kristiania,
Norway: H. Aschehoug, 1890), 78.
"luster of his fame": "A great gentleman," *Brown Bulletin*, February 1929, 3.
member of our club: Otto Mason, interview by John Allen, Berlin, New
Hampshire, July 9, 1980.

54 *enlarged in 1927:* Nansen Ski Club Fact Sheets, Nansen Ski Club, Berlin, New Hampshire. *Brown Bulletin* has many photos of the jump in the 1920s.

paid with his life: Letter from Henry Baldwin to author, Hillsboro, New Hampshire, November 3, 1991, Allen archive; Ron MacDonald, "Former Olympian One of the Last People to Receive the Death Penalty in Nova Scotia," *Cape Breton Post*, August 22, 2015, updated October 2, 2017.

leap of 172 feet: Brown Bulletin, March 1, 1923, 9.

"feet of the spectators": "America Cradles Scandinavian Sport," *Literary Digest* 117 (February 10, 1934): 22.

construction of the jump: Donna Horne, *The Nansen Ski Jump*, typed manuscript (hereafter TMS) for a University of New Hampshire Extension writing course, December 5, 1988, 2–4.

"Old Man Winter Himself": Quoted in Linda Laplante, "Nansen Ski Members are the Best Story," *Berlin Gorham Winterfest '85*, 5A. Held by the Berlin and Coos County Historical Society in the Moffet House Museum in Berlin, New Hampshire. My thanks to Walter Nadeau.

55 *inaugurate the jump:* Horne, *Nansen Ski Jump*, 5.

($9 million today): Ibid., 3

Nansen Ski Club: Ibid., 5.

56 *Miss Berlin presiding:* United States Eastern Amateur Ski Championship and Winter Carnival program, reprinted in E. John B. Allen, "The Development of New Hampshire Skiing: 1870s–1940," *Historical New Hampshire* 36, no. 1 (Spring 1981): 9.

carnival of 1930: Photo in *Brown Bulletin*, March 1930, 13.

"promoters of the world": Cited in Laplante, "Nansen Ski Members," 5A.

winter carnival: The event was picked up by the Boston papers: the *Boston Herald Traveler*, the *Boston Daily Globe*, and the *Boston Evening Globe* from February 7 to 13, 1926, with such eye-catching headlines as "Exhausted for Time, They Gain New Strength for Fight," and "Oakerlund, Blinded by Chill Blasts, Halts for a Time." See also Allen, "100 Miles of Hell," *Magnetic North* (Winter 1986): 37, 40.

57 *"a top-notcher on the hickory staves":* John J. Donovan, "Ski Runners All Set for Race," *Boston Daily Globe*, February 10, 1926.

before they went to bed: John J. Donovan, "Exhausted for Time, They Gain New Strength for Fight," *Boston Daily Globe*, February 11, 1926.

58 *"The blizzard conquerors":* "Skiers Finish the Third Stage," *Boston Daily Globe*, February 13, 1926.

"The Day Ski Jumping Died": Shawn Costello, "The Day Ski Jumping Died," *Conway Daily Sun*, December 27, 2018, updated January 2, 2019. The actual date of the last competition was January 20, 1985.

National Historic Register: For what follows, see John Koziol, "Nansen Ski Jump in Milan Readying for February 2021 Re-opening," *Union Leader*, April 16, 2020. Thomas Caldwell, "'Big Nansen' Awakening from Slumber," InDepthNH.org, accessed January 8, 2022, https://Indepthnh.org /2021/09/16/big-nansen-awakening-from-slumber.

59 *"correct amount of speed":* E-mail from Kim Bownes to author, April 18, 2020.

another ten years: Koziol, "Nansen Ski Jump."

Chapter 4: Fred Harris of Dartmouth College

60 *Ipswich, New Hampshire:* John C. Perry, *Diary*, December 12, 1885 (making skis), January 18, 1888 (going to school on skis), February 15, 1888 (going to the dentist on skis) in New Hampshire Historical Society, Concord, New Hampshire.

"depth of seven feet": Charlotte E. Wilde, "Reminiscences of the Snow-Shoe Section," *Appalachia* 18, no. 7 (June 15, 1952): 55.

toboggan chute: Dale S. Atwood, "Winter Sports at St. Johnsbury," *Vermonter* 29, no. 9 (1922): 217, 222.

61 *"on the brain evidently":* Harris, *Diary*, January 27, 1907.

while skating: Fred H. Harris, "How I Learned to Ski," *Outing*, January 1922, 158.

notable personage in town: Dr. Lawton's life can be followed in the *Brattleboro Daily Reformer*, May 10, 1922, on the occasion of his retirement, and his obituary can be found in "Obituary of Dr. Shailer Emery Lawton," April 1, 2006, *American Journal of Psychiatry,* accessed October 13, 2020, https://doi.org:10.1176/ajp.80.2.395.

62 *5-inch wide skis:* Harris, "How I Learned to Ski," 158.

63 *he enthused:* Fridtjof Nansen, *Paa Ski over Grønland* (Kristiania, Norway: H. Aschehoug, 1890), 78.

"Weakness Is a Crime": This was part of "The Physical Culture Creed," which began, "We believe . . ."; Bernarr Macfadden, "The Physical Culture," BernarrMacfadden.com, accessed January 9, 2022, bernarr macfadden.com/macfadden6.html.

"and their brains": Richard Hovey, *Alma Mater*, Dartmouth College, Hanover, New Hampshire.

64 *general rationalization of sport:* Allen Guttmann, *From Ritual to Record: The Nature of Modern Sports* (New York: Columbia University Press, 1978).

DOC's formation: Boston Globe, December 16, 1910.

"seemed interested": Elmer G. Stevens, "First College Meet," *Dartmouth Alumni Magazine*, February 1950, 19.

"Dartmouth Outing Club of Boston": Hans Paschen, "The Dartmouth Outing Club of Boston, Organization meeting December 10, 1930," *Dartmouth Alumni Magazine*, October 1931, 14–18, archive.dartmouth alumnimagazine.com/article/1931/10/1/the-dartmouth-outing-club-of -boston.

Dr. Lawton: Harris, *Diary*, January 2, 1904. Bending and making skis are mentioned in his diary twelve times in 1904, thirteen times in the 1904–5 season, six times in the 1905–6 season, and five times in 1907. The article referred to must be J. A. Gade, "Skeeing: A New Sport," *Country Life in America*, December 1903, 109–13.

rough-cut skis for him: What follows on skis, bindings, boots, poles, and general attitude to skiing comes entirely from Harris, *Diary*, 1904–11, and will not be noted individually.

66 *Ashland, Wisconsin:* "Mr. Holter Visits Norway," *American Ski Annual and Skiing Journal* 34, no. 2 (January 1950): 52.

69 *"wide wide territorie":* Harris, *Diary*, February 7, 1905.

70   "*spread at the rear*": Edwin Frost, *An Astronomer's Life* (Boston: Houghton-Mifflin, 1943), 38.

jumping over Rollins: Photo taken March 14, 1896, by H. G. Pender, *Dartmouth Alumni Magazine*, May 1941, 41. See also Herman Holt, *Diary*, 1896 and 1897, in Barbara Holt's possession, and notes by Barbara Holt in NESM, Franconia, New Hampshire.

from Maine: Robert Allen to Jay Rand, January 21, 1952, quoting letter from William Andrus, Rauner DOC Collection, box 3, file 23. Letter from J. B. Thomas to Dan Hatch, April 7, 1935, Rauner DOC Collection, box 14, file 20, cited in Stephen Waterhouse, ed., *Passion for Skiing* (Lebanon, NH: Whitman Communications, 2010), 5.

"*warm rooms*": John W. Ash, "Ski Letter," *Skiing Magazine*, March 1959, 46.

skis as payment: William E. Worcester, "The Early History of Skis in Vermont," *Vermont Life* 34 (Winter 1979): 58–61.

hillsides around Hanover: John W. Ash, *Skiing Magazine*, March 1959, 46.

71   "*American colleges*": Dartmouth, December 7, 1909.

"*Slept in a farm house*": Harris, *Diary*, December 10, 17, 1910.

Reservoir Pond: Harris, *Diary*, February 22, 1911. Harris, "Up Mount Washington on Skees," *Country Life in America*, December 1912, 63–65.

72   "*appalling from above*": Harris, "How I Learned to Ski," 160.

coming to a stop: Harris, "The Beginnings of Organized Skiing at Dartmouth," *Dartmouth Alumni Magazine*, March 1926, 421–22.

Lincoln's birthday in 1909: "Mountain Club Degrees" with Taylor's handwriting at top: "Scheme to get the boys going," in Taylor Papers, box T7, folder: Green Mt. Club 1911–1914, Vermont Historical Society, Montpelier, Vermont. Other information from Taylor Papers, box T7, folder: Green Mt. Club 1915–1919, Vermont Historical Society, Montpelier, Vermont.

Dartmouth in 1910: James P. Taylor, "The Blazing," 9, in Taylor Papers, box T7, folder: Green Mt. Club 1911–1914.

Outing Club from him: Copy of letter Jim Taylor to Hon. Frank L. Green, February 7, 1920, Taylor Papers, box T7, folder: Green Mt. Club 1920, January–March.

Normal School in New Hampshire: Saint Olaf, *Manitou Messenger* 2 no. 1 (1888): 3. The *North* reported on men and women skiing at the Minnesota college in 1891. *Mining Journal*, December 3, 1904. Plymouth Normal School, *Prospect* 2 (January 1907): 114.

"*outing club*": Harris, *Diary*, November 30, 1909.

"*justify its existence*": Fred Harris, "Beginnings of Organized Skiing," *Dartmouth Alumni Magazine*, March 1926, 423.

registered fifty-five men: Harris, *Diary*, January 10, 1910.

73   *Licklider ninety miles:* Dartmouth, May 1, 1911.

"*in a ski race*": Newport, New Hampshire carnival program reprinted in *75th Annual Newport Winter Carnival, 1991, Program Guide*. A few Finns settled in Newport and in Enfield, New Hampshire.

"*skeeing on the brain*": Harris, *Diary*, January 27, 1907. I used this as a title of a lecture at the DOC on their seventy-fifth anniversary.

"*skiing parties*": Fred H. Harris, "Skiing over the New Hampshire Hills," *National Geographic*, February 1920, 151–64.

74 *824 to 2,675:* David Bradley had confirmation of these figures in 1958. David Bradley, "Dartmouth in the Old Days," *Ski Magazine,* January 1959, 19.
against McGill University: Waterhouse, *Passion for Skiing,* 7–8.
fruition in 1924: An Eastern Intercollegiate Ski Association comprising one Canadian and four U.S. colleges was founded on February 27, 1921. *New York Times,* February 28, 1921. From that came the Intercollegiate Sports Union in 1924. *Ski Bulletin,* March 3, 1939.
February 19 and 20, 1926: Boston Daily Globe, February 15, 1926.
Dartmouth team: Letter from Fred Harris to the DOC, January 5, 1922, Rauner DOC Collection, box 2, file 33, 57. Letters from Fred Harris to Charles Throop, February 27 and March 3, 1921, in ibid., 52 and 53, cited in Waterhouse, *Passion for Skiing,* 28–29.
hardly a real coach: Waterhouse, *Passion for Skiing,* 28.

75 *first downhill in 1927:* Ibid., 29.
Buda and Pest: Oberleutnant Anton von Diettrich, "Der Skilauf in Ungarn," *Ski-Chronik* 5 (1913): 91–97.
"what his right doeth": Boston Herald, February 7, 1926.
own mountain descents: Letter from Harold H. Leich to father, Hanover, January 18, 1926, Jeffrey R. Leich Archive.
twenty-three-page booklet: Anton von Diettrich, *Skis and Skiing,* Lecture 1, *Equipment* (Hanover, New Hampshire: DOC, 1924).

76 *taken by his accent:* Waterhouse, *Passion for Skiing,* 28–29.
"where it belongs": Letter from Harold H. Leich to mother, Hanover, March 5, 1927, Jeffrey R. Leich Archive.
"crazy over Moosilauke": Letter from Harold H. Leich to mother and father, Hanover, February 18, 1927, Jeffrey R. Leich Archive.
Norge Ski Club: Steinwall's splendid ski jumping and cross-country record were at the fore when Dartmouth announced hiring him. "New Sports Head for D.O.C. Activities," *Dartmouth Alumni Magazine,* January 1928, 262.

77 *University of New Hampshire's team:* Phil Sherman, "Following the Green Teams," *Dartmouth Alumni Magazine,* February 1930, 274.
second in the Altersklasse: The Schwabian ski championships. *Der Winter* (1926–27): 428.
blitz on the English language: N. E. Disque, "Dartmouth Becomes Ski-Conscious as Faculty and Students Enjoy Outing Club Activities on Many Snowy Mountain Slopes," *Harvard Crimson,* November 7, 1931. *Appalachia* 21, no. 10 (January 1929): 285; and *Bulletin Appalachian Mountain Club* 23, no. 4 (December 1929): 408–9. *Boston Evening Transcript,* December 7, 1929.
surrounding colleges: Bob Frank and Bob Averill, eds., *A Way of Life: The Story of Otto Schniebs* (Warren, NH: Moose Country Press, 1995), 8, 12, 14.
"Otto problem": Ibid., 12.
ski equipment supplier: Ibid., 12–13, 18.
Garmisch-Partenkirchen: John Jerome, *The Man on the Medal* (Snowmass, CO: Durrance Enterprises, 1995).
after demobilization: "Prager Resigns, Merrill Ski Coach," *Dartmouth Alumni Magazine,* November 1957, 39.

78 *"around Hanover":* Nathaniel L. Goodrich, "A Pioneer Ski Ascent," *Mt. Mansfield Skiing* 9 no. 1 (1943): n.p.
    American skiing: Ellen F. Adams, *Baker Bulletin* 4 no. 5 (February 1960): n.p.
79 *in order to race:* Roger F. Langley, interview by Arthur F. March, Jr., Barre, Massachusetts, January 30, 1980, NESM Oral History Archive.
    next CEO: September 27, 2021, announcements from the U.S. Ski and Snowboard Association.

Chapter 5: The Lure and Lore of Mount Washington

81 *(first noted in 1940):* Charles F. Brooks, "The Worst Weather in the World," *Appalachia*, new series, 6, no. 12 (December 1940): 194–202.
83 *"scene of desolation":* Kathleen Erwin, "Transcription of Thomas Cole's 'Sketch of My Tour of the White Mountains with Mr. Pratt,'" *Bulletin of the Detroit Institute of Arts* 66, no. 1 (1990): 30, quoted in Robert McGrath, *Gods in Granite* (Syracuse, NY: Syracuse University Press, 2001), 11. Cole wrote in his diary on October 6, 1828, "The site of the Willey House . . . in gloomy desolation recalled to mind the horrors of the night." "The Willey Tragedy," Exploros.com, accessed January 12, 2022, exploros.com/summary/grade-7-the-willey-tragedy.
84 *"true account of it":* Henry David Thoreau, "Where I Lived and What I Lived For," *Walden; or, Life in the Woods* (Boston: Ticknor and Fields, 1854), accessed January 12, 2022, etc.usf.edu/lit2go/90/walden-or-life-in-the-woods/1538/where-i-lived-and-what-i-lived-for.
    "Arnica mollis": Ralph Waldo Emerson, "Thoreau," *Atlantic Monthly*, August 1862, accessed January 12, 2022, Atlantic.com/magazine/archive/1862/08/Thoreau/306418. Christopher McKee, "Thoreau: A Week on Mount Washington and in Tuckerman Ravine," *Appalachia* 30, no. 12 (December 1954): 172–75.
    Mount Washington: For what follows, see *"History of the Road,"* accessed January 12, 2022, HistoryoftheRoad.mt-washington.com/history.
85 *about forty-five thousand:* Ibid.
    glory of the road: For what follows, see Robert W. Bermudes, Jr., "Cog Railway: Mount Washington Railway Company," accessed January 12, 2022, whitemountainhistory.org/Cog_Railway.html.
86 *"monarch of mountains":* Boston Evening Transcript, May 1, 1877, cited in *Consuming Views: Art and Tourism in the White Mountains 1850–1900* (Concord: New Hampshire Historical Society, 2007), 76.
87 *Switzerland on skis in 1897:* Wilhelm Paulcke, "Eine Winterfahrt auf Schneeschuhen quer durch das Berner Oberland (18. bis 23. Jänner 1897)," *Österreichische Alpen-Zeitung*, May 13, 1897, 117–23.
    around the world: C. J. Luther, "Geschichte des Schnee- und Eissports," in *Geschichte des Sports aller Völker und Zeiten*, ed. G. A. E. Bogeng, 2 vols. (Leipzig: E. A. Seemann, 1926), 2:527.
88 *July 1899: New York Tribune*, July 31, 1899.
    September 9: Among the Clouds 23, no. 50.
    on a hunting trip: Bangor Daily Whig and Courier, December 3, 1899.
    of March 11, 1900: Max Wiscott, "Summit of Mt. Washington," *White Mountain Republic-Journal*, April 6, 1900; and *Boston Sunday Herald*, March 11, 1900. Information from Rob Bermudes with thanks.

August 1928: Günther Weinhold, "Schlesiens Kinderschuh," *Der Winter* 21, no. 15 (August 1928): 240.

89   *"full speed":* White Mountain Republic-Journal, April 6, 1900.

    Others: Gorham Mountaineer, March 7, 1900; and Chester F. Stiles, "Mount Washington in Winter," *Photo Era* 5, no. 2 (1900): 41–45.

90   *full of this feat: Gorham Mountaineer,* February 22 and March 8, 1905.

    "sport in this country": Portland Sunday Telegram, February 26, 1905.

    more ambitious: First noticed in the *Boston Globe,* March 12, 1907. For what follows, see *Among the Clouds,* July 17, 1907, and newspaper clippings, n.d. but c. 1907, in a scrapbook belonging to the late Susan Chandler, Brunswick, Maine.

92   *"say to Mooselac": Dartmouth,* December 7, 1909.

93   *necessarily all bad:* J. W. Goldthwaite, "Hanover and Outdoor Life," in *Dartmouth Out O' Doors,* ed. Fred H. Harris (Hanover, NH: Outing Club, 1913), 54.

    Boston Evening Record: "The Mountaineer," *Boston Evening Transcript,* March 15, 1913; and Carl Shumway, "Dartmouth Students Ski up Mount Washington," *Boston Evening Record,* March 15, 1913.

94   *"back and forth":* "The Mountaineer," *Boston Evening Transcript,* March 15, 1913.

    Notes by Carl E. Shumway: Notes by Carl E. Shumway, three-page, handwritten MS, NESM 2002.131.001.

    Dartmouth was doing: Letter from J. S. Apperson to C. A. Chandler, Schenectady, New York, February 23, 1912; and letter 14 036, from J. S. Apperson to Harold G. Rugg, Schenectady, New York, April 13, 1914; both in Apperson Papers, Adirondack Research Center, Schenectady, New York. Philip F. Palmedo, *Roland Palmedo: A Life of Adventure and Enterprise* (Portsmouth, NH: Peter Randall, 2018), 10. For Wendel L. Paul, see Harris, *Dartmouth Out O' Doors,* 107n.

95   *Charley Proctor in 1981:* Charles N. Proctor, presentation at Hanover, New Hampshire, September 23, 1981.

    "great natural ice-box": Ski Bulletin, October 1940, front cover.

    quarter hours down: A. H. d'Egville, "The Inferno Challenge Cup," *British Ski Year Book* 4, no. 9 (July 1928): 507–13.

    "ready not far away": Arthur C. Comey, "Skiing in Inferno," *Mountain Magazine,* October–November 1929, 7–8.

    of any responsibility: For what follows on the first Inferno, see Gwendoline Keene, "The Summit Race," *Bulletin Appalachia* 26, no. 10 (June 1933): 472–73.

96   *fourteen minutes and 41.3 seconds:* Ibid.; also Summer number 19, no. 3 (June 1933): 473.

97   *thirty-five seconds:* R. R. S. [Rockwell R. Stephens], "The American Inferno," *Appalachia* 20, no. 4 (June 1934): 121–22.

    "fortunately struck": Robert S. Monahan letter, in *Appalachia* 16, no. 10 (June 1933): 472n.

98   *"a good memory":* Edward Wells, interview by Jerry Urdang, January 21, 1980, NESM Oral History Archive.

    added another contestant: Al Sise, interview by Nick Brewster, November 5, 1979, NESM Oral History Archive.

"above your ears": Toni Matt tape, January 22, 1982, NESM 2012.031.158.

Walter Crandell of Hanover: Dr. Walter B. Crandell, 1939, *American Inferno*, 350 feet (about ten minutes) P 1980F.005001, and 1939 *American Inferno*, 800 feet (about twenty-four minutes) P 1980F.005.002 in NESM Film Archive.

Chapter 6: Cannon Mountain

99   *for sale at $400,000:* Meghan McCarthy McPhaul, *A History of Cannon Mountain: Trails, Tales, and Skiing Legends* (Charleston, SC: History Press, 2011), 9–10.

100   *Dixville Notch in 1917: Boston Globe*, December 4, 1912, and January 21, 1917.

    front page of February 16, 1911: Littleton Courier, February 16, 1911.

101   *extraordinary client list:* Peckett's guest list, Sugar Hill Historical Museum, Sugar Hill, New Hampshire. Allen Adler, "That Peckett Mystique," in *2002 International Ski History Congress Selected Papers*, ed. E. John B. Allen (New Hartford, CT: International Skiing History Association, 2002), 17–18. The descriptive additions to most names were not, of course, in the guest book.

102   *south of Luzern:* Adler, "That Peckett Mystique," 18.

    "Thomas Cook & sons": Jim Ring, *How the English Made the Alps* (London: John Murray, 2001), 135.

103   *for us to follow:* Adler, "Peckett Mystique," 18.

    hour west of Munich: Carolyn Harris, "How a Romanov Duke Popularized Skiing in Quebec's Laurentian Mountains," Royal Historian, accessed February 22, 2021, Royalhistorian.com//how-a-romanov-duke-popularized-skiing-in-quebecs-laurentian-mountains/.

    the duke, replaced him: Charles Proctor, "New Ski Trails," *Appalachia* (December 1933).

    Steinhauser from Munich: Ski Bulletin, January 13 and February 17, 1933.

104   *"snowplough position":* Roger Peabody, interview by Harry Stearns, Franconia, November 28, 1980, NESM Oral History Archive.

    after the war: Andreas Praher, *Österreichs Skisport im Nationalsozialismus: Anpassung—Verfolgung—Kollaboration* (Berlin: De Gruyter, 2022), 102–3.

    came to Peckett's: Letter from Liz Feuersinger Templeton to *Skiing Heritage* 16 no. 3 (September 2004): 6.

    season was Otto Lang: Otto Lang, *A Bird of Passage: The Story of my Life*, 2 vols. (Helena, MT: Falcon Press), 1994, 2:243–48, typed MS.

105   *Ski Trails Committee:* McPhaul, *History of Cannon Mountain*, 20, 23–24.

    National Forest: "New Ski Trails in New Hampshire," *New Hampshire Troubadour*, March 1934, 11–12.

    New Yorker *writer put it:* David Moffat, "Hotels Here and There: Peckett's," *New Yorker*, November 25, 1933, 68.

    "without a fall": A. H. B. [Alexander Bright], "Richard Taft Trail," *Ski Bulletin*, February 17, 1933.

106   *instructing at Peckett's:* "Out of the Banana Belt," *Ski Bulletin*, January 12, 1934.

New England Council: R. R. S., "The Proposed Franconia Notch Aerial Tramway," *Appalachia* 20, no. 9 (December 1934): 260–61. *Boston Evening Transcript,* December 9, 1933.

"whole season in New England": See Arnold Lowell, "The Bright Idea," *Ski Bulletin,* October 1938, 9–11.

Dartmouth's mountain: R. P. B. [Robert P. Booth] and John P. Carleton, "Aerial Tramway on Cannon Mountain," *Appalachia,* n.s., 1, no. 7 (November 1935): 459.

107   *"us in the gallery":* Ernest Poole, *The Great White Hills of News Hampshire* (Garden City, NJ: Doubleday, 1947), 426.

"vacations in Canada": "The Aerial Tramway," *Exeter News-Letter,* September 21, 1934.

top in five minutes: R. P. B. and Carleton, "Aerial Tramway," *Appalachia,* n.s., 1, no. 7 (November 1935): 459–62.

"The Tram": State of N. H. Archives and Records, Concord, N.H., box 14070: House Judiciary. Typed minutes for February 7, 14, 19, March 20 and June 13, 1935, box 13066: Senate Committee. Revision of laws. Typed minutes for April 20, 1937. See also *Journal of the House of Representatives, January Session of 1935* (Concord, NH: Rumford Press, n.d.), 99, 425, 935–51, 1026, 1935, 1067–68, 1106, 1124–28, 1172, 1183. *Journal of the Honorable Senate, January Session of 1935,* 421, 423, 427, 441–42, 445. *Laws of the State of New Hampshire, passed January Session 1935, Legislature Convened January 2, Adjourned June 21* (Concord, NH: 1935), 186–90, 295–98.

108   *remaining 45 percent:* Roland Peabody, "The American Bleichert-Zuegg on Cannon Mountain," *Appalachia,* n.s., 4, no. 7 (June 1938): 125.

top of the mountain: Ibid.

for the 1937–38 season: All the cable cars listed are mentioned in "Luis Zuegg," accessed January 15, 2022, https://second.wiki/wiki/luis-zuegg.

three towers: Roland Peabody, "American Bleichert-Zuegg," *Appalachia,* n.s., 4, no. 7 (June 1938): 125–26.

109   *"Ski Fun":* Ski Bulletin, December 9, 1938.

had urged in 1934: New York Times, August 23, 1934.

carried uphill: Cannon Mountain Aerial Tramway II (Concord: New Hampshire Department of Resources and Economic Development, 1980), 2.

Nuova Agudio: "New England Ski Lift Database: Tram II, Cannon Mountain," NewEnglandSkiHistory.com, accessed January 15, 2022, newenglandskihistory.com/lifts/viewlift.php?id=520.

forty and fifty years: "Cannon Seeking $10 to $30 Million for Tramway," NewEnglandSkiHistory.com, accessed January 15, 2022, newengland skiindustry.com.

110   *died two days later:* Richard Hough and Denis Richards, *The Battle of Britain* (New York: Norton, 1989), 188, 194.

"Cannon's greatest day": Dick Hamilton, interview by Meghan McCarthy McPhaul, October 28, 2010, quoted in McPhaul, *History of Cannon Mountain,* 116.

given their approval: For what follows, see Jeff Leich, "Cannon Mountain on the World Stage: North America's First World Cup, 1967," *Journal of the New England Ski Museum* 103 (Winter 2017): 1, 5–15.

112 *"alpine ski event":* Jean-Claude Killy to Yves Perret, *Skiing History*, April 5, 1917.

"than the Europeans": E-mail from Jean-Claude Killy to author, May 11, 2021.

Chapter 7: The Schneider Phenomenon

114 *Bis Wir Tot:* William L. Shirer, *The Rise and Fall of the Third Reich* (New York: Simon and Schuster, 1960), 333.

115 *judged Time: Time*, February 20, 1939, 24.

"as a ski teacher": Hannes Schneider, "Wie ich Skifahrer und Skilehrer wurde," *Feierabend Wochenbeilage zum Vorarlberger Tagblatt* 12 (1930): 44–46.

116 *Germany in 1913: Year-Book of the Ski Club of Great Britain* 1, no. 6 (1910): 34; *Allgemeine Sport-Zeitung*, February 2, 1913.

"before I do another": Quoted in Arnold Lunn, *A History of Ski-ing* (London: Oxford University Press, 1927), 384.

"military manuals available": Raimond Udy, *Kurze praktische Anleitung über den Gebrauch, die Konservierung und Erzeugung des Schneeschuhs für Militärzwecke* (Laibach, Slovenia: Udy, 1896). Hermann Czant, *Militärgebirgsdienst im Winter* (Vienna: Sterns, 1907). Georg Bilgeri, three articles, *Ski-Chronik* 1 (1908–9): 76–92; *Ski-Chronik* 2 (1909–10): 156–70; *Ski-Chronik* 3 (1910–11): 105–21.

117 *"Hannes Schneider":* "Die Heiligsprechung Hannes Schneider," *Ski* [Swiss] 20 (1925): 110–12.

"more papal than the pope": Quoted in Lunn, *A History of Ski-ing,* 384.

118 *after the Great War: La Montaigne*, November–December 1919, 275–76.

or the Arlberg technique: International Sport: Christian Rubi, "Ski Instruction in Switzerland," quoted in *Skiing: The International Sport,* ed. Roland Palmedo (New York, Derrydale Press, 1937), 115–42. "Arosa Notes," [1927?], typed MS, Deutscher Ski Verband, Carl Luther Archiv, Planegg, Germany, 6 Env. Wintersportsaison-Verlängerungen. Luther's archive is now at the Deutsche Sporthochschule Köln, Cologne, and is presently being accessioned.

"ugly and unnecessarily strenuous": "Arosa Notes," Carl Luther Archiv.

119 *"come to much":* Arnold Fanck, *Er führte Regie mit Gletschern, Stürmen und Lawinen: Ein Filmpionier erzählt* (Munich: Nymphenburger, 1973), 113–19.

"out into the world": Hannes Schneider, "The Development of the Ski School in Austria," in Palmedo, *Skiing,* 101.

Leni Riefenstahl: E. John B. Allen, "Leni Riefenstahl's Skiing World," in *L'Art et le Sport,* ed. Laurent Daniel (Biarritz, France: Atlantica, 2009), 2 vols., 1:222–30. *Der Winter* 28 (November 1934): 285.

120 *"cheated you all these years":* Friedl Pfeifer and Morten Lund, *The Making of the Aspen Dream,* 129, TMS.

"breath-taking skiing": Illustrated in E. John B. Allen, *The Culture and Sport of Skiing from Antiquity to World War II* (Amherst: University of Massachusetts Press, 2007), 269.

"never left me": Fanck, *Regie mit Gletschern*, 115.

"greatest importance": Der *Film Kurier*, n.d., cited in Fanck, *Regie mit Gletschern*, 130.

121 *warned in 1927*: Axel Eggebrecht in *Die Weltbühne* (Berlin), November 1, 1927, reprinted in Fanck, *Regie mit Gletschern*, 162.

Nazis could depend: Siegfried Kracauer, *From Caligari to Hitler* (Princeton, NJ: Princeton University Press, 1947), 112.

"beautiful and terrifying": Susan Sontag, "Fascinating Fascism," *New York Review of Books*, February 6, 1975, 23.

"Pre-Anschluss": F. Sandoz, "Le Bluff des méthodes nationales, *Neige et Glace* 17 (July 1939): 379.

Rudolf Gomperz: Hanno Loewy, "Wunder des Schneeschuhs? Hannes Schneider, Rudolf Gomperz und die Geburt des modernen Skisports am Arlberg," in *Hast Du meine Alpen gesehen?*, ed. Hanno Loewy (Hohenems, Austria: Jüdisches Museum Hohenems, 2009), 318–42.

122 *"preparation for* Anschluss*"*: *Nazi Conspiracy and Aggression* (Washington, DC: U.S. Government Printing Office, 1946), 2:944–45.

national socialists: Kitzbüheler Ski Club, Brochure: *75 Years Kitzbüheler Ski Club*, 1934. *Kitzbüheler Nachrichten*, February 1934.

Schneider had refused: Letter from Hannes Schneider to SS Reichsführer Himmler, Garmisch-Partenkirchen, November 14, 1938, Schneider Archive, NESM 2005.068.001.

devourer of Nazis: "Die zwei 'Herren' von St. Anton," *Der Rote Adler*, February 2, 1934, transcript in NESM 2005.068.008. Die Herrscher von St. Anton," *Das Schwarze Korps*, October 27, 1938.

123 *should not be run*: Arnold Lunn, "The Seventh Arlberg-Kandahar Meeting," *British Ski Year Book* 6 no. 15 (1934): 660.

instructing in Japan: Hannes Schneider, *Auf Schi in Japan* (Innsbruck, Austria: Tyrolia, 1935).

124 *"sensational upsets"*: Arnold Lunn, "The Tenth Arlberg-Kandahar Meeting," *British Ski Year Book* 9, no. 18 (1937): 153, 154.

"learning to ski": H. de Watteville, "On Ski-ing Schools and Styles," *British Ski Year Book* 6, no. 12 (1931): 219.

"it oozes at every pore": Ibid., 221–22.

125 *"tragic circumstances"*: A. L., "Hannes Schneider and the Arlberg-Kandahar," *British Ski Year Book* 9, no. 19 (1938): 217.

Nazi mayor of Saint Anton: For what follows, see *British Ski Year Book* 9, no. 19 (1938): 216–18.

Lunn's Kandahar Club: Arnold Lunn, "Obituary: Hannes Schneider," *British Ski Year Book* 16, no. 36 (1955): 326.

happier days of the 1920s: In the German Ski Championships of 1923, Rösen placed sixth, and Toerring, twelfth. *Der Winter* 16, no. 9 (February 1923): 133.

Hans Schneeberger: *Der Winter* 16, no. 10 (March 1923): 158

126 *such a success*: *Der Winter* 31, no. 12 (March 1938): 485–86.

Altersklasse the next year: *British Ski Year Book* 5, no. 11 (1930): 696; *British Ski Year Book* 6, no. 12 (1931): 286.

help if needed: "Aktennotiz über Besprechung Dr. Rösen-Reitinger in Sachen Hannes Schneider," 1938–1944, August 4, 1938, TMS, Marktarchiv Garmisch-Partenkirchen, Nr. 1814 EAPL: 02–025 Bürgermeister Scheck.

"obtain his amnesty": Denver paper, March 20, 1938, in Pachman Scrapbook, Denver Historical Society, Denver, Colorado.

if Schneider were released: Boston Globe, April 1, 1938.

127 *upcoming race:* New York Times, March 17, 1938.

one meet: David O. Hooke, "D.O.C. History," MS lent to me by David Hooke in the mid-1980s and returned to him.

work for the Nazis: Alice Kiaer, "Hannes Schneider," Ski (USA), October 1955, 46.

Rösen a favor: Otto Lang, A Bird of Passage: The Story of My Life, 2 vols. (Helena, MT: Falcon Press, 1994), 2:17, typed MS.

speak to Drabe: Marktarchiv Garmisch-Partenkirchen, Nr. 1814 EAPL: 02–025 Bürgermeister Scheck.

128 *impressed the Nazis:* Ibid.

presented a cup: Letter from Nancy Kinsey to Daisy Lloyd, Mount Stewart, Northern Ireland, July 1938, reprinted in Stephen Anderton, Christopher Lloyd: His Life at Great Dexter (London: Pimlico, 2011), 59–60.

released after five days: Letter from Hans Falkner to Lajko [Marcel Breuer], London, May 24, 1938, Marcel Breuer Papers, Special Collections Research Center, Syracuse University Libraries, Syracuse, New York.

"my Siegfried": Letter from Lady Londonderry to Hermann Göring, quoted in Circe: The Life of Edith, Marchioness of Londonderry, by Anne de Courcy (London: Sinclair-Stevenson, 1992), 271–72.

Bavarian Ski Association: Der Winter 21, no. 13 (April 1928): 474–75.

129 *Schneider from Garmisch:* Gerard Fairlie, Flight without Wings: The Biography of Hannes Schneider (London: Hodder and Stoughton, 1957), 206–7.

"use in such affairs": Marktarchiv Garmisch-Partenkirchen, Nr. 1814 EAPL:02–025 Bürgermeister Scheck.

Heinrich Himmler: Letter from Hannes Schneider to SS Reichsführer, Gasthof Melber, Garmisch Partenkirchen, November 14, 1938.

130 *occasional spelling mistakes:* "Mein Verhältnis zu Herrn Bürgermeister Moser," TMS, Schneider Archive, NESM 2005.068.002.

cordially received there: Fairlie, Flight without Wings, 206–7. British Ski Year Book 10, no. 20 (1939): 285.

long winter season: According to Lang, Bird of Passage, 2:22–23. A letter from Hilda Jaques (Auburn's secretary) to Mania Zborowska, London, April 19, 1938, listed $1,500 for four months, plus 10 percent of all gross receipts and room and board. This was information she might need if she connected with Schneider, then at Garmisch-Partenkirchen. NESM 2021.105.002.

"Hannes Schneider Ski School": Poster by Tyler Micoleau, c. 1938, NESM 1985P.002.020.

131 *Hjalmar Schacht:* Harvey D. Gibson, An Autobiography (North Conway, NH: Reporter Press, 1951), 306.

"financial wizard": Shirer, Rise and Fall, 112.

"will and German thought": Schacht speech to employees of the former Austrian National Bank on March 21, 1938. Nazi Conspiracy and Aggression 2, chapter 16, part 12: Hjalmar Schacht. "Hjalmar Schacht," Yale Law School, Lilian Goldman Law Library, Avalon project, accessed January 17, 2022, Avalon.law.yale.edu/imt/chap16_part12.asp.

taken ski lessons at Saint Anton: New York Times, February 10, 1939.

North Conway: Jaques to Zborowska, April 19, 1938.

132 leave Germany: Allen, Culture and Sport of Skiing, 268–74.
"nothing to say about it": New York Times, February 19, 1939.

133 "Two souls with one mind": "Zwei Seelen ein Gedanke" is a fairly common expression, first used by playwright Friedrich Halm in Der Sohn der Wildnis (Vienna: C. Gerold, 1843), accessed April 19, 2022, Austria-forum.org/af/Austriawiki/Friedrich_Halm. The play was first staged in 1842.

134 "bolt from the blue": Boston Herald, February 7, 1939.
to give him advice: Gibson, Autobiography, 302.

135 in March: Boston Globe, March 10, 1939.
Maine, in April 1939: Portland (ME) Sunday Telegram, April 16, 1939.
World's Fair: Photo in the Boston Globe, October 6, 1939.
"Here Comes Hannes": Ski-Week 2, no. 1 (December 2, 1939): cover. "Track! Here Comes Hannes!," Boston Post, January 9, 1942.
Schneider waxes: Unknown newspaper clipping, NESM Scrapbook 2005.069.003.
perfect English: Tacoma (WA) News, May 6, 1940.
Boston Globe: Boston Globe, February 7, 1939.

136 "on the golf course": Letter from Hannes Schneider, North Conway, New Hampshire, to Herta Bergmann-Richter, January 1, 1940, Schneider Archive, NESM 1981L.008.005.
his father died: Herbert Schneider, interview by Jeff Leich, Saint Anton, April 9, 2005.
"rush hour": Boston Herald, March 3, 1939.

137 recalled son Herbert: Herbert Schneider cited by Tom Eastman, "North Conway's Eastern Slope Inn," Hannes Schneider Meistercup Program 2008 (Franconia, NH: New England Ski Museum, 2008), 10.

138 "to earn a living": Letter from Hannes Schneider to Otto Lang, quoted in Jeff Leich, "Harvey Dow Gibson," Hannes Schneider Meistercup Program 2012 (Franconia, NH: New England Ski Museum, 2023), 27.
"I know of have fallen": Letter from Hannes Schneider to Herta Bergmann-Richter, December 1, 1941, NESM 1981L.008.005.
"no longer be in the USA" he wrote: Ibid.
"good I settle here": C. Lester Walker, "A Way of Life," New Yorker, February 28, 1942, 25.
"need it more": Schneider, interview by Jeff Leich.

Chapter 8: America's Holmenkollen?

140 "America's Holmenkollen": Postcard, NESM P80.10.19.

141 "rend the firmament": North, February 4, 1891, cited in Helen M. White, The Tale of a Comet and Other Stories (Saint Paul: Minnesota Historical Society Press, 1984), 144.

143 "Brattleboro's 750 feet": Vermont Phoenix, n.d., NESM, Fred Harris Memory Book L82.16.5
four three-foot "lips": Charles Edward Crane, Winter in Vermont (New York: Alfred A. Knopf, 1941), 242.
according to a friendly neighbor: Ibid., 239.
the rest pledged: Unnamed newspaper, December 1921, NESM, Fred Harris Memory Book L82.16.5.

half million dollars: Boston Evening Transcript, December 14, 1922; *Atlantic Coast Merchant*, January 20, 1923, NESM, Fred Harris Memory Book L82.16.6.

144 *replaced him:* Untitled newspaper clipping, NESM, Fred Harris Memory Book L82.16.5.

"ski into skiing": Berkshire Evening Eagle, March 2, 1922.

"amateur affair": Unnamed newspaper clipping, NESM, Fred Harris Memory Book L82.16.5.

145 *Ivar Dahl:* Jakob Vaage, *Holmenkollen* (Oslo: Sekkelsen & Sønn, 1971), 201–7.

and Greenfield: Unnamed newspaper clipping, NESM, Fred Harris Memory Book L82.16.5.

third in the jump in 1924: Skisport, 1924–25, 41.

146 *"grace and control":* NESM, Brattleboro Scrapbook L80.2.1.

"his run at the bottom": Score sheet of the Vermont Open Amateur Ski Jumping Championship, NESM, Fred Harris Memory Book L82.16.5.

"Day's Program": "More Than 40 Falls Add Thrills to the Day's Program," unnamed newspaper clipping, January 21, 1923, NESM, Fred Harris Memory Book L82.16.6.

147 *"about ten days": Boston Globe*, February 5, 1922.

"fame—or eternity": Letter from Rollin S. Childs to editor, Brattleboro, unnamed newspaper clipping, February 1, 1922, NESM, Fred Harris Memory Book L82.16.5.

"Flawless Jump": Unnamed newspaper clipping, March 1, 1922, NESM, Fred Harris Memory Book L82.16.5.

148 *"amateur record again":* Ibid.

149 *"St. Moritz of America": Lake Placid Club Notes* 78 (January–February 1915): 549.

"Eastern ski meet there": 1972 tape recording of Alf Halvorson, Berlin Historical Society. This tape cannot be found. E-mail from Walter Nadeau to author, February 4, 2022

150 *"Soc et tuum":* The First Kingdom of the Ski, Utica, New York, *Third Annual Report of the National Ski Association of America*, 1906–7, 32.

151 *reported the newsmen: New York Times*, February 5, 1924.

"style was atrocious": Lieutenant colonel H. de Watteville, "The Olympic Winter Games at Chamonix," *British Ski Year Book* 2, no. 5 (1924): 230.

one hundredth of a point: Skisport, 1924–25, 44; *Skier*, November 1974, 13, and December 1974, 6.

152 *reported to the Eastern establishment: Report by Fred Harris to Twenty-Second NSA Convention, February 13–14, 1926*, in USEASA minutes, 1926, n.p., NESM 1983R.023.001.

"entire world": Oscar T. Oyass, "Our Achievements," *Skisport*, 1924–25, 3.

153 *"good as in Brattleboro":* Newspaper clipping, February 14, 1925, NESM, Fred Harris Memory Book L82.16.5.

"throughout the East": Skisport, 1924–25, 38.

"Winged Trophy": Unnamed newspaper clipping, NESM, Brattleboro Accounts Book L80.2.1.

154 *"anywhere in the United States":* Fred Harris, "A Green Hill in Brattleboro," *Ski Bulletin*, November 1941.

Holyoke and Northampton: NESM, Brattleboro Accounts Book L80.2.1.

155   "*Ski Stars in Person*": NESM, Harris Scrapbook L80.2.1.

      "*189 feet*": *American Ski Annual*, 1939–40, 131.

156   *Dartmouth Carnival*: *Ski Bulletin*, February 14, 1941.

      foreign jumpers: For what follows on foreign jumpers, see the *Brattleboro (VT) Reformer*, February 1 and 16, 2009; *The Rutland Daily Herald*, February 17, 2012, and February 18, 2013; and *Commons* (Brattleboro, VT), February 15, 2018.

      Turk won the 2015 meet: *Commons* (Brattleboro, VT), February 18, 2015.

157   *standards in 2006*: *Brattleboro (VT) Reformer*, January 30, 2006.

      "*Step Up and Soar*": *Weekend Reformer*, n.d. [2006?], Dana Sprague Archive.

      ensured success: *Brattleboro (VT) Reformer*, February 29 2008.

      of great interest: E-mail from Dana Sprague to author, October 17, 2020.

158   *Oberstdorf in March 2021*: *FIS Newsletter*, March 3, 2021.

      "*famous name it bears*": *Ski Bulletin*, March 3, 1939.

      "*event held in Berlin*": *Ski Bulletin*, October 1940.

Chapter 9: Vermont Ski Towns

160   "*favorite pastime with the boys nowadays*": *Vermont Phoenix*, March 22, 1895.

      "*popular sport*": *Burlington (VT) Free Press*, February 24, 1899.

      "*snowshoeing and skiing*": *Brattleboro (VT) Reformer*, November 25, 1910.

      five miles away: *Brattleboro (VT) Reformer*, January 21, 1914.

      Winter Sports Club: Dale S. Atwood, "Winter Sports at St. Johnsbury," *Vermonter* 27, no. 9 (1922): 217.

      "*depth of seven feet*": Charlotte Endicott Wilde, "Reminiscences of the Snow-Shoe Section," *Appalachia*, n.s., 18, no. 7 (June 1952): 55.

161   *snows of Wilmington*: *Brattleboro (VT) Reformer*, February 24, 1916.

      "*the snowshoe and ski*": Fred H. Harris, "Skiing and Winter Sports in Vermont," *Vermonter* 17, no. 11 (1912): 677–81.

      hundreds out on skis: *Brattleboro (VT) Reformer*, January 22, 1918.

      "*adapted for skiing*": *Brattleboro (VT) Reformer*, December 22, 1917.

      "*popular lately*": *Express and Standard, Newport (VT)*, January 22, 1926.

      Outing Club flourished: *Express and Standard, Newport (VT)*, October 30, 1925.

      Hospital in Newport: *Express and Standard, Newport (VT)*, November 24, 1933.

162   "*specialization of cross-country*": Narada Coomara, "Green Mountain Skiing," *American Ski Annual*, 1935–36, 121–23.

      Brattleboro in 1924: *Skisport*, 1924–25, 38.

      Vermont Journal: *Vermont Tribune* (Ludlow, VT), May 12, and August 11, 1910; and *Vermont Journal*, February 22, 1924.

      soon after 1900: *Skier*, November 1963, 23.

      "*scant in Vermont*": Coomara, "Green Mountain Skiing," 123.

      "*winter sports enthusiasm*": A. W. Coleman, "Vermont Ski Runs," *Appalachia* 20, no. 9 (December 1934): 224.

      "*permanent factor*": "Winter Sports Development: Season of 1937–38," 1, 12, state of Vermont pamphlet, box UVW Wgw M4 58s, Bailey Howe Library, University of Vermont, Burlington, Vermont.

163 *"hotel in many ways":* C. W. J. Tennant, "Ski-ing in the States," *Year-Book of the Ski Club of Great Britain and the National Ski Union* 2, no. 10 (1914): 372.

"developed yet for skiing": Captain B. J. Marden," Wanderings through Eastern America," *British Ski Year Book* 4, no. 9 (July 31, 1928): 364.

164 *held for four years:* In Harris's copy, he penciled in, "This mark stood in N. E. for four years." Fred H. Harris, "How I Learned to Ski," *Outing*, January 1922, 189.

Alec Bright vice president: Woodstock Skirunners Club, Woodstock, Vermont, invitation to become a charter member, NESM L 80.33.1.

165 *Charley Proctor: Ski Bulletin*, February 26, 1933.

"unofficial cut off": Boston Evening Transcript, March 21, 1932.

vacation package: J. D. Francis, "Something New under the Winter Sun: Ski Cruise," *Country Life of America* 67 (December 1934): 51–55.

"ride and run": Woodstock, Vermont Winter Sports Map, n.d., NESM L84.43.3.

David Dodge: Jonathan Robinson, "David H. Dodd, Ski Tow Pioneer," *Journal of the New England Ski Museum* 114 (Fall 2019): 1, 4–9.

166 *were on hand: Rutland Daily Herald*, January 27, 1934.

they fixed it up: "New Ski Club Formed," *Harvard Crimson*, April 12, 1934.

"Unspoiled Vermont": American Ski Annual, 1937–38, 43.

"stampeded into skiing": Boston Herald, November 30, 1936.

Sundays would not be allowed: Boston Herald, December 3, 1937.

top to bottom: For what follows, see John C. Tobin, *The Fall Line: A Skier's Journal* (New York: Meredith, 1969), 57–58.

167 *came to mean Woodstock:* Sign of the times: plans for changing what is being called a "sensitive" name are under discussion. Lilit Marcus, "Vermont Ski Resort to Change 'Insensitive' Name," CNN, June 29, 2022, https://www.cnn.com/travel/article/suicide-six-ski-resort-vermont-name-change/index.html.

"100 miles per hour": American Ski Annual, 1942, 13.

168 *forty-three feet off it: Ski News*, March 7, 1936.

"no bindings, no poles": Manchester Journal, February 23, 1961.

coasting at Manchester: Brattleboro (VT) Reformer, February 24, 1916.

169 *Dorset Cave: Manchester Journal*, March 4, 1920.

"summer resort": Manchester Journal, September 23, 1920.

"or so at least": Letter from Edward Griffiths to James P. Taylor, Manchester, August 4, 1921, in Taylor Papers, box T7, folder: Green Mountain Club 1921 July–December in Vermont Historical Society, Montpelier, Vermont.

an hour away: Manchester Journal, April 21, 1927.

Lake Placid Club: Philip A. Pabst, *Fred A. Pabst, Jr.: A Pioneer of the Skiing Industry*, typed MS paper for History 485, April 16, 1989.

"the theory of downhill techniques": Ibid., 4.

"too much red tape or both": Ibid., 4.

170 *"chain-store management":* Ibid., 6.

171 *concentrate on Bromley:* Ibid., 8.

"area in the East": Ski Bulletin, January 2, 1942; *American Ski Annual*, 1943, 3.

"famed resort": Baltimore Sun, February 29, 1948.

"highest in the country": Boston Globe, December 4. 1949.

1940, and 1941: For mid-Vermont, see Ski Bulletin, February 24, 1939. For southern Vermont, see Ski Bulletin, February 17, 1939; December 12, 1939; and December 15, 1940.

172   wearing helmets: Ski Bulletin, March 27, 1942.

Bromley's Shincracker: Ski Bulletin, February 13, 1942.

(1936 German Olympic team): John L. Garrison, Sun, Snow, and Skis (New York: McGraw Hill, 1946), 207.

star in aviation circles: New York Times, September 29, 1982, and the well-sourced Wikipedia entry "Paul Kollsman," en.wikipedia.org/wiki /Paul_Kollsman.

173   eighth in the slalom: Post-Star (Glens Falls, NY), March 4, 1940; and Rutland Daily Herald, February 24, 1941.

taken into custody: Ski Bulletin, December 19, 1941.

"ski school there": Otto Lang, A Bird of Passage: The Story of My Life, 2 vols. (Helena, MT: Falcon Press, 1994), 2:196–98, typed MS.

"each of the resorts": Manchester Journal, December 31, 1942.

174   "between two mafia factions": Lang, Bird of Passage, 2:198.

in November 1941: Burlington (VT) Free Press, November 10, 1941.

Lake Placid: American Ski Annual, 1938–39, 44; 1939–40, 44; 1940–41, 38, 39, 45; 1942, 28, 50.

grounds of anti-Semitism: Peter M. Hopsicker, "Defying the Restrictions: The Adirondack Mountain Club Answers the 'Jewish Question,'" New York History, 91, no. 2 (Spring 2010): 132.

He was refused: Burlington (VT) Free Press, February 7, 1946.

"prize attraction": Rutland Daily Herald, December 5, 1941.

174–175   "Snow Man's Rest Lodge": "Snow Valley," accessed January 22, 2022, NewEnglandSkiHistory.com.

175   "YOU in '42": Ibid.

"to open very soon": Manchester Journal, January 1, 1942.

Chapter 10: Stowe

178   homemade skis: Craig Burt, History of Mount Mansfield, April 1962, n.p.

179   made them skis: Mrs. Slayton, "Reminiscences of Stowe," Stowe Reporter, March 22, 1962, 1–3.

February 1914: Nathaniel L. Goodrich, "A Pioneer Ski Ascent," Mt. Mansfield Skiing 9, no. 1 (1943): n.p.

prize attraction: Slayton, "Reminiscences," 7; Burt, History of Mount Mansfield, n.p.

World War I: Philip F. Palmedo, Roland Palmedo: A Life of Adventure and Enterprise (Portsmouth, NH: Peter E. Randall, 2018).

180   "New York City": Livingston Longfellow, "How the Club Grew," in Ten Winters, 1931–1941, ed. David Judson (New York: Amateur Ski Club of New York, 1942), 11.

winter excursions: Letter from Roland Palmedo to Postmaster of Stowe, February 19, 1931, reprinted in Palmedo, Roland Palmedo, 50.

was quite possible: Ski Bulletin, March 18, 1931.

Charlie Lord: For a good overview of this activity, see A. W. Coleman, "Vermont Ski Runs," Appalachia 20, no. 9 (December 1934): 224–28.

181   *"world to come"*: A. W. Coleman, "Skis over Vermont," *Appalachia*, n.s., 2, no. 7 (June 1936): 39.

"almost a scandal": *Ski Bulletin*, January 29, 1937.

182   *"but less difficult"*: Ford K. Sayre, "The Certification of Ski Teachers under the USEASA," *American Ski Annual*, 1938–39, 147.

not exotic enough: Fred Nachbaur, interview by E. John B. Allen, Gilford, New Hampshire, August 3, 1982, NESM Oral History Archive.

"candidate was accepted": Letter from Charles N. Proctor, Santa Cruz, California, to author, August 16, 1982.

183   *"expert out of every duffer"*: Lowell Thomas, "Let's Ski for Fun," *American Ski Annual*, 1937–38, 158.

"Prussian sergeant": Arthur Callan, interview by John Allen, North Conway, October 24, 1979, NESM Oral History Archive.

"you'll make it": "Crouch and You'll Make It," *Boston Evening Transcript*, December 7, 1929.

"essentially American": Thomas, "Let's Ski for Fun," 158.

"School for American Skiers": On Schniebs, see ibid., n.p.; on Lamere, see Paul Lamere, interview by Nick Brewster, Whitefield, New Hampshire, December 1979, NESM Oral History Archive; on Cyr, see *Ski Bulletin*, January 13, 1939.

Eastern-certified instructors: Ski Bulletin, February 20, 1942.

184   *teaching experience:* For what follows on Sepp Ruschp, see Morten Lund, "The Austrian Instructor," *Skiing Heritage* 17, no. 1 (March 2005): 29–34.

186   *"our Arnold Lunn"*: Letter from Helen McAlpin to author, February 24, 1985.

187   *"Where are the lifts?"*: Palmedo, *Roland Palmedo*, 56.

finance the chair: Ibid., 57.

"resort in the East": Ibid., 59.

188   *ASC's mountain:* Ibid., 77–78.

who had come to Stowe: Palmedo correspondence, NESM 1987 L.008.001.

189   *"side-show attractions"*: Palmedo, *Roland Palmedo*, 78.

lower forty-eight: Information from Eric Friedman, Mad River Chamber of Commerce, April 14, 2020. The oldest single chairlift is at Mount Eyak, Alaska.

Chapter 11: Southern New England

190   *"I know how to make snow"*: Mary Bellis, "Making Snow," The Inventors, accessed October 16, 2020, theinventors.org/library/inventors/blsnow .htm.

"As the Earth Turns": April White, "How Artificial Snow was Invented," *Smithsonian Magazine*, November 2019.

1938 and 1939: Photographs in Ingrid P. Wicken, *50 Years of Flight: Ski Jumping in California, 1900–1950* (Norco, CA: Vasa Press, 2017), 50, 51, 121, 122, 143.

191   *ice but snow:* Bellis, "Making Snow."

radio broadcasts: Boston Globe, March 16, 1950; Arthur R. Hunt, "Snowmaking Is 40 Years Old," *Ski Area Management* 29, no. 2 (March 1990): 59. See also Jeff Leich, "Skiing in New England's Southern Tier: Connecticut and Rhode Island," *Journal of the New England Ski Museum* 112 (Spring 2019): 5.

April 1954: For what follows, see letter from John Hitchcock to *Skiing Heritage* 3 (September 1999): 10.

192 *snow a day:* "Ide's VIM," accessed January 24, 2022, ide-tech.com/en/vim.

Pierce and his friends: Carol Lugar, interview by Jeff Leich, March 12, 2019, in "Skiing in New England's Southern Tier," *Journal of the NESM* 112 (Spring 2019): 5.

193 *February 1951:* "Walt Sprays 450 Tons of Ice over Bare Mohawk Slope, Breaks Even," *Eastern Skier*, February 1, 1950, 1.

"enough to check speed": *Ski Bulletin*, December 27, 1935.

Tourism Council: For Schoenknecht on governor's tourism council, his involvement in Camp Jewel, and in the Weik Recreation area at Morris, see remarks by Allen Beavers on Camp Jewel and by "Woodcore" on the Weik Recreation area at *New England Lost Ski Areas Project Connecticut:* "Camp Jewel, North Colebrook, Connecticut," and "Henry Weik Recreation Area, Morris, Connecticut," at Nelsap.org.

194 *Willis Hayes, in 1899:* Photo in E. John B. Allen, *New England Skiing, 1870–1940* (Dover, NH: Arcadia, 1997), 12.

"On Skis in Connecticut": Edwin C. Dickenson, "On Skis in Connecticut," *Illustrated Outdoor News* 6 (February 4, 1905): 17–18.

own skis in 1910: Letter from William L. Hagen, New Britain, Connecticut, to Axel Holter, March 11, 1911, in *Skisport*, 1910–11, 17.

"winter house parties": *Hartford Daily Courant*, October 20, 1911.

golf course: *Hartford Daily Courant*, January 12, 1912, and February 27, 1916.

skis in 1923: Photo in Archives and Special Collections, Thomas J. Dodd Research Center, University of Connecticut, Storrs, Connecticut.

Paterson, New Jersey: *Boston Daily Globe*, February 15, 1926.

skiing family: "Vestre Trysil Idrettslag," *Norske Skiløpere: Østlandet Nord* (Oslo: Ranheim, 1955), 505; "Ski Jumping—95 Years and Counting," Salisbury Historical Society, accessed 23 January 2022, info@salisbury association.org.

195 *"friendly manner":* "1928 National Ski Tournament," United States Eastern Amateur Ski Association, *Year Book,* 1928, 16.

five thousand spectators: *Ski Bulletin*, February 8, 1935.

196 *road at Winsted:* On Lekang, see *Ski Bulletin*, February 24, 1933, and his biography at the National Ski and Snowboard Hall of Fame, Class of 1977, Ishpeming, Michigan.

three hundred feet: Joseph A. O'Brien, "Ski Jumping over Winsted," *Register Citizen*, February 26, 1995, D1.

"flyer of the snows": *Reno (NV) Gazette-Journal*, February 29, 1932.

197 *Winter Sports Association:* For Mrs. Bigelow and what follows, see Joan Lyford Colt, "Skiing in the Hills of Norfolk," in *Norfolk, Connecticut, 1900–1975*, ed. Alice V. Waldecker (Norfolk, CT: Norfolk Historical Society, 1976), 228–30.

"snow station": Ibid., 229.

198 *Skidreiverein:* For Skidreiverein and what follows, see *Ski Bulletin*, February 28, March 6, and 13, 1936; and Arthur G. Draper, "Skidreiverein," *Ski Magazine*, November 1955, 35–37.

"New England colleges": *Ski Bulletin*, February 1, 1935.

three days later: Union Pacific Railroad, untitled report of American snow train statistics, c. 1936, W. Averell Harriman Papers, box 737, Early Studies, Library of Congress, photocopy, NESM 2011.045.002.

"thing of the past": Appalachia, n.s., 2, no. 7 (June 1936): 94.

"sun tan special": Boston Herald, March 9, 1939.

on to the Berkshires: For what follows, see *Ski Bulletin*, February 28, and March 13, 1936.

199 *six hundred feet: Ski Bulletin*, March 1, 1940.

in a variety of competitions: For more, see https://www.jumpfest.org /assets/pdfs/2022results/.

200 *Pomfret Landing:* For memories of Stein Eriksen at Brooklyn, Connecticut, see Mike Baker, "Brooklyn, Connecticut," at nelsap.org/ct/brooklyn.html. For White Mountain at Pomfret Landing, see nelsap.org/ct/whitemtn .html; accessed January 26, 2022.

nine sports suggested: Newport Mercury, December 27, 1913.

lower abdomen: Groton Times (Woodsville, NH), March 14, 1924.

January 18 that year: Newport Mercury, January 18, 1935.

"Memorial Park": Ibid.

201 *January 1938:* Mike Szostak, "Next Week's R.I. Giant Slalom Has a Long History," accessed April 4, 2021, riskirunners.com.

word here and there: Beth Pinkham memories, "Diamond Hill, R. I.," accessed April 4, 2021, nelsap.org/ri/ri.html.

Pine Top: "Pine Top Ski Area, Escoheag, R. I.," accessed April 4, 2021, nelsap.org/ri/pinetopri.html.

"straightaway run and ski jump": Appalachia, n.s., 2, no. 12 (December 1936): 279.

202 *south of Providence:* Check "Yawgoo," https://yawgoo.com, for up-to-date information.

Chapter 12: The Modernization of New England Skiing

204 *"glimpse of Hannes Schneider":* Nathaniel L. Goodrich, "A Ski Holiday in the Alps," *Appalachia* 23, no. 4 (December 1929): 336.

"considered a criminal," she reported: Wilhelmine G. Wright, "Going to Ski School in the Austrian Tyrol," *Appalachia* 18, no. 4 (December 1931): 372–77.

"Ski Pope": Pickel und Ski, a Swiss calendar for 1935, with photo of Lunn, with the caption "Der Kulissenmann: Skipapst Arnold Lunn" (Background Man: Ski Pope Arnold Lunn). Arnold Lunn, "FIS Panorama," *British Ski Year Book* 8, no. 16 (1935): 178.

"organization of the sport": Ski Survey 1, no. 9 (1975): 521.

"his personal stamp": Ibid.

205 *ski mountaineering:* For what follows, see E. John B. Allen, *The Culture and Sport of Skiing from Antiquity to World War II* (Amherst: University of Massachusetts Press, 2007), 99–102.

"obstacles such as flags": Arnold Lunn, "Style Competitions and Slalom Races," *British Ski Year Book* 1 no. 3 (1922): 393.

"left down the steep hill": Boston Evening Transcript, February 6, 1926.

"British Ski Year Book": British Ski Year Book 4, no. 9 (July 31, 1928): 472.

206 *"through heavy woods":* C. A. Proctor, "Notes on Ski-ing in the United States," *Ski Notes & Queries* 5, no. 44 (May 1931): 151.

"How about a nip?": Al Sise, interview by Nick Brewster, Norwich, Vermont, November 5, 1979, NESM Oral History Archive.

"Norwegian expert": Advertisement for Strand Mikkelsen and the Weldon Hotel in *American Ski Annual*, 1936, 28; and John Knudson, "The Birth of New England Skiing," *Skiing* (Spring 1974): 117E–118E, 121E–122E.

Arlberg technique: For what follows, see *Appalachia* 21, no. 10 (June 1928): 285.

207 *Hope Finishing Company:* "Revere Brass Company of Fall River," Union Pacific Railroad, untitled report of American snow train statistics ca. 1936, 10, W. Averell Harriman Papers, box 737, Early Studies, Library of Congress, photocopy, NESM 2011.045.002. Hope Finishing Company, Harriman Papers, 12; and *Boston Herald*, January 17, 1936.

over three hundred: USEASA minutes of November 9, 1931, NESM 1983R.023.001.

hour away to the south: Francis Head, "Early Skiing in the A. M. C." *Appalachia*, new series, 30, no. 12 (December 1964): 220.

"activity are at their best": Pamphlet *Announcing Boston's 1ˢᵗ Winter Sports Sunday Outing Train* (Boston: Boston and Maine Railroad, 1931), 1, Perkins Scrapbook, NESM 1997L.017.001.

"strenuous exercise": "An Account of the First Winter Sports Sunday Outing Train to Warner, NH," pamphlet, (Boston: Boston and Maine Railroad, 1931), 2, Perkins Scrapbook, NESM 1997L.017.001.

208 *"conveyance, and directions":* Ski Bulletin, February 13, 1931.

"New England skiing": Appalachia 28, no. 3 (June 1931): 311.

Greenfield in Massachusetts: Appalachia 19, no. 1 (June 1932): 151.

recalled a north-country shop keeper: George Marshall, interview by Jerry Urdang, Franconia, New Hampshire, January 21, 1980, NESM Oral History Archive.

"just engulf you": Selden Hannah in *Legends of American Skiing*, directed by Richard Moulton (Huntington, VT: Keystone Productions, 1982).

"ski larks": Ski Larks, film, 1939, video 1993. Brochure for Ski Lark Train c. 1948, copy in E. John B. Allen archive.

"ski trains depart": New York Times Magazine, February 18, 1940.

"glorious Sun-day": Cover by Lee Stout of Boston and Maine booklet, *The Snow Train*, 1937–38, NESM 2018 089.002. "Suntan" reference in *Boston Herald*, March 9, 1939.

209 *top of the trestle:* Dartmouth Outing Club minutes, February 5, 1915, Baker Library: box 10, T-10-5.

Shawbridge, Quebec: "Our First Funicular," *Canadian Ski Annual*, 1933, 50; *Ski Bulletin*, January 6, 1933.

Woodstock, Vermont: For what follows, see *Rutland Daily Herald*, January 28, 1934.

"as in coming down": David Judson, ed., *Ten Winters, 1931–1941* (New York: Amateur Ski Club of New York, 1942), 60.

"sport gone softy?": Ski Bulletin, January 6, 1933.

"Tow-Way": For what follows on Cooke's ski hoist, see *Ski Bulletin*, December 28, 1934. *Boston Traveler*, February 1, 1935. Ted Cooke, interview by Janet Young, Newbury, New Hampshire, January 31, 1980, NESM Oral History Archive.

210 *"improvements in the future":* Ted Cooke, "Ski Tows," *Appalachia*, n.s., 1, no. 7 (November 1935): 405.

"fifty at one time": Ski Bulletin, January 17, 1936.

"Swiss ski center": Ski Bulletin, February 7, 1936.

did not twist: American Ski Annual, 1938–39, 46.

handheld claw: There is an original in the New England Ski Museum (NESM 1980 E.010.001).

"tramway comfort": Ski Bulletin, March 18, 1938.

"immorality of the machine": American Ski Annual, 1936, 158.

211 *"sit-down variety":* Boston newspaper clipping, January 14, 1938, in Fred Nachbaur scrapbook (held privately).

212 *"But what have they lost?":* David R. Brower, "Beyond the Skiways," *Sierra Club Bulletin* 23, no. 2 (April 1938): 40.

214 *Garmisch-Partenkirchen:* American Ski Annual, 1935–36, n.p.

215 *"size of Zermatt":* Ted Ryan in *Legends of American Skiing,* 1982.

Chapter 13: Selling Venues, Transportation, and Equipment

217 *began in the East:* Strand: *Ski Annual* 18 (January 1922): n.p. Lund: *Ski Bulletin,* December 16, 1932.

"$1.25 to $2.00": Berkshire Evening Eagle, January 2, 1915.

"Skis in all sizes": Berkshire Evening Eagle, December 22, 1916; January 2, 1917; and January 31, 1920.

"sleds or toboggans": Berkshire Evening Eagle, December 22, 1917.

"one fine fellow": Acorn (Woodstock, VT), December 22, 1917.

cost $1.75: Bangor Daily News, December 16, 1917.

"Your Own Skis": Ski Bulletin, December 11, 1936.

218 *"Northland Skis":* Ski Bulletin, November 1939.

"Imported Ski Equipment": National Ski Association of America, *Year Book,* 1930–32, 107.

"Schniebs Ski": American Ski Annual, 1935, n.p.

219 *"faster, stronger":* American Ski Annual, 1936, 55.

"12 laminations": American Ski Annual, 1938–39, 22.

"World's Foremost Skier": American Ski Annual, 1939–40, 36.

broken skis in 1937: American Ski Annual, 1937–38, 31.

"Work our Specialty": American Ski Annual, 1939–40, 27.

"precisely attached": United States Eastern Amateur Ski Association, *Ski Annual,* 1934, back cover.

220 *"cold are encountered":* Berkshire Evening Eagle, December 21, 1916.

"Heavy Shoes": Berkshire County Eagle, January 9, 1924.

"type ski boots": Ski Bulletin, December 16, 1932.

"American price": American Ski Annual, 1936, 21.

"Hannes Schneider": American Ski Annual, 1937–38, 48.

"Boots for forty years": American Ski Annual, 1940–41, 30.

221 *"Antarctic Expedition":* American Ski Annual, 1939–40, 23.

"catching and jerking open": American Ski Annual, 1939–40, 30.

them in a list: Ski Bulletin, January 23, 1931.

"slithery, and watery": Theo. A. Johnsen Company, *The Winter Sport of Skeeing* (Portland, ME: Theo. A. Johnsen, 1905), 6–7.

222 *"snow conditions":* American Ski Annual, 1935–36, n.p.

"stays on the skis": American Ski Annual, 1937–38, 22.

"and 10th finishers": American Ski Annual, 1937–38, 59.

the Jerns climber: For the Jerns Ski Climber, see *American Ski Annual,* 1937–38, 55. For Alta, see *American Ski Annual,* 1938–39, 50.

223 *No Glare Ski Cap for sale:* For Eye Togs, see *Ski Bulletin,* January 19, 1940. For Blodjer, see *American Ski Annual,* 1939–40, 3; and for the No Glare Ski Cap, see *American Ski Annual,* 1939–40, 10.

for men only in 1939: For SarAnaC, *American Ski Annual,* 1935, n.p. For Morris-Shutts, see *American Ski Annual,* 1939–40, 3.

"American made": *American Ski Annual,* 1938–39, 47.

"Leather's Best Friend": *American Ski Annual,* 1937–38, 15.

224 *Absorbine Junior: Ski Bulletin,* January 23, 1931 (Nepto Lotion); *American Ski Annual,* 1939, 4 (Ultra Tan); *American Ski Annual,* 1939, 4 (Skoll:); *American Ski Annual,* 1940–41, 15 (Sports Gelée); *American Ski Annual,* 5 (Absorbine Junior).

(booklet of suggestions): Gorham of 5th Avenue and 47th Street, New York City, booklet containing one hundred trophy suggestions. United States Eastern Amateur Ski Association, *Year Book,* 1928, n.p.

regularly from 1934 on: To give the example of Balfour's, see United States Eastern Amateur Ski Association, *Year Book,* 1935, n.p.; 1938, 24; and 1939–40, 14.

"house that sports built": United States Eastern Amateur Ski Association, *Year Book,* 1929, 96.

"more as a club than a store": *Boston Herald,* March 13, 1936.

225 *"Lapland, and Switzerland":* *Ski Bulletin,* January 23, 1931.

"Everything for the skier": *American Ski Annual,* 1936, 3.

Tempo Ski Shop: American Ski Annual, 1940–41, 30.

"Corduroy Knickers": *Berkshire Evening Eagle,* December 19, 1922.

Vermont's Poultney Journal *in 1932: Poultney Journal* (Poultney, VT), February 5, 1932. For Katharine Peckett see *American Ski Annual,* 1935, n.p. For John Piane, see *Ski Bulletin,* December 11, 1936. For Sporting Tailor's, see *Ski Bulletin,* December 29, 1933.

226 *24,240: Appalachia,* n.s., 2, no. 7 (June 1936): 95.

up to 181: Thom A. Hook," Ski Clubs Boom throughout America," *Ski Annual,* 1960–61, 11–14.

227 *"wanted to be a competitor":* Roger F. Langley, interview by Arthur F. March, Jr., Barre, Massachusetts, January 30, 1980, NESM Oral History Archive.

Placid Club, Northwood: American Ski Annual, 1935, n.p. For Williston, see *American Ski Annual,* 1936, 57. For Northwood, see United States Eastern Amateur Ski Association, *Year Book,* 1928, n.p., and *American Ski Annual,* 1937–38, 61.

model cost $6.50: For Forbes see *American Ski Annual,* 1938–39, 43, and 1939–40, 43. For Groswold's model see *American Ski Annual,* 1936, 8; for Crandall Hicks Co., Boston, see *American Ski Annual,* 1937–38, 57.

228 *superb recommendation:* For slalom wear, see *Ski Bulletin,* December 16, 1932; for Charles Dudley, see *Ski Bulletin,* February 3, 1933; for the Byrd expedition, see *Ski Bulletin,* December 29, 1933.

"Daily outfit lots of ignorant ladies": Poem by Dot, illustrated by Max Barsis, *Ski Bulletin,* February 7, 1941.

229 *"even touching it":* For Bousquet's see *American Ski Annual,* 1939–40, 7. For Cooke's planned claw, see *Boston Evening Transcript,* December 21, 1934; the artifact is occasionally on view in NESM 1980E.010.001.

almost foreign skiing: American Ski Annual, 1935, n.p.

"Direct to Norway" excursions: USEASA, *Year Book,* 1928, n.p.

230 *Olympics at Garmisch-Partenkirchen:* For Sestrières, see *American Ski Annual*, 1935, n.p. For German shipping lines to the Olympics, see ibid. *"Austrian Ski Boat":* *American Ski Annual*, 1936, 7A.
"challenge your daring": *American Ski Annual*, 1937–38, 56.
South America too: For New Zealand, see *American Ski Annual*, 1937–38, 56. For Pan Am to Chile, see *Ski Bulletin* 7, no. 12 (February 12, 1937). For trip to South America, see *Ski Bulletin* 8, no. 13 (March 11, 1938).

Chapter 14: Closing Ski Tow Slopes

231 *"Keep Out Ski Area":* Also called Kallander Hill, Southboro, Massachusetts. All NELSAP citations are taken from the organization's website, Nelsap .org.
232 *three hundred feet:* At "Lyndon State College, Lyndonville, Vermont," Nelsap.org.
arm-stretching 3,100 feet: *Ski Bulletin*, March 29, 1935.
Annual *of 1938–39:* *American Ski Annual*, 1938–39, 26.
233 *Guptil's Pasture:* "Guptil Pastures, Jackson, New Hampshire," Nelsap .org.
"pretty good clip": Bob Humphrey report, "Topsfield Ski Club, Wheatland's Hill, Topsfield, Massachusetts," Nelsap.org.
"climb in and warm up": Ibid.
234 *about the same time:* "New Britain Stanley Quarter Park, New Britain, Connecticut," Nelsap.org. Tow ropes were cut according to the *New Britain Herald*, March 11, 1964, December 20, 1965. "Abell Ski Slope, Braintree, Massachusetts," Nelsp.org.
Londonderry, New Hampshire: Peter Misiaszek report, "Birchwood, Londonderry, New Hampshire," Nelsap.org.
Rotary Clubs: Examples of Parks and Recreation include Augusta, Maine; Jaycees, Wickham Park, East Hartford, and Manchester, Connecticut; Kiwanis, Gorham, Massachusetts; Lions, Richford, Vermont; Rotary Clubs, Bristol, Vermont; and YMCAs, Camp Jewel, North Colebrook, Connecticut. All references are on Nelsap.org.
until 1993: "Ark Ski Tow, Monadnock Bible Conference, Jaffrey, New Hampshire," Nelsap.org.
after the war: "High Point Tow, Augusta, Maine," Nelsap.org.
235 *club in 1940:* Phil Cooke report with accompanying typed letters, October 15, and December 19, 1940, "Newton Commonwealth Part 1, Newton, Massachusetts," Nelsap.org.
1937–38 season: *American Ski Annual*, 1937–38, 60.
"with ski tow": *American Ski Annual*, 1935–36, n.p.
service at Woodstock: "Zing– – –! 10 to 100 miles an hour on the level," advertisement for Underwood Tow, *Ski Bulletin*, March 28, 1941.
236 *twisting and turning:* *American Ski Annual*, 1938–39, 46.
"United States": *American Ski Annual*, 1940–41, 34.
copied it: Clark Griffiths, "Oak Hill: The First North American Overhead Cable Ski Lift," in *Passion for Skiing*, ed. Stephen L. Waterhouse (Lebanon, NH: Whitman Communications, 2010), 72–74; *Ski Bulletin*, December 27, 1935.
"immorality of the machine": "That Ski Tramway at Dartmouth," *American Ski Annual*, 1936, 158.

"he-and-she-sticks": The name originated with the British, and was used at Pico Peak. Charles Edward Crane, *Winter in Vermont* (New York: Alfred A. Knopf, 1941), 233–34.

"sit-down variety": Unnamed Boston paper, January 14, 1938, in Fred Nachbaur scrapbook, privately held.

237 *fifty would turn up*: Jeremy Davis, "Preserving 'Lost' Ski Areas of New England—The New England Lost Ski Areas Project," in *2002 International Ski History Congress, Selected Papers*, ed. E. John B. Allen (New Hartford, CT: International Skiing History Association, 2002), 273.

Russell Slope: John Hitchcock, "Bousquet Is Where Lighting All Began," *Ski Area Management* 9, no. 2 (Spring 1970): 56–57.

238 *ten meters*: "Elms Ski Tow Hill, Goff's Falls, New Hampshire," Nelsap .org.

239 *built into a hill*: Greg Kearney report, "Oak Grove School, Vassalboro, Maine," Nelsap.org. The school is now the Maine Criminal Justice Academy. Don Adams report, "Underhill Ski Bowl, Underhill Center, Vermont," Nelsap.org.

"dug into the ski slope": Kearney report.

241 *Lenox, Massachusetts*: For these three examples of Eastover Resort, Twin Town Inn, and Esquimo Lodge, see Steve Latham report, "Eastover Resort, Lenox, Massachusetts," Nelsap.org; "Twin Town Inn, Tilton, New Hampshire," Nelsap.org; Ned Bolle report, "Esquimo Lodge Tow, Dublin-Marlborough line, New Hampshire," Nelsap.org.

242 *"rush hour"*: *Boston Globe*, March 3, 1939.

"carry insurance": *Ski Bulletin*, January 27, 1933.

"Whose devotees need Dr. Shedd": *Appalachia*, n.s., 2, no. 7 (June 1936): 102.

243 *"negligent operations"*: *Ski Bulletin*, February 6, 1942.

awarded $1.5 million: *New York Times*, June 11, 1977.

quite out of reach: Owen R. Houghton report, "Franklin Pierce College, Rindge, New Hampshire," Nelsap.org. Dick and Christine Rudolph report, "Boy Scout Troop 286, Mount Rudolph, Spofford, New Hampshire," Nelsap.org.

Chapter 15: Assessing the Ski Heritage of New England

252 *after a visit in 2020*: Ian Aldrich, "Winter in Mount Washington Valley Winter's Playground," *Yankee Magazine*, January 2021, accessed August 20, 2021, newengland.com/yankee-magazine/travel/new-hamp shire/white-mountains/winter-in-the-mount-washington-valley-winters -playground/.

260 *started a trend*: Pote's photo of Siegfried Buchmayr's jump turn on the Headwall ended up as an advertisement for Camel cigarettes.

INDEX

advertising venues: foreign, and
domestic, 229–32, 250. *See also*
Sun Valley
Albizzi, Nicolo degli: in Canada,
103; at Peckett's, 103
Allgeier, Sepp, 118
alpine races, 10, 198–99, 246;
Arlberg-Kandahar (A-K),
124–26; critique of, 212;
development of, 205–7; FIS at
Cannon, 110–11
Amateur Ski Club of New York
(ASC and ASC of NY), 126–27,
165–66, 171, 179, 185, 209,
250; founding of, 8. *See also*
Palmedo, Roland
amateur vs. professional problem,
144–45
Amstutz, Walter, 204, 213, 221
Anderson, Ingvald "Bing": crimes
of, 54; jumping, 54, 141, 147,
152
Anschluss, 113–14, 124–25; events
leading to, 121–23
anti-Semitism, 40, 104, 149; *Arierparagraf*, 121
Appalachian Mountain Club
(AMC): early skiing, 15, 18, 39,
60, 161, 168–69; instruction
of members, 206–7; at Mount
Washington, 94, 102
Arlberg technique, 115; development of, 123–24. *See also*
Schneider, Hannes
Auburn, William Herbert, 131–32

Beattie, Robert, 110, 184
Bernays, Walter, 116
Bigelow, Mrs. R. Graham, 197–98
Black National Brotherhood of
Skiers, 7–8
Bodwell, C. T., 107
Bonnet, Honoré, 184

border tax, 121. *See also* Anschluss:
events leading to
Bright, Alexander H.: clubs, 164;
Inferno Race, 96; influence
of, 78, 96, 101, 105–7, 181,
211; racer, 161, 211; Winant,
friendship with, 106–7. *See
also* Hochgebirge Ski Club
British influence, 19, 45, 78, 95,
102, 104, 204–5. *See also* Lunn,
Arnold
Broomhall, Wendall "Chummy,"
255
Brown Company, 51
Buchmayr, Siegfried: imprisoned,
173; as instructor, 103–5, 167,
172–73, 182; renown of, 26, 184
Byrd Antarctic Expedition, 213,
218, 228

Canada: eastern venues, 23,
227; marathons in, 46–47;
McKinnon, Frank, 144,
147–48; Montreal Carnival,
71–72; rope tow, 209. *See also*
snowmaking
Carleton, John P.: at Dartmouth
105; in Europe, 74; on Headwall, 95; involvement with
Cannon Tram, 107; jumping
record, 141, 144, 146; renown
of, 101, 107, 144, 164; U.S. team
and coach, 151
Civilian Conservation Corps
(CCC), 28–31, 105, 108, 180,
188, 193
colleges and universities, 8, 18, 20–
21, 72, 97, 144, 197, 201
Connecticut: early skiing in, 193–
94; snow trains to, 197–98. *See
also* Bigelow, Mrs. R. Graham;
Eriksen, Stein; Satre brothers;
Schoenknecht, Walter

293